THE VALOIS TAPESTRIES

FRANCES A. YATES

THE VALOIS TAPESTRIES

ROUTLEDGE & KEGAN PAUL
LONDON

First published in 1959
by the Warburg Institute
Second edition published in 1975
by Routledge & Kegan Paul Ltd
Broadway House, 68–74 Carter Lane,
London EC4V 5EL
Set in Monotype Garamond
and printed in Great Britain by
BAS Printers Limited, Wallop, Hampshire

ISBN 0 7100 8244 4

To
R. W. Y.

CONTENTS

LIST OF ILLUSTRATIONS

The twelve plates at the end of the book, which are numbered in Roman numerals, are referred to in the text by these numerals only. The thirty-six plates which are interleaved throughout the text, and which have a separate numeration in Arabic numerals, are referred to in the usual way.

Plate 1

    a—Henri and Louise in the "Fontainebleau" tapestry (Photograph Soprintendenza alle Gallerie di Firenze)

    b—Henri III, Painting. Ambras Collection, Kunsthistorisches Museum, Vienna (Photograph Kunsthistorisches Museum)

    c—Louise de Lorraine. Drawing, Bibliothèque Nationale, Paris (Photograph Giraudon)

Plate 2

    a—Anjou in the "Barriers" tapestry (Photograph Soprintendenza alle Gallerie di Firenze)

    b—François, Duc d'Anjou. Painting, Ambras Collection, Kunsthistorisches Museum, Vienna (Photograph Kunsthistorisches Museum)

    c—Marguerite in the "Elephant" tapestry (Photograph Soprintendenza alle Gallerie di Firenze)

    d—Marguerite de Valois, Queen of Navarre. Painting, A. J. Seligmann Collection, Paris (Photograph Giraudon)

    e—Navarre in the "Whale" tapestry (Photograph Soprintendenza alle Gallerie di Firenze)

    f—Henri, King of Navarre. Engraving by François Rabel (Photograph Cabinet des Estampes, Bibl. Nat., Paris)

Plate 3

    a—Lorraine in the "Whale" tapestry (Photograph Soprintendenza alle Gallerie di Firenze)

    b—Charles, Duc de Lorraine. Engraving by Thomas de Leu (Photograph Cabinet des Estampes, Bibl. Nat., Paris)

    c—Anne, Duc de Joyeuse. Drawing, Bibliothèque Nationale, Paris (Photograph Giraudon)

    d—Joyeuse in the "Polish Ambassadors" tapestry (Photograph Soprintendenza alle Gallerie di Firenze)

Plate 4

    a—Catherine in the "Tournament" tapestry (Photograph Soprintendenza alle Gallerie di Firenze)

    b—Catherine de' Medici. Drawing, Bibliothèque Nationale, Paris (Photograph Giraudon)

    c—Catherine de' Medici. Drawing, Bibliothèque Nationale, Paris (Photograph Giraudon)

Plate 5

    a—French Court Lady and Gentleman and French Bourgeoise. Engraving. From A. de Bruyn, *Omnium poene gentium imagines*, Cologne, 1577

    b—French Court Costumes in the "Whale" tapestry (Photograph Soprintendenza alle Gallerie di Firenze)

    c—French Bourgeois Costumes in the "Whale" tapestry (Photograph Soprintendenza alle Gallerie di Firenze)

Plate 6

    a—French Women's Costumes. Engraving. From A. de Bruyn, *Omnium pene Europae, Asiae, Aphricae atque Americae gentium habitus*, Antwerp, 1581

PREFACE TO THE SECOND EDITION

When this book was first published reviewers spoke of it as "a fascinating detective story" and it is true that—whether "fascinating" or not the reader of this second edition must decide for himself—the book follows up many clues derived from many and various sources to establish through converging lines of evidence the historical meaning of the Valois Tapestries. In cases where there are no documents, the detective must use every other kind of evidence that he can find, and the Valois Tapestries are such a case. There are no written documents to account for the existence of this obviously very important work. Yet these tapestries are themselves historical documents, written in visual imagery, the deciphering of which can give us insight into the historical, artistic and spiritual movements of the late sixteenth century at a deeper level than can more conventional historical sources.

The book is not an art-historical study of tapestries in general. It is about one set of tapestries as a vision of life and history. Historical characters stand in the foreground apparently remembering the brilliant scenes of court festival in which they have taken part which are unrolled in amazing detail behind them. The detective story establishes that the foreground portraits are members of the French royal family as they were in the later part of the sixteenth century, the family of Catherine de' Medici. The festivals in the backgrounds are those which she designed and produced during her long regency, brilliant spectacles based on the exercises of chivalry and leading, as the century proceeded, to the emergence of new European art-forms. The story further establishes that the tapestries were made in the circle of William of Orange to celebrate the brief rule in the Netherlands of a member of the French royal family, François d'Anjou, well known in English history as the unsuccessful suitor of Queen Elizabeth I, and that, though based on French materials, they were designed by Lucas de Heere, a Flemish artist employed by Orange as propagandist for Anjou.

The larger historical issues emerge as the story unfolds. The splendour of the festivals was not mere extravagance and display but a part of the *politique* policy through which Catherine de' Medici strove to steer a middle course through the great crisis of the century, the division of Europe into hostile religious positions after the closure of the Council of Trent in 1564. She brought together Catholics and Protestants in these festivals, hoping to soften religious discord as both sides participated in chivalric pastimes in settings of opulent Burgundian-style splendour. She who had encouraged in the Colloquy of Poissy the eirenic efforts of the early part of the century, still continued her eirenic and *politique* policies—of which the great court festivals were one expression—one might almost say in defiance of Trent. The festivals at Bayonne in 1565 were actually attended by the terrible Duke of Alva with the object of inducing Catherine to publish the decrees of the Council in France and to set up the Inquisition for their enforcement. She replied with festivals, with the "magnificences" of Bayonne, with tournaments, running at the ring, barriers, and so on, the traditional pastimes of chivalry performed in brilliant costumes by her young son, Charles IX, and the courtiers. In one of the Bayonne settings a new art form, the

French *ballet de cour*, was born, expressing a gentle magic of nature through the movement of mythological figures to music, in the effort to counteract with the weapons of art the destructive religious passions of the age. Such festivals, of which Bayonne set the pattern, are reflected in the brilliantly-moving scenes behind the foreground portraits of the French royal family in the Valois Tapestries.

In 1567, two years after his interview with Catherine de' Medici at Bayonne, the Duke of Alva entered the Netherlands at the head of the armies of Philip II there to crush religious revolt by force and by those years of repression marked by cruelties so atrocious that they have left an ineradicable stain on the conscience of mankind. Surely festivals were better than this! Surely the eirenic and *politique* policies which strove to avert such disasters were those which should have been followed. Catherine de' Medici continued to proclaim through festivals her belief in the arts of developing Renaissance culture as the antidote to wars of religion. After every cessation of the French religious wars she produced a festival, and even the outbreak in the midst of one of her festivals of the Massacre of Saint Bartholomew (which was connected as is now known with the Spanish policy in the Netherlands) did not deter her.

In the Netherlands, the rich Burgundian civilisation had been developing during the earlier part of the century in new and significant directions. The trade of Antwerp was opening up the world, and wide cosmopolitan interests stimulated the work of Netherlandish geographers, cartographers, mathematicians and scientists, of whom Ortelius was a leading representative. The title which Ortelius gave to his monumental atlas was *Theatrum orbis terrarum* (1570) and this wide interest in the countries of the world and their peoples stimulated a large topographical literature and many publications on the costumes of many nations, such as could be seen in the great cosmopolitan port of Antwerp. The traditional interest of Burgundian artists in costume was carried on in this specifically topographical sense by artists such as Joris Hoefnagel and his friend Lucas de Heere. The disastrous Spanish policy broke the port of Antwerp and brought desolation to the once prosperous Netherlands. The costume books, and the cult of the costumes of many nations, became, perhaps almost unconsciously, a symbol of the wide and liberal cosmopolitan outlook which the Spanish tyranny had tried to suffocate.

The interest in costume of the Flemish designer of the Valois Tapestries is shown in the way in which the portrait-figures stand in the foregrounds, almost like costume figures in a landscape. This interest is also expressed in the exuberance with which the figures in the festivals are clothed in the costumes of many nations. The world of the tapestries is a free world, or a would-be free world, in which festivals are preferred to the Inquisition and a wide outlook on the theatre of the world in all its variety is preferred to a narrow rigidity. It is also, in a sense, a world deliberately returning to a Burgundian type of chivalric magnificence as a counterpoise to the narrowness of persecuting orthodoxy. This was exactly the spirit which William of Orange tried to encourage when he placed the French Valois prince, François d'Anjou, in the position of ruler of the Southern Netherlands which his long campaigns had at last freed from Spanish tyranny.

Thus in the Valois Tapestries, different liberal traditions converge. The splendours of the Burgundian-type magnificences with which Catherine de' Medici had sought to maintain a middle way, are illustrated by a Flemish-Burgundian school of costume and topography artists, exempli-

fied in Lucas de Heere, the propaganda expert employed by William of Orange to build up
François d'Anjou as ruler of a state in which religious toleration would be practised. The Valois
Tapestries belong into the atmosphere of the propaganda for Anjou, and they have the closest
links with Catherine de' Medici.

There are also close, though unspoken, links with Elizabethan England behind the tapestries.
It was from England, after the festivals there in his honour and his unsuccessful courtship of
Elizabeth, that Anjou came to Antwerp to make his "Joyeuse Entrée" as the new Duke of
Brabant. And the designer of the propaganda for Anjou, Lucas de Heere, had spent long years in
England as a refugee artist and poet. The stream of religious refugees to England of which Lucas
de Heere was one—he arrived in England in about 1567, the year in which Alva's régime in the
Netherlands began—carried Burgundian influences into the early Elizabethan period. Lucas
de Heere when he returned to his native country after its liberation by Orange, had behind him a
long experience of life in England. The festivals for Anjou in England were the chivalrous type
of magnificences with *politique* background, such as we see in the Valois Tapestries in one of
which Anjou performs at a "barriers". Though Orange's plans for a liberal bloc in Europe were
not completed by the marriage of Elizabeth with Anjou for which he had hoped, yet his establishment of Anjou in the Netherlands was a move of deep significance for England. The portrait of
Anjou in the tapestries belongs in English history as that of one of the most significant of the
failed suitors of Elizabeth, significant because he symbolised the *politique* approach to religious
questions.

Since I wrote *The Valois Tapestries* other books and articles have appeared to which the reader
of this foreword to its second edition must be referred for further light on the historical and
religious situation behind the tapestries. Important among these is *The Radical Arts* by Jan Van
Dorsten (Leiden, 1970) which studies the influence of the Flemish refugees on the early Elizabethan
period. This included, almost certainly, an influence of the secret sect, known as the Family of
Love, which had arisen in the Netherlands under the stress of the religious wars and persecutions.
The Familist held that commitment to any definite religious confession was unimportant. What
mattered was an intense inner mysticism centred on charity. This enabled a member of the secret
sect to pass from Catholicism to Protestantism, or vice versa, as changing governments dictated.
This was a useful outlook in the sixteenth century and it enabled secret adepts of the sect, like
Christopher Plantin, the printer, Justus Lipsius, the classical scholar, Ortelius, the geographer,
to pass through the difficulties of the age. Van Dorsten indicates that Familist influences were
particularly strong among the refugee artists and scholars in early Elizabethan England. Such
secretly liberal views could be associated with intensive cultivation of the arts and sciences, as
forces making for toleration, and peace from religious wars.

Among the refugee artists, Lucas de Heere is particularly extolled by Van Mander for his skill
as a portrait painter, though no existing portrait has as yet been successfully attributed to him.
His costume studies have, however, survived, and many of them are reproduced in this book. In
the light of possible Familist influence on De Heere, many of whose friends and associates were
certainly Familists, one can think over again the curious story about the "costume gallery" which
Lucas had painted for Admiral Clinton, in which the Englishman was painted naked, but with stuff

and scissors, ready to change into any style required. When the Admiral showed his costume gallery to Queen Elizabeth, she is reported (by Van Mander) to have said that it was quite right thus to satirise the changeability of the English.

This story may gain an added meaning when one considers the career of Admiral Clinton who was a strong supporter of the Protestant régime under Edward VI, but under his successor, Catholic Mary, he retained favour and his position of admiral (see the article on Clinton in the *Dictionary of National Biography*). He placed the services of the fleet at her disposal for carrying messengers and messages between her and her fiancé, Philip II. These messages probably included the exchange of portraits for which Lucas de Heere might have been employed (see E. Auerbach, *Tudor Artists*, London, 1954, p. 90). Lucas's favoured position as the protégé of admirals on both sides of the water (a Burgundian admiral was also his patron) would have made it easily possible for him to make unrecorded visits to England in the ships of his employers before his documented arrival as a refugee in 1567. On the accession of Elizabeth, Clinton switched again and became one of the new queen's most trusted favourites and councillors, particularly after the important part which he played in quelling the Rising in the North in 1569.

Is it possible that Van Mander when he tells the "costume gallery" story in his account of Lucas de Heere is hinting at a Familist meaning?

Though no definite statement can be made about this elusive subject, it can be said that the Valois Tapestries belong into the period when Familism was spreading, that Familist influences have been suggested behind the intervention of Anjou in the Netherlands, which is the theme that the tapestries celebrate, and that their designer, Lucas de Heere, whether or not a Familist himself, certainly moved in Familist circles. It is thus possible to view these great tapestries as expressive of the atmosphere of that movement, even though nothing definite can be proved. I knew nothing about Familism when I wrote *The Valois Tapestries*, though I always thought that the Man with the Mask (Pl. 36) had a secret.

Since portraits signed with the HE monogram, formerly believed to be by Lucas de Heere, are now assigned to Hans Eworth (see R. Strong, *The English Icon*, London, 1969) the only painting of his English period which is now claimed for him is the well-known "Family of Henry VIII". King Henry sits on the central throne flanked by his daughters; on one side, Mary and her husband Philip, representing War; on the other side, Elizabeth with allegorical figures representing Peace and Plenty. One recognises in this picture a mind working on similar lines to the mind behind the Valois Tapestries, and one can see in it the emergence of the allegorical portrait of Queen Elizabeth I as a *politique* figure representing an imperial *pax* from wars of religion. Closely associated with this picture is the famous one of "Queen Elizabeth I and the Three Goddesses" in which the Queen stands under a portico, with Windsor Castle in the distance, whilst the three goddesses, amongst whom Paris had to choose for the award of the golden apple, indicate that the prize is to be given to Queen Elizabeth. This picture was attributed to Lucas de Heere in an old catalogue; the most recent suggestion (made by Van Dorsten) is that it is by Joris Hoefnagel who was in England in 1569, the year in which it was painted. The splendid topographical background certainly reminds of Hoefnagel's landscape studies, with the classical figures of the goddesses instead of the costume figures. I would like to think that it is by Hoefnagel *and* Lucas de Heere, with Lucas as the propaganda expert suggesting ideas to his close friend Hoefnagel. The costume and topographical school, to which both Lucas and Hoefnagel belonged, is perhaps here seen in the act of evolving an allegorical study of Queen Elizabeth I.

The doubt attaching to the attribution to Lucas de Heere of portraits painted during his English period must not obscure his importance as a leading Burgundian expert, both in art and letters, during that early formative period in England, before the appearance of the so-called English Renaissance with Sidney, Spenser, and, eventually, Shakespeare. Though his artistic side is so obscure, the literary side is well-attested by the considerable volume of Dutch poetry which he wrote and in which he was in many ways a pioneer. Lucas's poetry and its connections with the work of his friend Van der Noot, and so with the early Spenser, is discussed by Van Dorsten. Lucas's experiments with the sonnet form in Dutch were continued by Van der Noot and by Janus Gruter, the bulk of whose work was lost in the sack of Heidelberg, after the defeat of the Winter King of Bohemia in 1620. Leonard Forster (in his book *Janus Gruter's English Years*, Leiden, 1967) discusses the importance of the "new" Dutch poetry in its influence on German poetry in the early seventeenth century. In his work as a poet, Lucas de Heere was thus a significant transition figure in an important European movement. The most recent study of Lucas as a poet is that by W. Waterschoot (*Levens en Betekens van Lucas d'Heere*, Ghent, 1974) who discusses the pictorial side of the poetry and its importance for Lucas's art as a portraitist. He concludes that Lucas's masterpiece, expressive of both his poetic and artistic sides, was the Valois Tapestries.

And indeed we can see in the portrait figures of the tapestries the quick seizing of a likeness which Van Mander says was characteristic of Lucas's portraits. We see his skills as a costume artist. And we feel the poetic and profound understanding of vast movements of history which is expressed through these extraordinary tapestries.

Another book published since the first edition of *The Valois Tapestries* is my own, *Astraea: The Imperial Theme in the Sixteenth Century* (London, Routledge, 1975). The much enlarged essay in this volume on the Magnificences for the Joyeuse wedding of 1581 is relevant for the Valois Tapestries which allude to the Joyeuse wedding festivals in the portraits of Henri III and his Queen, and of Joyeuse himself. These festivals held at the French court in the year before Anjou became ruler in the Netherlands represent the final explosion of Catherine de' Medici's tradition of Burgundian magnificences. They were almost contemporary with William of Orange's attempt at a Burgundian revival under Anjou as Duke of Brabant. The new essay in *Astraea* on the festivals for the Joyeuse wedding attempts to bring out further the intensive cultivation of all the arts and sciences—poetry, music, painting, mechanics—in these final Magnificences in the intensive effort to allay divisive religious passions with the magic of art. The poetry and music of the poets of the Pléiade (with whom Lucas de Heere was in sympathy and who influenced the Dutch poetic movement) were here brought into play on a grand scale. The effort was to prove unsuccessful and the renewed outbreak of the wars would finally destroy the French Renaissance culture of the court of the Valois. This tragedy was parallel to the tragic failure to establish a tolerant Burgundian state in the Netherlands under Anjou. Both disasters form the dark background to the later history of the tapestries as objects, as recounted in the later chapters of this book.

Following the essay on the Joyeuse Magnificences in *Astraea* is one on religious processions in Paris in 1583–4. The House of Christian Charity towards which the processions of knights and penitents move may possibly have been a centre of the Family of Love, suggesting a Familist atmosphere behind Henri III's Counter Reformation, such as has been suggested behind Anjou's movement. In my discussion in *The Valois Tapestries* of Christopher Plantin's rôle in printing the account of Anjou's entry into Antwerp, I was unaware of Plantin's secret Familist connections.

Catherine de' Medici appears in the Processions as a warm supporter of Nicolas Houel's House of Christian Charity and one may suppose that she would have been in sympathy with the interpretation of her festivals in the tapestries. In fact one may go further and suggest that she herself may have had an influence on their design. In *The Valois Tapestries* I made no attempt to enquire how the Flemish designers of the tapestries obtained the French materials which they used—the Caron drawings of the festivals, the printed accounts of the festivals, the portraits of the French royal family. The most reasonable answer to such a query would be that Catherine herself must have sent them the materials.

An interesting parallel is the set of embossed and gilt leather hangings which Catherine ordered in 1570 through the French ambassador in Madrid. The documents concerning this order have been printed and discussed by Eugénie Droz ("Les tapisseries de cuir de Catherine de Médicis", *Gazette des Beaux Arts*, 1965, pp. 137–4). Catherine sent designs with her order for these Spanish "leather tapestries", also "poésies" to be inscribed on them. These hangings have long since disappeared but Mlle Droz suggests that the brightly coloured leather tapestries may have decorated the walls of rooms in which French festivals (after 1570) were held.

It is thus not impossible that Catherine de' Medici and Lucas de Heere, who had worked for Catherine in his early youth on designs for tapestries, may to some extent have collaborated on the designing of the Valois Tapestries, she sending the French materials with hints as to their use, he providing his own visionary understanding and the exuberant execution influenced by the Flemish tradition to which he belonged. The presence of Louis of Nassau in the tapestries, their connection with William of Orange and his propaganda for her son, Anjou, would not have displeased Catherine whose true position as an Erasmian *politique* in sixteenth-century religious history has been distorted. The Valois Tapestries may show her in her true colours as always secretly in sympathy with the side of liberalism.

As the great artist who designed the festivals, it would be fitting that she might have had some part in the design of the great tapestries which are a monument to her work of reconciliation through art.

The review-article of my book by G. T. van Ysselsteyn ("Wilhelmus" in *Spiegel der Historie*, Vol. 2, February 1967) must be mentioned here for Dr. van Ysselsteyn is a noted tapestry expert. She stresses the important nature of the undertaking to weave tapestries of such size and complexity. She estimates that eighty to ninety workers would have been required to execute them in time; she suggests Oudenarde as the place where they were made; and she emphasises that this series was the last large project carried out in the old country before the collapse, the end of a great tradition. She makes knowledgeable suggestions as to how William of Orange might have raised the money for this very expensive diplomatic gift. She accepts my interpretation of the historical meaning of the tapestries and of their purpose as belonging to Orange's French policy. She makes, however, some other suggestions concerning the identification of some of the portraits which tend to be rash rather than convincing. Her most interesting idea is that the third man in the foreground group in the "Journey" tapestry, standing with Louis of Nassau and his brother (Pl. 26), is Marnix de Sainte Aldegonde. This thought somehow stays in the mind, and may be accepted on historical and other grounds as a better suggestion as to the identity of this figure than my guess that he might be Christopher of the Palatinate.

I am glad to have this opportunity of criticising some of my other portrait suggestions. The worst of these is Sheffield in the "Elephant" tapestry (Pl. 35). Not only are the portraits of Sheffield reproduced for comparison not in the least like the unknown young man in the tapestry, but the suggestion is at variance with the principle that the portrait groups are members of the French royal family (unless they are members or friends of the Nassau family). If I were starting to look for that young man again, which I shall not do, I would try to find a portrait of Charles de Valois, "le bâtard" to whom Catherine left half her property. Another comparison which I now find quite unconvincing is Philip of Nassau for a youth in the "Barriers" (Pl. 33), though I would like to try to keep Maurice as the page (also Pl. 33).

A German reader of *The Valois Tapestries* suggested to me in a letter that the Knight in the "Barriers" (Pl. 32) is the Prince Dauphin (François de Bourbon-Montpensier) a prince of the French royal blood who was with Anjou in the Netherlands. He had been present at all the great festivals and was with Anjou in England. He was also the brother of William of Orange's third wife, Charlotte de Bourbon Montpensier. On all these counts he seems highly suitable for appearance with Anjou in the tapestry; the Knight of the "Barriers" is more likely to be an allusion to him than to Orange, who kept himself in the background.

It should be said of the portraits in the tapestries in general that though the majority of them can be certainly identified, others are less certain.

The drawing of Queen Elizabeth (Pl. 17a) is a later interpolation into a manuscript by Lucas de Heere and so cannot be used as evidence of his style. This is indicated in the footnote on p. 23 but should be emphasised again here.

It is as an historical document, written in images, that one should read the Valois Tapestries. They throw light in many directions, not only on Franco–Flemish relations in the sixteenth century, but also on Elizabethan England in which the revival of chivalry in the Accession Day Tilts was such an important feature of the cult of the monarch. *The Valois Tapestries* belongs with *Astraea* with its comparative studies of French and English images of monarchy. And as a record of a failed movement for religious toleration it belongs with *The Rosicrucian Enlightenment* as a previous attempt at the establishment of an "enlightened" state. The supporters of Anjou's movement belonged into much the same traditions of European liberalism as those who were afterwards to support the ill-fated Elector Palatine. To enter the world of the tapestries is to gain new insights into elusive movements running from the past into the future.

Frances A. Yates

Warburg Institute
University of London
1975

PREFACE TO THE FIRST EDITION

This book could not have come into being without the co-operation of many people in many countries, and it is my pleasant task in this preface to try to express my thanks. Permission for the taking and reproduction of the photographs of the Valois Tapestries with which the book is illustrated was kindly given by Professor F. Rossi, the Sopraintendente of the Florentine Galleries, to whom my warmest thanks are due. New photographs of the tapestries as a whole were made for the plates at the end of the book, and the many details shown in the plates in the text have never been photographed before. The excellent photographs were taken by the official photographer to the Uffizi, Signor Tronci. I was also assisted by the Uffizi authorities in tracing the recent history of the tapestries, and I hope that this book will be some small return for all the kindness which I received in Florence through making more widely known one of the treasures of the Gallery.

Some of the portraits used are in Holland. I have to thank Her Majesty Queen Juliana of the Netherlands for gracious permission to reproduce a portrait in her possession. Other portraits are reproduced by permission of the Rijksmuseum, Amsterdam, and the Mauritshuis, The Hague. Invaluable assistance in the tracing of portraits and in answering enquiries was given by the Rijksbureau voor Kunsthistorische Documentatie at The Hague. I also received kind help at The Hague from Miss van Schaick of the Koninklijk Huisarchief, from Dr. P. J. H. Vermeeren of the Koninklijke Bibliotheek, from Dr. Japikse of the Rijks Archief, and from Dr. G. T. van Ysselsteyn. I am glad that this book has been printed in the town of Leiden, with its many associations with William of Orange.

In Ghent, I was generously welcomed and guided by the late Professor H. F. Bouchery, and I have to thank Ghent University Library for permission to reproduce Lucas de Heere's drawings. The photograph of his painting in St. Bavon Cathedral was supplied by the Institut Royal du Patrimoine Artistique of Brussels.

I am indebted to my friend Monsieur Jean Ehrmann for his permission to reproduce a painting by Caron in his possession, and also for the stimulus of his paper on the Valois Tapestries, delivered at one of the conferences on festivals organised by Monsieur Jean Jacquot of the Centre National de la Recherche Scientifique, and for all his other articles on this subject. I have also to thank the present owners of the six Caron drawings for their permission to reproduce them; these owners are, the Louvre, the National Gallery of Scotland, the Courtauld Institute of Art (University of London), the Pierpont Morgan Library, and the Fogg Art Museum, Harvard University. Several portrait drawings are reproduced by permission of the Bibliothèque Nationale, and the Cabinet des Estampes has supplied photographs of many prints and drawings used in the search for the originals of the French portraits in the tapestries. Permission to reproduce paintings and drawings in their possession has been given by the Kunsthistorisches Museum, Vienna, and by the Berlin State Museums.

Needless to say, without the library of the British Museum the research necessary for this book would not have been possible, and the Museum possesses one of the collections of Lucas de Heere's drawings, two of which are here reproduced by kind permission of the Trustees. New photographs of these drawings were taken by Mr. O. Fein of the Warburg Institute. I have made great use of the historical sections of the London Library, to the staff of which I am, as always, deeply indebted. I should also like to thank the staff of the library of the Victoria and Albert Museum. The photographic collection of the Courtauld Institute has been invaluable, and I am most grateful for all the help which I have received there.

An exhibition organised by Professor Sir Anthony Blunt was the starting point for the new approach to the Valois Tapestries. The Director of the National Portrait Gallery, Mr. C. K. Adams, and Mr. David Piper have allowed me to use the photographic files of the Gallery. Professor E. K. Waterhouse has patiently answered several letters of enquiry. Professor F. Wormald has taken an encouraging interest in the progress of the book. Dr. D. P. Walker made some useful suggestions.

As a member of the staff of the Warburg Institute I have had the enormous advantage of being able to enjoy the facilities for research there so generously supported by the University of London, and the use of the rich library founded by Warburg. The Valois Tapestries were one of Warburg's special interests, and he was a pioneer in the serious study of festivals. It is thus as some small expression of gratitude for all that I owe to his foundation that I am most glad that this book should be published in the series of Studies of the Warburg Institute, edited by G. Bing. It was Professor Bing who encouraged me to develop what was at first to have been an article into a book. She has read all the successive versions of the manuscript, and the proofs. To her constructive criticisms, her enthusiastic interest in the subject, and her inspiring friendship the book owes more than can be expressed.

Professor E. Gombrich read the book in manuscript and has been constantly stimulating and encouraging. Mr. Charles Mitchell helped by lending me his copy of the *Beschrijving der Britsche Eilanden* for a very long time. To all my colleagues of the Warburg Institute my warmest thanks are due for their unfailing comradeship. The librarians of the Institute have born with my importunities with endless patience, and so has the staff of the photographic collection. The book has been seen through the press by Miss Anne Marie Meyer.

My sister has given untiring assistance in countless ways and has lived with me in the Valois Tapestries.

Frances A. Yates

Warburg Institute,
University of London
June, 1959.

INTRODUCTION

In the galleries of the Uffizi hang eight famous and splendid tapestries, usually known as the Valois Tapestries. Every visitor to the great Florentine gallery has passed in front of them, and those who pause and gaze find themselves transported into a strange and dazzling world. A marvellous series of court festivals is evidently in progress, combats in masquerade costumes and in fantastic settings, water festivals, a court ball. Groups of people, sumptuously attired, stand in the foregrounds, resplendent beings whose amazing festival-life unrolls itself behind them.

Shakespeare's Costard, when suddenly introduced into a brilliant company, orientated himself by enquiring, "Which is the head lady?". The head lady in the Valois Tapestries is immediately recognised by the passing crowds. Catherine de'Medici in her black widow's weeds stands out amidst the throng of gay court ladies and gentlemen in their many-hued and bejewelled garments. Dignified and compelling, she dominates her surroundings, and her dark figure is set off by the magnificent richness of the tournament behind her (II).

Twice we encounter the enigmatic gaze of her son, Henri III. Wearing the distinctive "bonnet Henri III", he stands in one tapestry in front of a water festival; with him is his elegant and beautiful young queen, Louise de Lorraine (I). In another, he is in masquerade attire, mounting his horse to take part in the exotically costumed festival (VI). The lively features and sparkling black eyes of the elaborately dressed girl in front of the "Elephant" show (VIII) undoubtedly belong to Catherine's difficult daughter, Marguerite. The youth beside her, in a court suit of wonderfully patterned material, is a portrait, made as flattering as possible, of her brother François, Duke of Anjou, Catherine's youngest son. Anjou also appears in great splendour in the "Barriers" tapestry, where he holds an immensely long lance with a somewhat uncertain attempt at regal dignity (VII).

Having picked out these familiar faces, we are already in a position to recognise that one of the leading purposes of the Valois Tapestries is to present the family of Catherine de'Medici in all its glory.

Though the Queen Mother appears only once in the foreground, in nearly all the other tapestries a tiny figure in widow's weeds can be detected presiding over the shows. She watches from a centre seat in pavilions; or is seated in a barge; or contemplates the dancers from her chair. This is as it should be, for the identifiable festivals in the tapestries are the ones with the production of which she was particularly associated. These were the series of "magnificences" which she deployed at Bayonne in 1565, on the occasion of her meeting with her daughter, the Queen of Spain, at the celebrated Bayonne Interview; and at her splendid reception at the Tuileries in 1573 of the ambassadors from Poland who came to confer the crown of that country on her son Henri.

Aby Warburg was the first to point out how closely the festival scenes in two of the tapestries (II, III) correspond to written descriptions of the shows given at Bayonne in 1565.[1] The writer

(N. Ivanoff) of an article in the *Revue du seizième siècle* made independently the same discovery.[2] Another tapestry (IV) undoubtedly depicts Catherine's entertainment for the Polish ambassadors in 1573; this vital identification, first made by Guiffrey,[3] was usefully followed up by Ivanoff. The major festivals particularly associated with Catherine are thus reflected in the tapestries. Their double purpose would seem to be to glorify, in the foregrounds, the members of the Queen Mother's family, and, in the backgrounds, the brilliance of her festivals.

The dates of these festivals, however, bring us face to face with a major problem, namely the time-gulf between the foreground figures and the festivals behind them. All the hitherto identified festivals took place in the reign of Charles IX, yet there is no likeness of that king in the tapestries. Why are the foreground portrait figures, so unmistakeably "Henri III" in period, standing in front of festivals of the preceding reign? Why are the family groups, representing members of Catherine's family as they were at some time during the reign of her son Henri III, assimilated to spectacles which the Queen Mother had produced during the reign of his predecessor, her son Charles IX, whose part in them is totally suppressed and eliminated?

An entirely new light on this problem has been shed in recent years through J. Ehrmann's publication of six French drawings (IX-XI) which bear a remarkable resemblance to six of the Valois Tapestries.[4] On stylistic grounds, these drawings can be certainly attributed to Antoine Caron, a well-known French court artist. The designer of the tapestries had undoubtedly seen these Caron designs, in some form, and had used them as his basis. The foregound portrait figures are not in the Caron designs, but have been inserted by the artist who revised these for the tapestries. We thus have to deal with two artists behind the tapestries; the first is Caron, making a set of straight records of the festivals of the reign of Charles IX; the second is the artist of the tapestries, who anachronistically placed portraits relating to a later period onto these designs, which he also altered in many other ways.

The Valois Tapestries were made in Flanders; this is attested, not only by their style and colouring, but by the fact that they bear upon them the famous mark of Brussels. They are of supreme quality, a superb example of Flemish tapestry-art, and they must have been extremely costly. Only personages of the very highest rank could have afforded to order works of such princely splendour; or, if they were presented as a gift to some person of the highest rank, the givers must have been able to draw upon considerable subsidies.

No documentary evidence has so far come to light, in either French or Flemish sources, to indicate who ordered these tapestries; no payments relating to them have been traced; no documents describing a commission to an artist, or connecting any artist's or weaver's name with them. That works of such obvious importance should be so totally undocumented is in itself curious.

They appear to have been in Florence from time immemorial, and to have reached the Uffizi from the old grand-ducal collections. Ivanoff conjectured that they might have been taken to Florence by Catherine de' Medici's granddaughter, Christina of Lorraine, when she went thither from the French court in 1589 as the bride of the Grand Duke Ferdinand I. That this was almost certainly the case is indicated by a document published by J. Ehrmann from the Florentine archives.[5] It is from an inventory of articles stated to have been given to Christina by Catherine de' Medici which was made after Christina's arrival in Florence. Among the objects mentioned in it is a set of eight Flemish tapestries, with "figures" and a border of "grotesques", white and of various colours. Their measurements are given, and they correspond almost exactly with those of the Valois Tapestries, which are surrounded by borders decorated with the type of ornaments technically known as "grotesques" and which, moreover, give an effect of "white and of various colours" owing to the white ground of the designs and of the borders. There seems little doubt, therefore, that the eight tapestries described in this inventory are the Valois Tapestries.

This solitary piece of documentary information tells us a fact of great importance. Since the goods in the inventory are expressly stated to have been given to Christina by Catherine de' Medici, we know that the Valois Tapestries must have been for a time in Catherine's possession. They had reached her from the Flemish atelier where they were made, either because she herself had ordered them, or as a presentation from some person or persons unknown.

The first of these alternatives was the one which used to be taken for granted, and until recently no other possibility was considered. With her well-known princely magnificence and lavish expenditure on works of art, who but the Queen Mother herself could have commissioned these marvellous records of the splendours of her court? [6] This supposition has, however, been questioned by J. Ehrmann on the grounds that Catherine, who always carefully supervised the artists working for her, would not have sanctioned what appear to be the historical errors in the Valois Tapestries, their anachronistic confusions, their possible blunder in taste in presenting a journey (V), in which Catherine appears to be travelling in her litter in front of the Château d'Anet, the palace built by her husband for his mistress, Diane de Poitiers. The discovery of the Caron drawings points, Ehrmann thinks, to the probability that the design of the tapestries was evolved at a distance from the French court by persons not quite fully informed as to its doings, and who assembled them from various materials at their disposal. Pointing to the prominence of François, Duke of Anjou, in two of the tapestries, he suggests that the occasion of their making was to commemorate Anjou's triumphal entry into Antwerp in 1582 as Duke of Brabant. He fancies that a theme based on an elephant used at that entry is reflected in the "Elephant" tapestry. His hypothesis is that the designs of the tapestries were assembled in a Brussels atelier by some cartonnier attached to it who had at his disposal the Caron designs, printed accounts of French festivals, portraits, albums of fashion, traditional motifs used in the atelier, and perhaps also drew on personal memories of Anjou's Antwerp entry. Working at the Flemish end, and not the French end, and working with this assemblage of second-hand evidence and material, the designer of the tapestries made (Ehrmann supposes) his historical and other blunders through ignorance. He suggests that the City of Antwerp, or some other Flemish organisation, may have financed the making of the tapestries as a tribute to the accession of a prince of the House of Valois to the position of titular ruler of the southern Netherlands.[7]

Here the matter stands at present, the result of the cumulative efforts of a long line of scholars who have interested themselves in the Valois Tapestries. In the pre-Caron epoch, the festivals and many of the portraits[8] were identified, and the time discrepancy between foregrounds and backgrounds was pointed out.[9] In the post-Caron epoch, Ehrmann has propounded his stimulating theory that the designs of the Valois Tapestries were assembled in the Flemish atelier where they were made, the occasion which brought them into existence being the brief and disastrous intervention into the affairs of the Netherlands of Catherine de' Medici's youngest son. Our attention is now strongly directed upon the two appearances of Anjou in the tapestries (VII, VIII). This curious-looking personage, the unsuccessful suitor of Queen Elizabeth I of England and still more lamentably unsuccessful as Count of Flanders and Duke of Brabant, becomes the Valois prince upon whom the meaning of the Valois Tapestries now—perhaps—turns.

In spite of these great advances, there remain many problems. Some of the portraits have not yet been identified, particularly the group of three men who stand on the right in the foreground of the "Journey" (V). Unlike those in nearly all the other tapestries, this group contains no member of the French royal family. Who are these mysterious strangers and why are they given such prominence? This tapestry is also unique in being the only one which does not have a festival for its subject and in its radical divergence from the Caron design (XI, a) which the unknown artist who composed it was using. Here the second artist, the man who was using the Caron designs, departed wildly from his French model and seems to have been giving himself a free rein. Gazing meditatively at the winding cavalcade which he imposed on Caron's sketch of a scene at the Château d'Anet and at the three cloaked men whom he placed in the foreground, we feel that this fascinating tapestry may hold the key to the mind and purposes of the second artist. Until it is explained, and the three men identified, we cannot assume that the reviser of the French designs was working in a haphazard manner, or in ignorance. He perhaps had a plan, even in what appear to be his historical innaccuracies, but one which we do not understand.

The more we compare the Caron drawings with the tapestries, the more we feel that the second artist is a man with a vigorous personality. The French designs are his raw material, certainly, but he is transforming them with some energetic purpose of his own. It is in the *alterations* which he makes in the Caron designs that the significance of the tapestries lies. Unless we can discover the identity of the second artist, the man who made the alterations, we are still in the dark.

We believe that we can prove that this second artist was Lucas de Heere. His name has already been pronounced by G. T. van Ysselsteyn in connection with the Valois Tapestries, on the grounds that Carel van Mander in his life of Lucas de Heere mentions that this Flemish artist designed tapestries for Catherine de' Medici.[10] It was not, however, because very early in his life he worked for Catherine but because, in his last years, he was in the employment of William of Orange and engaged in propaganda for Anjou in the Netherlands that Lucas de Heere became involved with the Valois Tapestries. Our arguments will confirm Ehrmann's hypothesis that the tapestries were designed at the Flemish end, and in connection with Anjou; but we hope to show that their Flemish designer, Lucas de Heere, was working in accordance with a carefully laid plan based on profound knowledge of the complicated history of Franco-Flemish relations in the sixteenth century.

These marvellous tapestries are an interpretation of French festivals, and of the history bound up with them, made by an artist in the confidence of William of Orange as a plea to Catherine de' Medici and Henri III to support Anjou's venture in the Netherlands.

PART I

THE MAKING OF THE TAPESTRIES

CHAPTER I

THE CARON DESIGNS AND THEIR ALTERATION IN THE TAPESTRIES

In the winter of 1949-50 an exhibition on "Landscape in French Art" was held at the Royal Academy; many little known French works from British collections were selected and catalogued by Anthony Blunt for this exhibition, amongst them a hitherto unknown drawing (IX, a) depicting a "Water Fête; Combat, Assault on an Island" which had been unearthed by E. K. Waterhouse in the National Gallery of Scotland at Edinburgh. The catalogue attributed the drawing to Antoine Caron on the ground of its stylistic likeness to his designs for the "Histoire d'Arthémise" and pointed out that it is a "study for a tapestry in the Uffizi . . . in which, however, large figures have been added in the foreground" [1]. This was the first inkling which those interested in the Valois Tapestries had of their connection with Caron.

In 1955, five other drawings (IX, b; X, a, b; XI, a, b,), which obviously belong to the same series as the drawing in the National Gallery of Scotland, turned up in the sale-rooms of Messrs. Colnaghi [2]. The five drawings are numbered in a late hand one to six, the missing number two being the already known Edinburgh drawing. One of the five is now in the Louvre, one in the Pierpont Morgan Library, two in the Witt Collection at the Courtauld Institute, and one in the Winslow Ames collection. This set of six small drawings, roughly the same size (probably sketches for cartoons), look as though they must all have been made at the same time.

Five of them represent festivals at the French court; two certainly refer to shows at Bayonne in 1565, and one alludes to the entertainment for the Polish ambassadors in 1573. One drawing is not of a festival but appears to depict a hunting scene at the Château d'Anet. The style of the costumes and other points suggest that these drawings all belong within the reign of Charles IX, who died in 1574. They were probably made in 1573, soon after the festivals for the Polish ambassadors.

Six of the Valois Tapestries are undoubtedly based, either on these actual drawings or on derivatives from them, as a rapid glance will suffice to demonstrate. In four cases, the tapestries correspond very closely indeed to the drawings; compare the "Fontainebleau" tapestry (I) with the relevant drawing of the island festival (IX, a); the "Tournament" and "Whale" tapestries (II, III) with the drawings of those subjects (IX, b; X, a); the "Polish" tapestry (IV) with the drawing of the festival for the Polish ambassadors (X, b). In two cases, the tapestries have deviated very considerably from Caron; the "Quintain" (VI) reproduces the figures running at the quintain dragon as we see them in the relevant drawing (XI, b) but has swept away its foreground and introduced an entirely new group of riders; the "Journey" (V) is based on the winding road leading to the Château d'Anet of the drawing (XI, a) but has imposed on that road a new cavalcade.

So far, only six of the set of Caron drawings have come to light; it is possible that there were originally two more such designs which formed the basis of the "Barriers" and "Elephant" tapestries. In the case of the latter, the existence of a painting of a festival with an elephant attributed to Caron (XII) [3] renders it extremely probable that this tapestry also was based on a French design.

We are now able to see clearly that the vivid foreground portraits of the Valois Tapestries were imposed on the French designs by the artist who revised these to form the tapestries. Caron's vaguely defined spectators of the festival scenes, turned inwards to watch them, have been transformed into portraits turned outwards, away from what is going on behind them. Usually the artist has stood these figures on ground or platforms existing in the French design; in one case, the "Whale" (III), he has added this ground. It is this change which gives these tapestries their unusual character. There seems to be no earlier example known of tapestries with foreground groups like these which are not participating in the scene depicted. [4] Though we can now perceive the mechanics of how they were evolved by imposition on an already existing design, this does not detract from their remarkable effect. Looking forwards from the scenes behind them, these people seem to stand outside time. And in fact they do belong to the present—to the moment at which the tapestries were designed—so that there is more than one time-level suggested. People of the present stand in front of festivals of the past looking out towards the future.

The artist of the tapestries did not make his anachronistic introduction of the foreground figures through ignorance of the dates of the festivals depicted by Caron, for he had consulted a printed account of the festivals at Bayonne in 1565, the *Recueil des choses notables faites à Bayonne*, and from this drew details which he added to the Caron designs. In the "Tournament" he has shown on the shields of the knights devices which are illustrated in the Bayonne *Recueil* (Pl. 22) but which do not appear in the Caron drawing (IX, b). In other ways, also, to be discussed later, he has made this tapestry a more accurate delineation than Caron's sketch of the festival as described in the printed account.

In the "Whale" (III), he followed closely Caron's arrangement of the mythological creatures of this festival at Bayonne but the topography of the scene, as shown in the tapestry, conforms more closely to the printed account than do the vague parallel planes of the Caron design (X, a). The account describes how the royal party crossed the river in a barge to an island on which they landed, and then walked up a specially prepared and turfed avenue to the banqueting-hall in a wood on the island [5]. This island, with its reedy margin, is much more clearly outlined in the tapestry than in the drawing, giving to the whole scene the character of a topographical view in place of the formalised classical composition of the French design. This change is revealing as to the mentality of the artist, who is reinterpreting the elegant vagueness of the design as a naturalistic view which he has taken care to make as topographically accurate as possible by studying the printed account.

The most obvious of the preoccupations of the artist of the tapestries, as compared with Caron, is his intense interest in costume. The vaguely elegant French spectators of the festivals in the Caron drawings become, in the portrait figures of the tapestries, fashion plates in which every detail of the wonderful creations worn by these royal personages of the Valois court is rendered with loving care. These figures are not only portraits of the French court, but a presentation of French court costume for men and women. Similarly in the "Polish" tapestry (IV) the artist has turned the faintly exotic Polish spectators of the scene in the Caron drawing (X, b) into rich studies of Polish costume. His passion for all the varieties of different national costumes also comes into play, with glorious effect, within the festival scenes in the masquerade costumes worn by the participants. In the "Fontainebleau" tapestry (I) for example, one boat-load wears Turkish costume whilst the defenders of the island are dressed as savages, perhaps American Indians; the generalised classical costumes of Caron's masqueraders in the relevant drawing (IX, a) have been transformed, through the dominant interest of the artist of the tapestries, into costumes of different quarters of the world. In the "Quintain" tapestry (VI) the group which the artist has superimposed on the Caron design (XI, b) was probably built up from the description in the Bayonne *Recueil* of a masquerade in which the performers wore costumes of many different nations [6]; this subject has given him full opportunity for a magnificent display of his special gift.

The Valois Tapestries are thus the result, not of a collaboration between two artists, but of a total revision and reinterpretation of the designs of one artist by another. Antoine Caron, a late product of the neo-classical school of Fontainebleau [7], worked for the French court in the later sixteenth century, particularly as a designer of cartoons for tapestries and as a painter of decorations for festivals and entries. The six designs used by the artist of the Valois Tapestries show Caron's usual characteristics, a certain formal elegance and decorative quality, elongated and uncharacterised human figures, coldness and lack of spontaneity. Caron's designs contribute a firm underlying French classical structure to the Valois Tapestries, but all their peculiar originality and charm are the contribution of the second artist. His introduction of the foreground portraits, through which he hits on an originality in composition, gives them their haunting human quality. His animatedly moving figures in the festivals give life and excitement to these marvellous scenes. His brilliance in costume imparts an incredible richness of effect to the whole.

All the stylistic evidence suggests that this second artist was Flemish. Apart from his intentionally planned deviations, it is through his training as a Flemish designer of tapestry-cartoons that he almost mechanically or instinctively transforms the French scenes. His treatment of trees and distant views, his foregrounds studded with various kinds of plants, his passion for rich materials, all mark him out as a Flemish artist practised in the drawing of motifs common to many Flemish tapestries of the sixteenth century.

It was a Flemish hand which transformed the French designs, and made of them a view of the French court and its festivals seen from the Netherlands.

CHAPTER II

THE FRENCH PORTRAITS

The artist was using yet another class of French materials, namely French portraits, so astonishingly abundant in this period, from which he copied the likenesses of members of the French court which form so significant a part of his design. In some cases, it is possible to identify, not only the personage portrayed, but the actual portrait type from which the likeness was taken.

A charming head of Louise de Lorraine is certainly the type whence the portraits of Louise have been taken (Pl. 1, a, c). The clear-cut features, the "Louise de Lorraine" hair style, even the necklace, have been copied by the tapestry artist from a portrait of Louise which must have been of exactly the type which we see in the drawing. An engraving of this queen[1] of a somewhat similar type and wearing the same necklace is dated 1581, which is probably also the date of the drawing. The likenesses of Louise in the tapestries thus show her as she was in about 1581, the beautiful and distinguished-looking young Queen of France, who had been married for some years (she was married to Henri III in 1575).

A portrait of Henri III at Vienna is very close to his appearances in the tapestries (Pl. 1, a,b). The small beard and moustache, the lie of the hair on the high forehead, the backward tilt of the "bonnet Henri III", even the ornament in the bonnet are repeated in the tapestries from a portrait of this type. In the "Quintain" (VI) the head—identical in other respects with the one in the "Fontainebleau"—has been turned in the opposite direction. Henri is of about the age that he was around 1581, not the very young prince nor the prematurely aged man, but Henri in the prime of life, dark and subtle, Catherine's favourite son as King of France before the storms gathered about him.

A good portrait of his sister Marguerite appears in the "Elephant" tapestry (Pl. 2, c). This is the oddly chubby face, full of character, with the black eyes and lively expression with which we are familiar in the many portraits of Marguerite (Pl. 2, d), though the exact type which was used by the tapestry artist, wearing the heart-shaped little cap on the carefully frizzed hair, has not been traced. He used it three times[2]; once in the "Elephant" (VIII); again in the "Tournament" (II), where exactly the same head of Marguerite wearing the same little cap can be seen looking out from behind her mother; and yet again in the "Whale" (III) where the same face, wearing the same cap, and looking in the same direction, is that of the lady who stands with two gentlemen in the foreground group. As he did for one of his two uses of his portrait of Louise (the one in the "Tournament") he has varied his Marguerite portrait here by putting a ruff around her neck.

The Marguerite of the tapestry artist's portrait was not the very young girl, nor even the young Marguerite as she was at the time of her ill-fated wedding in 1572, but Marguerite as she might have been around 1581 or 1582, the mature and fascinating "reine Margot". We are beginning to grasp the idea that the Valois Tapestries are a family group taken at the same time,

Pl. 1

a   Henri and Louise in the
    "Fontainebleau" (p. 6)

b   Henri III (p. 6)

c   Louise de Lorraine (p. 6)

c Marguerite in the "Elephant" (p. 6)

a Anjou in the "Barriers" (p. 9)

e Navarre in the "Whale" (p. 7)

d Marguerite (p. 6)

b Anjou (p. 9)

f Navarre (p. 7)

or rather fitted together from those photographically accurate likenesses, which were always being taken of these people, to look like a family group.

The man who stands with Marguerite in the "Whale" tapestry (III), and who is shown in profile looking towards her, is her husband, Henry of Navarre [3]. The thick lips, the Bourbon nose, the faint grin, are all recognisable as belonging to the famous physiognomy of Henri IV, whom we see here, however, years before he became King of France. We may compare him as he appears in the tapestry, wearing the "bonnet Henri III", with an engraving of him as King of Navarre (Plate 2, e, f). It has not been possible to trace the actual portrait type of Navarre which the tapestry artist was using. It was in profile, since it is again in profile that we see him in the "Tournament" (II), where he stands on the left beside Catherine and in front of Marguerite. Thus in both the "Whale" and the "Tournament" tapestries, Navarre is shown with his wife.

Who is the striking looking man who gazes out from between Marguerite and her husband in the foreground group of the "Whale"? A comparison of this face with the engraved portrait of Duke Charles of Lorraine (Pl. 3, a, b) proves his identity beyond a doubt [4]. The man in the engraving is the man in the tapestry, and furthermore the tapestry artist was using a portrait head of Charles of Lorraine of exactly the same type as the one on which the engraving was based; the position of the head, the hair, the eyes, the moustaches and beard, even the little white collar—all correspond.

Why should Charles of Lorraine appear in the Valois Tapestries? Because, like so many of the foreground personages, he was a member of the family of Catherine de'Medici. He was the husband of her second daughter, Claude, by whom he had three sons and three daughters—one of the daughters was the Christina of Lorraine to whom the tapestries were given by her grandmother. His wife had died in 1575 and therefore does not appear with him, for the principle governing the foreground portraits is that they show only members of Catherine's family who were alive when the tapestries were made. The group of three in the "Whale" is a family group, held together by the relationship of each to Catherine. Her widower son-in-law, Charles of Lorraine, stands with her son-in-law, Henry of Navarre, and his wife, Marguerite, her daughter.

The portrait of the Matriarch herself in the "Tournament" tapestry could have been taken from any of the innumerable likenesses of Catherine in her widow's weeds (Pl. 4, a, b, c), the details of which have been carefully rendered. It is from this tapestry, and from the figure of Catherine in it, that we should start to read round the gallery of family portraits in all their various permutations and combinations. In the "Tournament"(II), Catherine is with a daughter, Marguerite; a son-in-law, Navarre; a daughter-in-law, Louise. If we follow Louise from here we find her in the "Fontainebleau" (I) with her husband Henri III, who appears again in the "Quintain" (VI). If we follow Marguerite and Navarre we find them again in the "Whale" (III) with their brother-in-law, Charles of Lorraine. Marguerite in her third appearance in the "Elephant" (VIII) stands now with her brother Anjou, whom we see again in the "Barriers" (VII). The main foreground figures are a family, consisting of two sons, a daughter, two sons-in-law and a daughter-in-law; they are arranged and rearranged in different groupings which are picked up and understood as all held together by the mother figure, provided that the beholder reads off the foreground portraits as a whole, following them from one tapestry to another and recognising the family relationships in which they stand to one another.

Who is the man in the velvet hat in the "Polish" tapestry (IV)? A good suggestion as to the identity of this man was made by N. Ivanoff who pointed out that Henri, Duc de Guise, was appointed to receive the Polish ambassadors on their visit to Paris in 1573 and to attend the head ambassador, Prince Laski[5]. The man in the velvet hat certainly looks as though he were receiving the head Polish ambassador.

The very historical excellence of this suggestion, however, militates against the principle guiding the foreground portraits, namely that they do not belong in date to the festival represented. The artist of the tapestry took over the position of the head Pole from the Caron design, but the portrait of Velvet Hat which he inserted is more likely to have been of someone well-known about 1581 or 1582, than of Guise receiving the ambassadors in 1573.

Velvet Hat looks not unlike Anne, Duc de Joyeuse (Pl. 3, c, d) one of the principle favourites of Henri III and noted for his dandyism and extravagance in dress, which would fit the exquisite appearance of the velvet-hatted one in the tapestry. Moreover, Joyeuse has a claim to enter the family group. In 1581, he married Marguerite de Lorraine, who was the half-sister of Queen Louise de Lorraine, and thus became the brother-in-law of the King.

The marriage of Joyeuse to the sister of the Queen was the occasion of festivals at the French court of unprecedented splendour. Outstanding among them was the ballet which Queen Louise gave for her sister, the bride, at which they both danced together. The text of this performance, with an introduction describing Louise's part in it, was published in 1582, entitled *Le ballet comique de la reine*. Since we know that the artist of the tapestries made it his business to consult published *livrets* about French festivals, it is not impossible that the *Ballet comique* came into his hands[6].

Looking again at Louise as she appears in the "Tournament" tapestry (II), we notice the prominence of the lady who stands beside her, with her back to us. She wears a dress as splendid as the Queen's, whose hand she holds and towards whom she turns. They might both be about to take part in some grave and majestic dance. Is it possible that the allusion is to the famous ballet of 1581, and that we are intended to see here Louise with her sister, the Duchesse de Joyeuse?[7] The idea is an attractive one, and would work well into that plan of the foreground portraits as a whole which we have been unravelling. For, through the presence of the Duchesse de Joyeuse in it, the central "Tournament" tapestry would now be linked with the only festival tapestry not as yet drawn within its family mesh—namely the "Polish" tapestry (IV), containing Louise's sister's husband, the Duc de Joyeuse.

It is thus as a family group that the foreground portraits hang together; they present the Queen Mother with her children and their respective connections by marriage. The artist's plan was to show a present day family group placed in front of the festival designs which he was using. The anachronisms between foreground portraits and background festivals are, therefore,

a   Lorraine in the "Whale" (p. 7)

b   Lorraine (p. 7)

c   Joyeuse (p. 8)

d   Joyeuse in the "Polish Ambassadors" (p. 8)

a   Catherine in the "Tournament" (p. 7)

b   Catherine (p. 7)

c   Catherine (p. 7)

deliberate, and not made in ignorance. The artist knew perfectly well the date of the Bayonne festivals—he had carefully consulted the livret about them—and who was present at them. But he placed in front of them, not the dead members of Catherine's family who were there (Charles IX and the Queen of Spain) but living members. The portraits are a gallery of the living members of the family as they are now, at the time the tapestries were made. Henri III is married to Louise de Lorraine and interested in the marriage of Louise's sister to Joyeuse, which he has celebrated with splendid festivals. Anjou is at the height of his career, and has recently been entertained with festivals in London, as suitor of Queen Elizabeth, and in Antwerp, as sovereign of the southern Netherlands. Marguerite and Navarre are at the age they are now, around 1582. The widower son-in-law, Charles of Lorraine, is at his present age; he had recently been an important figure as head of the house of Lorraine, at the Joyeuse-Lorraine wedding. The difficulty of the time gap between foregrounds and backgrounds disappears once we realise that the artist is deliberately placing contemporary portraits of the French royal family in front of designs of earlier French festivals which he is assimilating to the present.

For the most part, the artist was probably using only portrait heads for his foreground figures, onto which he fitted bodies clothed in suits and dresses. The figures of Henri and Louise in the "Fontainebleau" (I) are revealing for this technique; the artist has copied his portrait heads with great fidelity, but the figures have a stuffed look and Henri's stiff gesture is like the conventional arrangement of a costume figure. Navarre in the "Whale" (III) gives a similar impression of a portrait head on a suit of clothes making a display gesture, whilst the head of Marguerite in the same group is completed by a brilliant dress rather than by a body. Joyeuse in the "Polish" tapestry (IV) and his wife in the "Tournament" (II) both make identically the same fashion plate gesture, with hand on hip, and in general the stiffness of the bodies of the foreground figures beneath their marvellous clothes suggests an artist accustomed to making costume studies onto which he has fitted portrait heads.

An exception to this rule is formed by the portraits of Anjou in the "Barriers" and "Elephant" (VII, VIII). The head is rather close in type to the portrait at Vienna (Pl. 2, a, b,) though not identical with it, and in this case we feel that the artist may have been using a full length study. Anjou in the "Barriers" (Pl. 30) stands out from among the other portraits, not only because the foreground figures are larger in this tapestry than in any of the others, but also because there is character in the personage as a whole, and not only in the portrait head. The weak legs in their uncertain stance, the attempt at regal grandeur in the whole position, may reflect, one feels, the real Anjou posing for his portrait at the height of his glory, when he was hoping to become the husband of Elizabeth of England and had actually become Count of Flanders and Duke of Brabant. The figure is almost exactly repeated in the "Elephant" (Pl. 34) though, instead of half-armour, Anjou is now seen in the leather jerkin worn under armour.

Anjou is the only one of the French royal family who could have been studied at first hand in Flanders. During the year of his tenure of his position there — the year 1582 — he lived in Antwerp. Flemish artists were engaged in painting portraits of their new ruler; among them was the first-class portrait painter Peter Pourbus who, according to Van Mander, painted from the life in Antwerp an admirable portrait of the French prince[8]. This portrait is not now known to exist. The Anjou of the tapestries probably represents, either a portrait actually made from life by the artist, or some reflection of state portraits of the Duke being painted in Antwerp.

We have seen that the designer of the tapestries, working at a distance, built up his tribute to the magnificence of Catherine's festivals, not from personal observation but from secondary sources. And his tribute to the unity of her family shows what at first sight seems to be a curious unawareness of the strains and stresses operating upon these people. The Flemish outsider makes mistakes in his grouping of the family which, when one reflects upon them, begin to seem one of the most curious and puzzling features of the Valois Tapestries, infinitely stranger than the anachronisms, and indicating either a clumsiness much more serious than anything hitherto encountered or a plan much deeper and bolder than anything hitherto envisaged.

Let us look, for instance, at Marguerite and Navarre as they stand in the "Whale" (III), dressed as though for a festival and almost as though about to take hands for the dance, and then call to mind the history of their marriage. The wedding of Navarre, the leader of the Protestant party in France, with Marguerite de Valois, was the occasion of the most terrible tragedy of the French wars of religion. The Protestants, assembled in Paris for their leader's wedding festivals, were massacred by the Catholics on the dreadful St. Bartholomew's Night. A rumour widely current among the Huguenots maintained that the massacre at the wedding was a long-prepared trap, planned years before at the Interview of Bayonne. How strange that this pair should stand in the tapestry in front of a festival at Bayonne!

How strange, too, to see Henry of Navarre placed cheek by jowl with Charles of Lorraine! The House of Lorraine, of which Duke Charles was the head, was identified with the party of the extreme Catholic reaction in France, and his relatives, the Guises, were Navarre's most bitter enemies. Lorraine and Navarre were certainly both sons-in-law of Catherine de'Medici, but in every other respect they were at opposite poles, utterly divided from one another by the sixteenth-century ideological iron curtain.

Again in the "Tournament" (II) Marguerite and Navarre are seen in front of a Bayonne festival, whilst on the opposite platform stand members of the House of Lorraine, Queen Louise and her sister. The Navarres were not at the French court at the time of the Joyeuse wedding but far away in the kingdom of Navarre. After the massacre which followed his wedding in 1572, Navarre was for a time a prisoner in Paris but escaped down to his own country and his Protestant followers in 1576. His wife remained at the French court, but in 1578 Catherine—anxious to keep Navarre within the family influence and fearing the Protestant disaffection in the south—made a special journey down to Navarre taking her daughter with her to reunite her to her husband. In 1581 Marguerite was still down in Navarre, ostensibly living with her husband, but early in 1582 she came back to Paris without him.

The group in the "Tournament", where Marguerite is with her mother and her husband, perhaps reveals something of Catherine's anxious efforts to keep this husband and wife together in the interests both of family peace and of peace with the Protestants. And the artist seems to be again trying to bring the Navarre side of the family into proximity with the Lorraine side, for Queen Louise de Lorraine stands on one platform, opposite to her Protestant brother-in-law on the other. It is the figure of the Matriarch which unites the occupants of the two platforms into one family.

We may think, too, of the situations of the two royal brothers who dominate the tapestries— Henri III and François, Duc d'Anjou. In 1581-2, Henri was undergoing that religious crisis, expressed in his many devotional activities, which seemed to indicate his affiliation to the Counter Reformation and the Catholic reaction. He had married into the house of Lorraine, and he made the marriage of his favourite, Joyeuse, into that house the occasion of festivals which seemed the expression of solidarity with the ultra-Catholic faction of his subjects. Nevertheless, he was secretly much afraid of the Guises, and of the possible danger to himself of the nascent Catholic League.

The politico-religious position of Anjou was neither the Protestant one nor that of the Catholic reaction, but the intermediate line of the "politique". He maintained good relations with Navarre and the Protestants, yet he remained a Catholic, a "politique" or tolerant Catholic. It was this position which made him a possible candidate for the hand of the Protestant Queen of England, and possible as the titular ruler of Flanders and Brabant, the mixed Catholic and Protestant populations of which William of Orange was trying to unite on a basis of "politique" toleration. Is it, therefore, in this position that we should place ourselves for the understanding of the presentation of the French royal family in the tapestries? Ought we to take our stand with Anjou, and with his backer William of Orange, in Antwerp, and look from thence towards the other members of his family in France? Is it possible that the designer of the tapestries in his juxtaposition of apparently incompatible members of the family is not being tactless through ignorance, but deliberately making the point that the family relationships are holding religious opposites together?

There are still some people in the foregrounds whom we have not yet discussed and who cannot be made to fit into the French royal family group.

The very important figure of the dignified Knight in the "Barriers" (VII), who looks deferentially towards Anjou, is not very strongly characterised as a portrait. He is evidently a noble and significant figure, and his significance lies in his relationship towards Anjou. He might almost be an ideal portrait of a Knight looking towards his overlord, and there are not sufficient individual character traits in this dark bowed head through which to recognise it. The youth who stands behind him, however, is certainly a likeness of someone; and the young man who stands between Marguerite and Anjou in the "Elephant" (VIII) is also a portrait, though there is no member of the French royal family to fit him.

Most significant of all the unknowns are the three men in the "Journey" tapestry (V). They have been imposed onto the Caron design (XI, a) like the other portraits, but are set further back than usual, as though belonging into the imposed cavalcade going on a journey. They are dressed as though for a journey, in cloaks and mantles, and not in festival attire like the other portraits. The leading figure, leaning sadly on his heavy sword, wears a hat with an upturned brim, tipped backwards. Since costume details are always so accurately rendered by this artist one wonders whether the apparel of these three marks them out as not French. They are evidently in close connection with one another, but in no relationship that can be discerned to the other people in the tapestries. As we pass along the gallery of interconnected French royal family portraits it is always with a shock of surprise that we come upon these three. Why are these unknown yet evidently highly significant figures thrust in amongst the House of Valois and its connections by marriage? Unless the problem of their identity can be solved, we shall never know the historical meaning of the Valois Tapestries.

CHAPTER III

COSTUME AND TOPOGRAPHY

The interest of the artist of the Valois Tapestries in costume was warmly shared by his contemporaries as is apparent from the very large number of costume manuals published during the latter part of the sixteenth century. The normal costume manual consists of a series of figures, grouped under different countries, showing costumes worn by men and women and by various classes of society in these countries. The illustrations in these books tend to repeat the same types again and again rather than to make original observations. Typical of the class are the many costume manuals engraved by Abraham de Bruyn [1].

As J. Ehrmann has pointed out [2], the French costume figures (Pl. 5, a) in one of De Bruyn's manuals, published at Cologne in 1577 [3], are strongly reminiscent of costumes in the tapestries. Ehrmann compares the couple in this group with Henri III and Louise in the "Fontainebleau" tapestry (I), and in effect the costumes are very similar. The French gentleman in the fashion plate makes almost identically the same display gesture with his right hand as does Henri in the tapestry.

We would take this comparison further, and place the De Bruyn group beside the foreground figures of the "Whale" (Pl. 5, b, c). Here Marguerite and Navarre wear the court fashions; and there is another couple on the right, standing not with the court group but at a respectful distance behind it, as the smaller size of the figures shows. The woman wears a flat-topped bonnet which is exactly like that of the woman in the De Bruyn group who is holding a flower. We know from the captions to the De Bruyn group that his three figures represent respectively a French court lady and gentleman and a French merchant's wife—that is to say French fashions of different classes of society, noble and bourgeois. It is therefore clearly the explanation of the woman in the "Whale" in the flat-topped bonnet that she is dressed as a French bourgeoise, standing with her man after and behind the French court lady and gentleman. This is highly revealing as to the mentality of the artist; he is thinking in terms of a costume manual with its rows of figures showing the dress of different classes.

In 1581 there was published at Antwerp a greatly enlarged edition of De Bruyn's manual. [4] The 1577 edition had confined itself mainly to European countries but now costumes from all the four quarters of the earth—Europe, Asia, Africa, America—were included, and the European costumes were enriched by many more figures. Particularly was this the case for the French costumes; the three figures of the 1577 edition were now replaced by two plates (Pl. 6, a, b) showing a brilliant display of French costumes for women and men. The top rows give costumes for noble ladies and gentlemen; the lower rows those for bourgeois and other types including a bourgeoise of Paris wearing the flat-topped bonnet. The court costumes correspond most closely to those worn by the French foreground figures in the tapestries. Compare, for example, the noble ladies' styles (Pl. 6, a, top row) with the gowns worn by Marguerite and Louise de

Lorraine in the tapestries; and compare the styles for gentlemen (Pl. 6, b, top row) with those of the men in the tapestries. The elegant short cloak with patterned lining is worn by Navarre in the "Tournament" (II) and by Anjou in the "Elephant" (VIII). Clearly, it is upon styles for French noble ladies and gentlemen that the artist of the tapestries has imposed his portrait heads of the French royal family.

There were a few Polish costumes in De Bruyn's manual of 1577 and more of these in the edition of 1581 (Pl. 7, a). The lower row of five figures on this plate shows first a "Nobilis Polonus" in a fur-edged cap with feather, long cloak and boots; then come other ranks wearing different clothing. Looking now at the Poles in the foreground of the "Polish" tapestry (IV), we recognise here also the costume conventions. The tall figure on the left, with feathered cap, long cloak and boots is a Polish nobleman, followed by other types which are probably all variations on noble costume.

De Bruyn was also the engraver of plates for a manual, first published at Cologne in 1577, depicting riders of different countries[5] in their respective riding costumes and with horses accoutred in accordance with the various national fashions. Here are German, Belgian, French, English, Spanish, Muscovite, Turkish and many other riders. Like most of De Bruyn's work, these types are mostly derived from earlier sources. Care is taken to depict with accuracy the national methods of riding, particularly the length of the stirrup, which is short for oriental riders, and also for Polish riders, necessitating the bending of the knee, whilst western nations ride with long stirrups and fully extended leg. Compare for example the noble Polish rider (Pl. 7, b) riding with a short stirrup (and wearing a patterned robe of a cut like that of the noble Pole in the "Polish" tapestry) and the German rider (Pl. 7, c) with long stirrup and extended leg[6].

The two scenes which the artist of the tapestries added to the Caron designs are both groups of riders. In the "Quintain" (VI) he added the masquerade of riders of many nations; in the "Journey" (V) he added a cavalcade which also, perhaps, includes riders of different nationalities. The central figure is a French prince, riding with long stirrup; preceded by riders using a short stirrup. Here too, then, the artist may be thinking in terms of costume, envisaging his cavalcade as riders of different nations.

The intense interest in costumes of many countries is related to the advance in geographical studies made in the latter half of the sixteenth century. The atlas of Abraham Ortelius, the *Theatrum orbis terrarum*, first published by Plantin at Antwerp in 1570, with its wonderful maps engraved by Francis Hogenberg, was a landmark in such studies[7]. Hogenberg was also the engraver of a large geographical undertaking in which Ortelius was interested and which aimed at presenting views and plans of all the cities in the world. The first three volumes of the *Civitates orbis terrarum* by G. Braun and F. Hogenberg were published at Cologne and Antwerp between 1572 and 1581[8]. It is a fascinating experience to make a tour of all the cities of the world as they were in the late sixteenth century by turning over the pages of these books. The most attractive of the plates are those which are signed by the well known artist George Hoefnagel, a friend of Ortelius and like him a native of Antwerp.

The majority of the views and plans of the cities of the world are enlivened by groups of

a   De Bruyn, French Court and Bourgeois Costumes (p. 13)

b, c   French Court and Bourgeois Costumes in the "Whale" (p. 13)

Pl. 6

a De Bruyn, French Women's Costumes (pp. 13–14)

b De Bruyn, French Men's Costumes (pp. 13–14)

Pl. 7

a   De Bruyn, Hungarian and Polish Costumes (p. 14)

b   De Bruyn, Polish Rider (p. 14)   c   De Bruyn, German Rider (p. 14)

a, b   Plans of Chartres and Orléans with Costume Figures (p. 15)

c   G. Hoefnagel, View of Orléans with Costume Figures (p. 15)

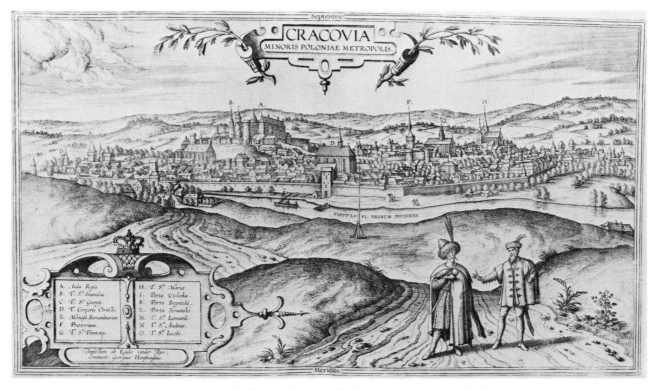

d   G. Hoefnagel, View of Cracow with Costume Figures (pp. 15–16)

human figures standing in the foregrounds. These figures are dressed in the local costumes, and the groups often show costumes for both men and women and for different classes of society. It is possible that this was something of an innovation for G. Braun draws attention to it in his preface to the first volume (1572) where he points out that figures have been introduced into the views to illustrate local customs and costumes, adding the curious reason that this has been done to prevent the Turk, whose religion prohibits the representation of the human figure, from acquiring and making use of the work to the detriment of Christendom [9]. The plates of the *Civitates orbis terrarum* show very clearly how the interest in costumes of many countries belongs into the sphere of geographical and topographical interests, for the foreground groups standing in front of the cities are like figures from a costume manual.

Let us look at a few examples of French cities. Standing on a platform in front of the plan of Chartres (Pl. 8, a) are a man and woman, the latter wearing the flat-topped bonnet of the French bourgeoise. The plan of Orléans (Pl. 8, b) has in the foreground a man and woman in French noble or court costume. The costume figures also appear in the plates which are views rather than plans, as for example in the view of Orléans (Pl. 8, c). This is signed by Hoefnagel and was probably drawn by him about 1561 when he was travelling in France; it was published in 1575 in the second volume of the *Civitates*. It is a charming view of the town on the banks of the Loire, with, in the foreground, a couple in local costume.

To see these costume figures in foregrounds and facing outwards from the picture is revealing for the Valois Tapestries. We have already seen that the foreground figures are related to costume manuals, and we now realise that their foreground placing could be related to topographical art. We feel ourselves to be drawing very near to the preoccupations and the visual formation of the artist who altered the Caron designs to form the tapestries. He saw those designs with eyes which had been trained in an entirely different milieu, the geographical milieu with its interest in costume as a part of topography. The spectators of Caron's festivals are seen by an artist accustomed to looking at costume figures in front of a view.

Consider the "Whale" tapestry (III) from this angle. Compare the bourgeoise on the right and her man, with the bourgeois couple in Hoefnagel's view of Orléans (Pl. 8, c). As we look from the Orléans view back to the "Whale" tapestry and the Caron drawing (X, a) on which it is based we learn to see how Caron's festival scene has been re-focussed in the tapestry as a naturalistic topographical view with costume figures in the foreground. We noticed earlier that the artist seemed to have consulted the description in the Bayonne *Recueil* of the island in the river which formed the setting of the festival and had taken care to make his representation of it much closer to the description than the vague Caron drawing [10]. We recognise this care now as the preoccupation of a geographically-minded artist, bent on delineating a locality correctly, and associating with a view of a place in France a row of foreground figures in French court and middle-class costumes. We now begin to understand the formal constituents of this magnificent tapestry. Based on a design by a French artist of the school of Fontainebleau, it imposes on the classicism of that design the outlook of Flemish topographical art; and the formal origin of its foreground figures is to be found in costume figures placed in front of views and plans.

Returning to the *Civitates orbis terrarum*, it is also instructive to look at its view of Cracow

(Pl. 8, d). This plate did not appear until 1618, in the sixth volume, but it was based on a design by the long dead Hoefnagel, as the inscription states. It shows figures in Polish costume in front of the city of Cracow, with its great square castle. The Polish costume figures in the "Polish" tapestry (IV) are in front of a festival at the Tuileries, but was it the topographical training of the artist which caused him to insert, in the right background, a square castle which is not in the related Caron design?

The foreground figures in the Valois Tapestries are a highly original feature to be found in no other tapestry of the period[11]. We now begin to understand something of at least one side of their formal origin. The foreground spectators of the festivals in the Caron designs have been seen anew and reformulated as costume figures in front of a view. Portrait heads have been added to these figures, and thus we arrive at foreground portraits in a landscape, as in the "Whale" (III), or in the "Fontainebleau" (I), where Henri III and Louise de Lorraine in French "noble" costume have behind them the gardens of the famous French palace with its waters. Henri's conventional fashion plate gesture betrays one of the influences behind this work in which different traditions have fused to produce something new.

We now know a good deal about the Flemish artist for whom we are seeking. He must be good at portraiture, a costume expert, and in touch with the topographical school. Yet first and foremost, of course, he must be a trained tapestry cartoonist.

CHAPTER IV

LUCAS DE HEERE

Lucas de Heere, says Carel van Mander in his lives of the northern painters[1], was born at Ghent in 1534. He learned drawing first from his father and then was apprenticed to the celebrated Frans Floris under whom he made rapid progress, particularly in making designs for glass and for tapestries which passed as being by Floris himself. He then travelled abroad and went to France, "where he executed many cartoons for tapestries for the queen, mother of the king. He went frequently to Fontainebleau where there are many fine things to see, antique figures, pictures and so on".

He excelled in portrait painting, posing his models well, and could even do portraits from memory "so much like that it was possible to recognise the personages". He painted various pictures of religious subjects for churches in Ghent and many other pictures by him, particularly portraits, existed in Van Mander's time. He would certainly have left more works behind him "if he had not lost a good deal of his time in the company of exalted personages who sought him out for the pleasure of his society, and for his talent not only as artist but as poet, for these two arts often go together. He was so highly thought of by certain princes that they gave him splendid offices".

One day, when Lucas was in England, the "admiral of London" asked him to decorate a gallery with representations of costumes of different peoples. He painted them all in their costumes, except for the Englishman whom he showed quite naked, holding various kinds of stuffs and a pair of tailor's scissors. The admiral enquired what he meant by this, and Lucas replied that he had not known what costume to give to the Englishman since he changed his fashions every day, being now attired in the French style, now in the Italian, now in the Spanish, now in the Flemish. "So I contented myself with giving him the stuffs and the utensils so that everyone can make out of them what he pleases". The admiral showed this novelty to Queen Elizabeth who remarked that it was quite right thus to satirise the changeability of the English which makes them the laughing-stock of foreigners.

Van Mander now indulges in a long digression on costume which takes up a considerable part of the biography. The English and the French are not the only peoples who can be reproached with love of change; the Flemish also copy the fashions of their neighbours. The Germans and the Swiss are more conservative. How absurd are the exaggerations of fashion! Sometimes it encourages us to have vast stomachs, hanging over our belts; sometimes it restricts us so violently that we can hardly breathe or move. Women achieve the height of the grotesque with their huge *cache-enfant* which makes it impossible to pass through a door, whilst at the same time they are pinched unnaturally at the waist. The Italians are wiser; both in ancient times and to-day they have wished to see their matrons plump and well-covered, and the women's dresses are so free that with one shake they can slip them off.

"To return to Lucas de Heere", continues Van Mander. He has left behind him a good deal of poetry, some of his own composition and some translated from the French of Marot. He also undertook to write the lives of the painters in verse, which Van Mander would have published if he could have found the manuscript[2]. He was a man of great learning and judgment, a lover of antiquities of which he had a collection. His device was an anagram of his name, "Schade leer u", which means "Misfortune teaches you". He died on August 29th, 1584, aged fifty.

Van Mander's life of Lucas de Heere presents us with a man who might very well be the artist of the Valois Tapestries. Here is a Flemish artist, thoroughly trained in the Flemish tradition of tapestry-cartoon design. His specialities are portraiture and costume. Not only does Van Mander dwell on the costume gallery which Lucas painted for the English admiral, but his curious digression in the midst of the biography shows how strongly the name of Lucas was associated in his mind with the subject of costume.

These, however, were not the points which caused G. T. van Ysselsteyn to connect Lucas de Heere with the Valois Tapestries in her book on the tapestries of the North Netherlands, published in 1936[3]. The point which she takes up is Van Mander's statement that Lucas had been in France where he had designed cartoons for tapestries for the Queen Mother. She suggests therefore, that the Valois Tapestries were amongst those designed by Lucas for Catherine de' Medici during his stay in France.

Though Van Mander knew Lucas de Heere very well indeed—he mentions that Lucas was his teacher—he is curiously vague, or purposely reticent, in the telling of his life's story. The date of his stay in France is not given; we are not told when he was in England, or why; nor are the names revealed of the "princes" who so much enjoyed his society and gave him splendid offices. In the sequence of his narrative, however, the visit to France comes very early, before Lucas' marriage; we are given the impression that it was near the beginning of his career that he was in France designing tapestries for Catherine and studying at Fontainebleau. Internal evidence has suggested the year 1582, when Anjou was reigning in Antwerp, as the most probable date for the design of the Valois Tapestries. This date falls near the end of Lucas' life, only two years before his death.

A document exists which reveals the date of Lucas' visit to France, and proves that it was in his early years as Van Mander seems to suggest. Though the existence of this document was pointed out long ago by Lionel Cust[4], it has never been used to establish the date of the visit to France.

In August, 1582, Lucas de Heere designed the decorations and wrote the welcoming verses for the state entry into his native town of a certain prince. This prince was none other than François, Duc d'Anjou, who was making his entry into Ghent as Count of Flanders and Duke of Brabant. A printed description of the entry was published in the same year, in both French and Flemish[5]; and the manuscript of the French version exists at Berlin[6]. This manuscript has illustrations which are not in the printed copies; and a dedication to Anjou signed by Lucas de Heere. This dedication is also not in the printed copies, nor has any modern student of De Heere printed it. It is as follows:

fresche manen ende vrouwe

Edel-vrouwe   *Burghers vrouwe*   *Wilde ier*

a   Lucas de Heere, Irish Costumes (p. 20)

Een burghers wijf   *Een burghers wijf*   *Een ionghe dochter*   *Een boerinne*

Lucas de Heere, English Bourgeois and Peasant Costumes
(pp. 20, 22)

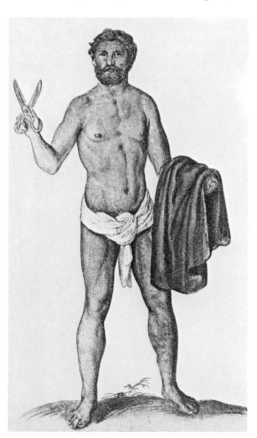

c   Lucas de Heere, Naked Englishman (p. 21)

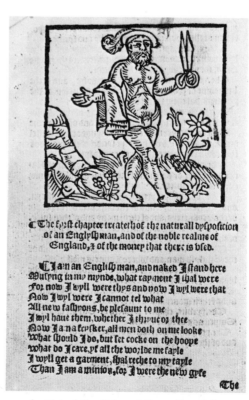

d   Naked Englishman. From Boorde's
Introduction of Knowledge (p. 21)

a   Lucas de Heere, English Gentlemen (p. 22)

b   Lucas de Heere, English Ladies (p. 22)

c   Lucas de Heere, French Demoiselle and Bourgeoise (p. 22)

d   Lucas de Heere, Polish Man and Woman (p. 22)

"A son Alteze.

Monseigneur, Me resentant obligé toute ma vie a la France, nourrice de vertu, et consequem-
ment a Vostre Alteze, pour les benefices que iy ay receu soubs la protection du feu Roy
Francois 2, vostre frere, et estant alors au seruice de la Royne vostre Mere, je me suis tant
plus volontiers employé a la charge et conduite de l'entree de V.A. en la Ville de Gand.
Et mesmes en attendant quil en soit faict un plus ample discours enrichi de figures selon
qu'elles sont pourtraites en ce liure ay faict imprimer ladicte briefue description pour donner
contentement a ceux qui sont desireux de scauoir ce qui s'est passé en ladicte entrée. Aussi
pour mieux faire cognoistre a chascun de quelle affection et integrité vostre Alteze a este
receu a ladicte ville. Et fay present a V.A. de ce mien labeur la suppliant de prendre en
bonne part et, comme procedant dun tres affectionné desir qui me commande a vous dedier
tout ce que Dieu a mis en ma puissance, pour en disposer a vostre Voulonte, tant ie prie
le Createur de preseruer vostre Alteze en toute felicité. De Gand ce   7 de
Septembre 1582

Le moindre seruiteur de Vtre Alteze

L. d'Heere"

This dedication gives us the date at which Lucas was in France. He is grateful, he tells Anjou,
for benefits received in France "under the protection of the late King François II, your brother,
when I was in the service of the Queen, your Mother". François II reigned for seventeen months,
between July 10, 1559, and December 5, 1560. It must therefore have been between these dates
that Lucas was in France designing tapestries for Catherine, when she had just entered upon
her long ascendancy as Queen Mother and he was a young man of twenty-four. This agrees
with Van Mander who implies that the French episode came early in Lucas' life.

The evidence of this dedication makes it impossible that Lucas de Heere should have designed
the Valois Tapestries for Catherine de'Medici, for if he had been working for her in recent
years, or at the time he wrote the dedication, he would surely have mentioned this to Anjou.
That he goes back to such ancient history, to the time of François II, for his reminiscences of
Catherine would seem to prove conclusively that he had not worked for her at any time after
1560.

On the other hand, the dedication reveals Lucas de Heere in exactly the milieu where all the
internal evidence suggests that the artist of the Valois Tapestries will be found, namely in the
circle of Anjou in the Netherlands in 1582. Lucas thus has a remarkably good case for qualifying
as the missing artist. He is a trained Flemish tapestry cartoonist; he is a specialist in portraits
and most particularly noted for costume; in 1582 he is found engaged in propaganda for
Anjou in the Netherlands. He had French leanings, had studied at Fontainebleau, had known
Catherine and worked for her and so would have gained some insight into her mind and tastes
and how to please her by feeding her passion for family and festivals. Surely this is the very
man who might have drawn up that survey of the French court seen from Flanders, the Valois
Tapestries.

Fortunately, though much is in doubt concerning the works of Lucas de Heere, the ones which we most need for comparison with the tapestries—namely his costume sketches—are indubitably his.

It was as a Protestant refugee that Lucas de Heere went to England, about 1567, fleeing thither like many other of his Flemish co-religionists from the proscriptions and persecutions of the tyrannical Spanish régime in the Netherlands[8]. Whilst there he wrote, between about 1573 and 1575, a treatise in Flemish on the geography, institutions, manners and customs, and history of the British Isles, entitled *Beschrijving der Britsche Eilanden*. It is illustrated by water-colour drawings of the costumes worn in the British Islands, both ancient and contemporary—ancient Britons, Irishmen, mediaeval English costumes, and contemporary types of English dress of all classes of society, knights, judges, aldermen, women's dress, and so on. The manuscript is in the British Museum[9] and it was published in full, together with an admirable introduction and notes, by T. Chotzen and A. Draak in 1937[10]. The editors suggest that the work is a kind of guide book to the country of their exile for the use of Flemish refugees. It is a remarkable product of the new schools of geographical, topographical, and local antiquarian studies; and it is a point of considerable significance for placing it that it contains a map of the British Isles which has been cut out of Ortelius' *Theatrum orbis terrarum*[11].

The illustrations reveal Lucas de Heere as a costume artist of no mean ability. They are much richer, more vigorous, and more varied than the normal run of costume manual types. Consider, for example, the Irish men and women (Pl. 9, a). Yet these and the many other striking studies belong into the sphere of costume manual conventions, as can be clearly seen in the group of four women (Pl. 9, b) depicting the costume of merchants wives, or English "bourgeoises", of an unmarried girl, and of a peasant woman with basket on arm and holding a fowl.

There is also a manuscript in Ghent University Library containing costume sketches by Lucas de Heere[12]. It contains very little text, but over one hundred and eighty water-colour drawings of figures in costumes of many countries, or indeed of all countries if we are to believe the proud claim of its title; "Theatre de tous les peuples et nations de la terre auec leurs habits, et ornemens diuers, tant anciens que modernes diligemment depeints au naturel par Luc Dheere Peintre et Sculpteur Gantois". Some of its illustrations are reproduced by Chotzen and Draak in their edition of the London manuscript by Lucas, and a few have appeared elsewhere, but the series has never been published as a whole. The Ghent "Theatre" is undoubtedly one of the most remarkable collections of sixteenth-century costume studies in existence.

It opens with Aaron as High Priest, followed by some ancient Roman costumes. Then come figures in the dress of the main European countries, Italy, Germany, Russia, Poland, (Pl 10, d) the Netherlands, France (Pl. 10, c), the British Isles (Pl. 10, a, b), Spain. Next is a set of ecclesiastical costumes and the dress of religious orders, and some figures in armour; the New World is represented only by an Eskimo, stated in an inscription to have been the one brought to Europe by Frobisher in 1576. The collection aims at showing, not only contemporary costumes but those of other times, "tant anciens que modernes". The various countries are very unevenly represented; the British Isles has by far the largest number of illustrations, no fewer than nine-

Pl. 11

b   Lucas de Heere,
Wild Scotsman (p. 21)

a   Masqueraders in the "Elephant" (p. 21)

a, b, c, d   Lucas de Heere, African, Turkish, Muscovite and German Riders (pp. 21–2)

e   The Cavalcade in the "Journey" (p. 22)

teen pages of figures; about half this number of pages are assigned to Italy, Germany, the Netherlands; Spain has seven pages; France and Turkey, five; other countries have only one or two
pages each. Many of these figures are derivative.

The Turks are the types created by Pieter Koeck van Aelst which passed through all the
costume manuals. For his antique types, Lucas had studied the illustrated work of the French
antiquarian, Guillaume du Choul [13]. The Italian section and the one on ecclesiastical costumes
are close to normal costume manual figures. As H. van de Waal has shown, the "ancient"
German costumes are related to the illustrations in a book by W. Lazius published in 1557[14].
The most interesting and apparently freshly observed of the figures are those of the British
Isles which are very like those in the London manuscript, though far more numerous.

The last picture in the series is that of the "naked Englishman" (Pl. 9, c) holding the stuff
and the tailor's scissors exactly as Van Mander describes him. From which it seems reasonable
to assume that there may be some connection between the Ghent "Theatre" and the costume
gallery which Lucas executed in England, so Van Mander tells us, for the "admiral of London",
otherwise Edward Clinton, Earl of Lincoln, and which was shown to Queen Elizabeth. The
"naked Englishman" was not, however, such a "novelty" as the admiral supposed for he had
appeared as the first wood-cut (Pl. 9, d) in an illustrated book on customs and costumes of
different countries written by Andrew Boorde and published about 1547 [15], more than ten years
before Elizabeth came to the throne. We do not know the date at which Lucas painted the
costume gallery for Admiral Clinton, and the date of the Ghent "Theatre" manuscript also
presents a puzzle, for it is dedicated to Lucas' Flemish patron, Adolphe de Wackene, who died
in 1568, yet it contains material which is certainly later than that date, for example the Eskimo
drawing which is dated 1576. Possibly, therefore, the manuscript represents a collection of
sketches which was begun before 1568 and added to in later years[16].

The London and Ghent manuscripts reveal Lucas de Heere as a costume artist of considerable
power. We have now to discover by comparison of some of the drawings in these manuscripts
with figures in the Valois Tapestries whether we can substantiate by stylistic evidence the other
lines of evidence which have pointed to Lucas as the artist.

We look first at the "Escossois Sauvage" (Pl. 11, b) from the Ghent manuscript. Though a
Scottish highlander appears in a costume manual of 1562 [17], he is of an entirely different type to
the one shown in this Lucas drawing which seems to be a new creation. It is rather a striking
figure, with the shaggy hair and beard, the heavy cloak flung over the shoulder, the tunic of
criss-cross design to suggest the plaid. In the "Elephant" tapestry, the group of wild looking
masqueraders in the left foreground (Pl. 11, a) can be certainly identified, by comparison of
their costume with that of Lucas' sketch, as intended to be "Wild Scotsmen". We would also
go further and suggest that stylistically these figures are so close to the drawing that we would
say that Lucas de Heere's was the hand which drew them.

There are several riders in the Ghent "Theatre", illustrating national differences in riding
costume, in the caparison of horses, and in modes of riding with short or long stirrups; they
are very close to figures in De Bruyn's collection of riders to which we referred in the last
chapter. We collect a little cavalcade of riders by Lucas—a German rider or "reître" (Pl. 12, d),

a Muscovite rider (Pl. 12, c), the Great Turk on horseback (Pl. 12, b), a galloping African rider (Pl. 12, a)—for comparison with the cavalcade (Pl. 12, e) in the "Journey" tapestry, or with the galloping horses in the "Elephant" (VIII).

Amongst the French costumes in the Ghent manuscript are those of a "Damoiselle et Bourgeoise" (Pl. 10, c), the latter wearing the flat-topped bonnet familiar to us from the "Whale" (Pl. 5, c). Since there are not many French costumes in the "Theatre" we add to this some of the English costumes to show Lucas as a fashion plate artist. The English ladies (Pl. 10, b) stand with hand on hip and hands linked rather like Louise de Lorraine and her sister in the "Tournament" tapestry; one of the English gentlemen (Pl. 10, a) is wearing the latest thing in velvet hats, an English dandy, the counterpart of Joyeuse in his velvet hat in the "Polish" tapestry. There is only one page of Polish figures (Pl. 10, d) in the "Theatre"; the man's costume is not quite like that of any of the Poles in the foreground of the "Polish" tapestry (IV), though the whiskered facial type can be seen amongst them.

Lucas' antique types are lively adaptations from Du Choul; we show a page from them (Pl. 13, b) for comparison with Henri III in antique costume (Pl. 13, a) in the masquerade of peoples of many countries in the "Quintain" . The sketch explains the bâton held by Henri as that of a Roman tribune.

The evidence from Lucas de Heere's costume drawings certainly does not contradict, but rather corroborates and confirms, the evidence from other quarters which points to him as the artist of the Valois Tapestries.

We saw in the last chapter that the artist of the tapestries might have hit on the idea of placing his costume portraits in the foregrounds by analogy with the foreground placing of costume figures in topographical views. Is there any evidence that Lucas de Heere was in touch with the topographical school, and therefore in a position to have had this idea suggested to him? This question can certainly be answered in the affirmative, for there are curious and close connections between some of Lucas' costume sketches and costume figures in Hoefnagel's views in the *Civitates orbis terrarum*.

This fact has already been noted, by Chotzen and Draak[18], in respect of Hoefnagel's 'Palace of Nonesuch' (Pl. 14, a). The band of figures illustrating English costumes for women of various classes was added to Hoefnagel's view of this palace, taken when he was in England in 1569[19], when it appeared in the fifth volume of the *Civitates*[20]. The peasant woman in the high-crowned hat, and holding a basket and fowls, in this row of figures is very close to Lucas de Heere's English peasant woman (Pl. 9, b). There is also a strong resemblance between the English ladies in this row and Lucas' English ladies (Pl. 10, b).

The charming view by Hoefnagel of the little town of Blamont in Lorraine (Pl. 14, b) has two women in Lorraine peasant costume in the foreground; one has a sheaf under her arm, and the other has drawn up the purse which hangs from her girdle and is fingering it. Compare these women with Lucas' old peasant woman of Lorraine (Pl. 15, b) with a sheaf under her arm and with her hanging purse drawn up in exactly the same way. The conclusion seems inescapable that there is a connection.

a   Henri III in Antique Costume in the "Quintain" (p. 22)

b   Lucas de Heere, Antique Costume (p. 22)

a   G. Hoefnagel, The Palace of Nonesuch; and English Costume Figures (p. 22)

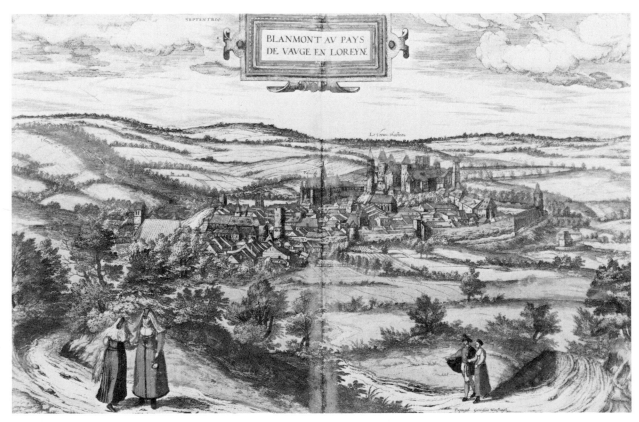

b   G. Hoefnagel, Blamont in Lorraine with Lorraine Costume Figures (pp. 22–23)

a   G. Hoefnagel, Biscaia and Spanish Costume
Figures (p. 23)

b   Lucas de Heere,
Lorraine Peasant (pp. 22–23)

c   Lucas de Heere, Women
of Bayona (p. 23)

a   Lucas de Heere, Flemish Sailors (p. 23)

b   Lucas de Heere, Men in Armour (p. 23)

c   Lucas de Heere, Dominican and Cordelier (p. 23)

d   Lucas de Heere, Monk of Grandmont and Knight of
Rhodes (p. 23)

The Blamont view appeared in the second volume of the *Civitates*, published in 1575, whence Lucas could have copied the Lorraine woman for inclusion in his "Theatre" collection. But there are also in the "Theatre" copies of Spanish costume studies by Hoefnagel in Spanish views by him which were not published until the fifth volume of the *Civitates*, which did not appear until long after Lucas' death. Compare Lucas' "Femmes de Bayona allant a la Messe" (Pl. 15, c) with the almost identical figures in one of Hoefnagel's Spanish views (Pl. 15, a). Lucas de Heere had therefore seen Hoefnagel's Spanish material long before publication, probably when the latter was in England between 1568 and 1569,[21] after his visit to Spain.

It is impossible to attempt to unravel here the meaning of these connections between Lucas' costume drawings and figures in the *Civitates orbis terrarum*.[22] It is sufficient for our purposes to have indicated that they exist, which means that Lucas must have been familiar with Hoefnagel's work, and would therefore have had every opportunity of studying the process of placing costume figures in topographical views. This makes him still more eligible as the artist of the Valois Tapestries, who may have arrived at his brilliant foreground placing of the costume portraits partly through the influence of the "costume and topography" school.

According to Van Mander, Lucas painted many portraits and was skilled in seizing likenesses, even from memory. Some of the Ghent drawings show Lucas' costume figures tending towards portraits. The "Mariniers Flamangs, Chastieurs des Espaignols" (Pl. 16, a) are dramatic figures; the bearded man might be a likeness of some real "sea beggar" noted in the struggle against Spain. These sailors have been raised from costume types into personages fraught with the stresses of contemporary history. The "Dominican" (Pl. 16, c) is more than an ecclesiastical costume figure; it is a somewhat satirical portrait. The "Knight of Rhodes" and his companion (Pl. 16, d) have character and dignity. One of the men in the study of tournament armour (Pl. 16, b) could be a sketch for a portrait, perhaps of some rather tough Elizabethan Englishman. These figures suggest for us Lucas, the costume artist, combining with Lucas, the portrait painter.

No existing painted portrait has as yet been certainly identified as the work of Lucas de Heere, with the exception of the likeness of Philip II in the "Solomon and the Queen of Sheba" (Pl. 18, a). There is, however, in his *Beschrijving der Britsche Eilanden* a tinted drawing of a half-figure of Queen Elizabeth (Pl. 17, a). This is a type of the Queen often used, as for example in Crispin de Passe's engraving of 1592; Lucas may be its creator or he may be copying it. For our purposes it is sufficient to point out that we have here a sketch, undoubtedly drawn by Lucas de Heere, in which a likeness of the Virgin Queen has been seized in outline, and lightly tinted to suggest the colours in a manner which reveals the hand practised in the tapestry cartoon technique. The dress and ruff are studied with meticulous precision. Stylistically, this drawing of Elizabeth is closely related to some of the portrait heads in the Valois Tapestries, for example the Louise de Lorraine (Pl. 1, a). It proves conclusively that Lucas de Heere could have done the business of placing the portrait heads of royal personages onto the costume figures to form the foreground portraits of the Valois Tapestries.

Though we have dwelt on the way that these portraits were put together and on the conventions which may have influenced their foreground placing, these techniques do not in themselves

Note.   Since this book went to press my attention has been drawn to the fact that the leaf of the *Beschrijving* with the portrait of Elizabeth (Pl. 17, a), and the blank leaf conjoint with it, do not have the same water-mark as that found in the rest of the volume. This may, but need not, affect the argument presented in the last paragraph of this page.

explain the most important thing about them, which is their quality. Only a gifted portrait painter, with a feeling for human beings, could have formed out of the materials at his disposal the wonderful series of figures which look out at us from the tapestries. Once more we have to fall back on Van Mander, who tells of how Lucas posed his models well, and whose gift for taking likenesses, even from memory, suggests the intuitive sympathy with his subjects of a good artist. Perhaps it may be added to Van Mander's evidence that it is thought that Lucas de Heere's influence as a teacher may have been felt by the generation of portrait painters working in England from about 1577 onwards who specialised in costume pieces.[23] If such was the nature of Lucas' influence, it might be inferred that his own practise was in the direction of costume pieces. In the costume portraits of the Valois Tapestries we may therefore perhaps see a reflection of his style as a portrait painter.

Of Lucas' style in large compositions we have some faint indications in his sketches for the decorations for Anjou's entry into Ghent in 1582. These have never been used as a stylistic basis for the attribution of works to Lucas.[24] One of these sketches (Pl. 17, b) depicts Gideon and the Angel; Gideon has that active, running motion so characteristic of many figures in the tapestries. Another (Pl. 17, c) is even more significant; Anjou, in French court attire, is standing between two conflicting armies appeasing them with a pacificatory gesture. Here we have an opportunity of studying Lucas' handling of large groups in movement and it is reminiscent of the crowds in the tapestries; we may compare it particularly with the "Elephant" (VIII) where Anjou also stands in front of many figures moving towards one another from opposite directions.

Slight though these sketches are, their stylistic evidence tends towards further confirmation of our thesis. We reserve for later discussion the study of their subject matter, which also has a bearing on the argument, since they are a glorification of the "politique" Anjou made at the same time as the tapestries which have a similar theme.

We therefore conclude that the Flemish artist who revised the Caron designs to form the Valois Tapestries was Lucas de Heere of Ghent. The possibility cannot be ruled out that he might have been assisted in this enormous work by other artists, but the main credit belongs to him. The reputation of this artist need no longer rest only on the importance attached to him by Carel van Mander in his long biography, nor on works signed with the monogram "HE" formerly attributed to him and now taken away from him. A famous masterpiece, the Valois Tapestries, is now restored to him and the way to a reassessment of him and a fresh review of other problems of attribution is open.

True, a part in the honour of the design of the Valois Tapestries belongs to Antoine Caron. Nevertheless, their most distinctive features were introduced by the Flemish artist. Lucas de Heere made a discovery when he placed costume figures evolved into portraits in front of the French festival scenes, and it is this discovery which gives the Valois Tapestries their peculiar distinction, their power to make a direct and immediate human appeal to the spectator, and to evoke timeless rêveries. Lucas was a poet as well as an artist, as Van Mander reminds us, and these figures impart to the tapestries an unforgettable poetic quality, as of seeing human beings in the setting of the world of their imagination.

b   Lucas de Heere, Gideon and the Angel, 1582 (pp. 24, 36)

a   Lucas de Heere, Queen Elizabeth I (p. 23)

c   Lucas de Heere, Anjou as Peacemaker (pp. 25, 35–6)

CHAPTER V

LUCAS DE HEERE LEADS TO WILLIAM OF ORANGE

We now have something, or rather someone, to take hold of, a guide to lead us towards the mysterious and undocumented origins of the Valois Tapestries. Let us take Lucas de Heere by the hand and accompany him for a while along the paths of his life, for these must be the paths which will lead, in the end, to the hour and the circumstances which gave birth to the tapestries.

When Lucas was a youth, the peoples of the Netherlands were still living in the old opulent traditions of the Duchy of Burgundy, and Charles v, who loved his Burgundian provinces more than any other part of his vast realms, wore the imperial crown. As the pupil of Frans Floris, whose studio was in Antwerp, Lucas would have seen that life at its richest. Floris, who had studied in Italy and belonged to the new Italianate school of Flemish art, kept open house and great Burgundian noblemen and knights of the Order of the Golden Fleece, amongst them the Prince of Orange and Counts Egmont and Horn, often came to drink with him.[1] Those were the days in which young Lucas de Heere might first have seen William of Orange.

The first years of Lucas' life [2] as a practising artist are somewhat of a blank, which used to be filled with the supposition that he paid an early visit, or visits, to England. This rumour should not be dismissed without careful examination of the pages in the *Beschrijving der Britsche Eilanden* in which he shows a curiously detailed knowledge of events in England in the reigns of Edward vi, Lady Jane Grey, Mary, and early Elizabeth.[3] In 1559, however, his presence at Ghent is attested. In July of that year, a chapter of the Order of the Golden Fleece was held at Ghent. Philip ii was now lord and master of the Netherlands but had not yet shown his hand and the horrors to come were still undreamed of. The chapter was attended by most of the main actors in the future tragedy. Philip himself was present at it; also the Duke of Alva. Amongst the noblemen of the Netherlands who attended were William of Orange and Egmont and Horn, the two unfortunates whose execution was later to inaugurate Alva's reign of terror. Decorations for this chapter, which was held in the cathedral of St. Bavon, were undertaken by Lucas de Heere and his father.[4] Coats-of-arms still to be seen on the cathedral walls are said to have been painted by Lucas, and a manuscript in Brussels relating to this chapter has been associated with his name.[5] His painting of "Solomon and the Queen of Sheba" (Pl. 18, a) in St. Bavon, which is signed *Lucas Derus inv. fecit* 1559, probably also relates to this occasion for Solomon is a portrait of Philip ii. This was perhaps not the first time that Lucas had painted Philip.[6] The picture is not without charm, and is interesting for its evidence of the influences operating on Lucas as an artist. On the one hand, it is closely related, particularly for the figure of the Queen of Sheba with her gesticulating hands, to a treatment of this subject by his master Frans Floris; on the other hand, in the idea of turning Solomon into a portrait and in parts of the composition, this work presents striking analogies with the design by Holbein in which Solomon is Henry viii.[7]

This chapter at Ghent was, as it turned out, the last chapter of the famous Order founded by the great Duke of Burgundy which was ever held. There, in St.Bavon, were Philip II, Alva, William of Orange, Egmont and Horn, all together and arrayed as Knights of the Golden Fleece—a scene marking the end of an era and containing within it the seeds of the terrible future.

It was presumably at some time after this that Lucas went to France to work as designer of tapestries for Catherine de' Medici, since, as we now know,[8] his stay in France took place in the reign of François II (July 10, 1559 to December 5, 1560). It was thus the early Catherine whom Lucas had known personally, Catherine as she was when she was first a widow, at a time before that of any of the festivals shown in the tapestries, none of which are earlier than the reign of Charles IX. In that time, Catherine, suddenly and unexpectedly confronted with responsibility, was feeling her way towards a personal policy of her own.

Her late husband, Henri II, had initiated the repression of heresy by forcible measures, in which he was supported by his ardently Catholic mistress, Diane de Poitiers. William of Orange relates in his Apology that when out hunting one day with Henri II, the French King revealed to him a secret plan for the extermination of all heretics in the Netherlands and in France, to which Orange listened in silence, without revealing his disgust.[9] His famous epithet of "William the Silent" is said to derive from this story, which typifies his extreme dislike of religious persecution in any form.

Even during Henri's lifetime, it was rumoured that his wife was more tolerantly disposed, and after his death Catherine seemed to be developing considerable leanings towards the Reform party.[10] She encouraged psalm singing in French, and even allowed it to be suggested in a letter to her that her husband's accidental death at the tournament was a judgment upon him for his persecution of the Gospel. Meanwhile the Guises—the first generation of troublesome Guises, the uncles of the young king's wife, Mary Stuart—were all for continuing the persecution policy with increased zeal. The Catherine whom Lucas de Heere had seen and watched was the young Queen Mother, who allowed herself to be exhorted to merit divine benediction by singing the "beaux psalmes Davidiques" and daily reading of the Gospel, a Catherine distinctly recalcitrant towards the extermination policy for heretics and working with the "politique" chancellor, Michel de l'Hôpital, though carefully watching her step in the Guise-infested labyrinth of the French court.

We do not know at exactly what date Lucas returned to Ghent. He was now married, and his wife was a Protestant. It has been suggested that this was the cause of Lucas' own change of faith[11], but it would seem equally probable that it was through having himself already become a Protestant that he met his wife. A manifestation of his views was his publication, in 1565, of a Flemish translation of the French psalms of Clément Marot. He also wrote an introduction to the psalms of Peter Dathenus, a fanatical camp preacher who was drawing thousands of listeners to his open-air sermons against "idolatry" in these years.

Lucas, however, had too many other interests to become fanatical. His literary side was in full play and he was writing a good deal of Flemish poetry. He was a member of the Chamber of Rhetoric known as "Jesus with the Balsam Flower",[12] another member of which was Abraham

Ortelius, whom he could thus have known well in Ghent. It was among the duties of the Netherlands Chambers of Rhetoric to assist in the design of local pageantries and festivities. In 1562, the dashing and popular Count Egmont brought down the popinjay at the annual shoot of the Guild of the Cross-Bowmen of St. George. There were rejoicings in Ghent, including water-tourneys on the canals. Documents in the town archives prove that Lucas de Heere and his father were employed for these festivities, and received payment for judging the water-tourneys.[13] It was thus an expert in water-tourneys who adapted the Caron design for the "Fontainebleau" tapestry, even though he had probably not seen with his own eyes any of the major French festivals. The young queen of France, Louise de Lorraine, who reigns with such high distinction and elegance in this tapestry was, strange to say, the niece (through her mother) of Lamoral Egmont, who little knew what the future held in store for him when the town of Ghent, with the aid of Lucas de Heere, was *en fête* in 1562 over his popinjay triumph.

Lucas' life and movements in these years are not very clearly or consecutively documented: possibly the volume of Flemish poetry which he dedicated to Adolphe de Wackene (the patron to whom the Ghent "Theatre" is also dedicated) in 1565 might yield more information. He certainly kept his school of art in Ghent at some time during this period; it was being attended by Carel van Mander in 1566.[14]

The times were very troubled. The iconoclastic outburst of 1566 was followed by the arrival, in 1567, of the Duke of Alva to practise the extermination policy on the Netherlands. The names of Lucas de Heere and his wife were on the proscription lists as heretics and they fled to England.

Now begins the certain and documented visit of Lucas de Heere to England. He was certainly here by 1567, when his name appears in the registers of the Dutch Church in Austin Friars[15], and may have arrived a little earlier[16]. At the Dutch Church he would meet the numerous colony of Flemish refugees in London. He seems to have been thrown particularly into contact with the Antwerp world in exile. He knew the Antwerp merchants Emanuel van Meteren, the historian, and Jan Radermacher (or Rotarius), who were both refugees in London.[17] The former was a relative of Ortelius; the latter, a close friend of Hoefnagel. Emanuel van Meteren kept an *album amicorum* in which his friends signed their names, wrote verses, and drew their devices. This album is in the Bodleian Library,[18] and its pages introduce us to the friends of Lucas de Heere. The signature and device of Ortelius is followed by those of Georg Hoefnagel; next comes the device of Lucas de Heere, a singing Siren, together with a poem on the anagram of his name "Schade leer u". Then come Henry Goltzius, Jan Radermacher, Marnix de Sainte Aldegonde, the close friend and adviser of William of Orange, and Philip Galle, the Antwerp engraver and print-dealer. Radermacher, or Rotarius, also kept an *album amicorum*, now in Ghent University Library,[19] in which there are several poems by Lucas, one being addressed to Thomas Gresham in honour of his foundation of the Royal Exchange. Gresham was the principal English agent for business transactions with Antwerp.

Three specimens of Lucas' device of the Siren are known. He drew it for Emmanuel van Meteren in the album already referred to; he also drew it in the album of Joannes Vivianus[20];

and another example (Pl. 18, b) is addressed to Georg Hoefnagel, and gives as the Latin version of his motto "Damna docent." The Siren is surrounded by ship-wrecked drowning men, whilst the ship of Ulysses is seen safely passing through the danger. We have chosen to reproduce this version of the device here, both because it is the most pleasing of the three examples and also because it affords final evidence of close contact and friendship between Lucas de Heere and Georg Hoefnagel. It was drawn, as the inscription states, in London in August, 1576.

Rather an unusual feature of Lucas' Siren is the man clinging to its tail; this motif is also present, though less obviously, on one of the other versions of the device. On the stern of the barge (Pl. 29, a) in the "Whale" tapestry there is a Siren holding a lute and with a figure clinging to its tail. The formal resemblance of this tiny decoration to Lucas' Siren is most striking. It is almost as though he is signing himself with his device on the tapestry.

The presence of the Flemish artist, Lucas de Heere, in England has given rise in the past to a mass of conjecture, and the many portraits and other works signed with the monogram "HE" were once assigned to him. Since Cust's article of 1912, the "HE" pictures have been attributed to Hans Eworth, an artist who is not mentioned by Van Mander and of whose work nothing is known, though his existence is attested by some entries in an English inventory and by a few other documents. The problem of the "HE" pictures is much too complicated a one to enter upon here, but it may be pointed out that, though the dating of the pictures seems to present difficulties in respect of Lucas de Heere, we have in his case known work which might be used for purposes of attribution, a good deal of literary material which has not been fully explored, and a known patron, Clinton, whose career and affiliations might provide a useful base for a new attack on the question of what artistic work Lucas did in England.

We can at least be certain of one work which he did in England; he painted the gallery of costumes, with the "naked Englishman" in it, for Clinton and which was shown to Queen Elizabeth. The full publication of the Ghent "Theatre", and examination of its problems, might throw some further light on this. Clinton is revealed as the employer of painters to decorate a banqueting-house for the reception of Elizabeth on her summer progress of 1559 by an entry in Henry Machyn's diary[21]. It appears from the Revels Accounts that this banqueting-house, evidently a temporary structure, was at Horsley in Surrey[22], where Clinton is known to have resided.[23] The date 1559 is earlier than that at which Lucas is supposed to have been in England; moreover it seems to conflict with his known presence at Ghent in that year. Nevertheless, though it seems unlikely that it can have been for the Horsley banqueting-house of 1559 that the costume gallery was painted, we learn from it that it may have been for some such state visit of the Queen to the Admiral that Lucas was employed to show his skill as a costume artist.[24]

It was probably not only as an artist that Lucas employed his skills in England, but also as a poet and designer of shows for entries, progresses and the like, and of masquerade costumes for revels and tournaments. A minor occupation which he evidently enjoyed was the painting of *impresa* shields for tournaments, since he took the trouble of introducing into the "Tournament" tapestry devices on the shields (Pl. 22) which were not in the corresponding drawing.

At the English court, the cultivation of the decorative pastimes of chivalry was pursued

a   Lucas de Heere, Solomon and the Queen of Sheba, 1559 (pp. 23, 25)

b   Lucas de Heere, Siren Device, 1576 (p. 28)

with as much fervour as in France. At the Accession Day Tilts, the knights assumed various characters; to these their devices corresponded, and also the costumes of the pageants of servitors who accompanied them.[25] There are indications that masquerade costumes of various countries were sometimes a feature of these tilts. An eye-witness account of an Accession Day Tilt in 1584 states that the tilters entered the tilt-yard, which adjoined the palace of Whitehall at Westminster, in pairs; trumpets or other musical instruments sounded as they entered. The combatants had their servants clad in various colours. Some of the servants were disguised like savages; others like "wild Irishmen".[26]

This tilt took place long after Lucas de Heere had left England, yet, when we look at his "Wild Irish" and "Wild Scottish" costume drawings, we may wonder whether the work on costume which he did in England may not have been a source of inspiration for English masqueraders. We have seen that his "Wild Scotsman" is transformed into a masquerader in the "Elephant" tapestry. Such figures might similarly have been copied for masquerade costumes in England.

Whilst Lucas was in England, the revolt of the Netherlands from the Spanish tyranny under the leadership of William of Orange was taking place on the other side of the water. The exile followed events abroad with passionate interest, as is revealed by the record of contemporary history at the end of the *Beschrijving der Britsch Eilanden*. This chronicle, which reads almost like a news-letter, breaks off suddenly at the end of the year 1574. The more striking entries are in larger script. Amongst those given head-line prominence are the execution of Egmont and Horn, and leading events in the subsequent campaigns of Orange and his brother, Louis of Nassau, against Alva. As an example of these urgent head-lines, we quote the following:

"COUNT LODOVIC AND COUNT CHRISTOPHER, THE PALSGRAVE'S SON, WITH OTHER GERMAN NOBLEMEN CAME OVER THE RHINE TO GOVIC."[27]

There was a misprint in this stop-press, for, as the editors note, "Govic" should be "Mook". The entry records the attempted liberating invasion of the Netherlands by Louis of Nassau ("Count Lodovic") in 1573; he was accompanied by Christopher, a German Protestant prince, the son of the Protestant Elector Palatine ("Count Christopher, the Palsgrave's son"). The campaign was to be a disastrous failure, for Louis of Nassau was defeated by the Spaniards at the Battle of Mook, or Mookderheyde, and there lost his life; there perished with him his brother Henry, and the German Count Christopher. The loss of his brother Louis was both a heavy personal blow to William of Orange and also crippling to the cause of the liberation of the Netherlands, for Louis was his ablest captain.

Lucas also shows deep interest in events in France, which had a close bearing on the fortunes of the Netherlands. Amongst entries in his news diary given head-line prominence are the pact of the King of France (Charles IX) with the French Protestants in 1570; the engagement of the King of Navarre to the King of France's sister (Marguerite de Valois) in 1572; and later in the same year the attack on Coligny made during their wedding "feeste", which was followed by massacres of Protestants in Paris and other French cities.[28]

Lucas might indeed have heard a good deal at first hand about that disastrous "feeste". His patron, Clinton, now Earl of Lincoln, was the head of the special English embassy which arrived in Paris in June, 1572, to confirm the league between Elizabeth and Charles ix. Philip Sidney went with this embassy, and he, with Clinton and the rest, therefore saw the wedding festivals, their interruption by the attack on Coligny and the subsequent horrors of the Massacre of St. Bartholomew's Night. There exists in the Bibliothèque Nationale in Paris a list of the members of this embassy, dedicated to Charles ix, headed by the name of Edward Clinton, Earl of Lincoln, and including that of Philip Sidney.[29] It is embellished with painted coats-of-arms of the leading members. It is not impossible that Clinton might have used the services of Lucas de Heere for painting the coats-of-arms on this list for presentation to the King of France; we know that Lucas had experience in such work. However that may be, when the embassy returned to England it spread the news of the shocking events in Paris, the treacherous reversal to the extermination policy by those who, just previously, had been treating with the French Protestants, with the Queen of England, and with Louis of Nassau. It is important for the understanding of the Valois Tapestries to know that Lucas de Heere in England might have been in touch with some of those who had been present at the deadly Parisian festivals of August, 1572.

We now come to evidence of actual contact between William of Orange and Lucas de Heere; in July, 1576, Orange wrote a letter to Lucas. In it he says that he has heard from Marnix de Sainte Aldegonde of Lucas' affection for himself and of his zeal for their common cause. He asks Lucas to deliver a private message to Walsingham concerning the enterprise against the town of Nieuport. The letter never reached Lucas because it was intercepted by the Spaniards but a copy of it exists in the Brussels archives.[30] Marnix de Sainte Aldegonde had been in London just previously, where he must have been in touch with Lucas. In the Rotarius album at Ghent there is a letter from Marnix to Lucas, dated 1576. It is an affectionate letter in verse, containing a poem on the psalms and another on a silver cup which Marnix had given to Lucas.[31] Evidently Lucas is a trusted friend of the right-hand man of William of Orange who has recommended him to the Prince himself.

In October, 1576, there occurred one of the most ghastly of all the horrors which had fallen upon the Netherlands, namely the appalling sack of Antwerp by the Spaniards, accompanied by nameless cruelties, and which reduced the great and opulent city to a smoking ruin. The news of the "furie espagnole" in Antwerp must have profoundly shaken the Flemish refugees in London. Nevertheless, it marked a turning point for the better in the fortunes of William of Orange, for it was the last cruel throw of a defeated enemy. The Spaniards began to retreat from the country which they had ruined but not subdued. Orange, whose hold on the freed northern provinces of Holland and Zeeland was secure, now began to acquire great influence in the southern provinces of Flanders and Brabant who were accepting him as leader. The Sack of Antwerp drew Catholic and Protestant inhabitants of the Netherlands together as never before in determination to throw off the hated rule of Spain.

It has been said of William of Orange that, in the midst of the violence of religious passions by which he was surrounded, he always remained faithful to Erasmian tolerance and to the gentler religious attitudes of the earlier humanist generation[32]. He disapproved of the sectarianism of the "Gueux", and of the Protestant clergy and refugees by whom he was surrounded. Even after his profession of Calvinism in 1573, religious liberty remained his ideal. He was faithful to this ideal from personal conviction and also because it was indispensable for his aim of welding together in national unity the Catholics and Protestants of the Netherlands.

At the time when the national resentment against Spain had reached boiling point, after the "furie espagnole", an accord of union between Protestants and Catholics of the Netherlands was drawn up. Peace, accord, and unity were sworn by the contracting provinces who were to make a common effort to free the land from the intolerable Spanish yoke; this treaty was proclaimed at Ghent in November, 1576, and was known as the Pacification of Ghent. It was a kind of truce of religion which allowed freedom of worship to both religious parties, though without expressing as fully as William of Orange would have wished the principle of religious toleration.[33] He earnestly tried in the following years to make it work by discouraging both Catholic and Protestant manifestations of intolerance.

It was at the time of the Ghent Pacification that Lucas de Heere returned to his native land and his native city.[34] Perhaps he went back in answer to a call from Orange and Marnix, for we know that at some time after his return he was in their employment. A taxation list in the Ghent town archives, dated 1585, describes Lucas de Heere as (in the French translation of the entry) "greffier de la chambre des comptes et pensionnaire du prince d'Orange et de Sainte-Aldegonde."[35] This statement constitutes all that is known about these appointments. The registers of the accounts of the House of Nassau during this period are lost, [36] so there seems little possibility of discovering further evidence about Lucas de Heere as "pensioner" of William of Orange or at what date he received this appointment. Even more impossible is it to trace records of his employment by Marnix de Sainte Aldegonde, nor is it clear whether the office of "greffier de la chambre des comptes" is distinct from those of "pensioner" to Orange and to Marnix. But the information is enough to prove what mainly concerns us here, the contact between Lucas and William of Orange which we now know actually took the form of a paid position. We ought no doubt to connect these appointments, as Hymans and others do, with Van Mander's remark in his life of Lucas concerning those "high personages" who sought him out for the pleasure of his society, and with his statement that "he (Lucas) was so highly thought of by certain princes that they gave him splendid offices." [37]

One of his first tasks after his return (whether or not already officially in Orange's service) was to design the decorations and compose the speeches for that Prince's entry into Ghent in December, 1577. In the description of this entry, published at Ghent in 1578, [38] Lucas de Heere is named as the author, working in connection with the Chamber of Rhetoric "Jesus with the Balsam Flower". It must have taken him back to the old pre-Alva days and the triumphs for poor Egmont.

The themes of this entry reflect the new hopes inspired by the Pacification of Ghent. William of Orange as the national champion was presented in the character of the Hebrew patriot,

Judas Maccabaeus, attired in full armour.[39] Patriotism, Freedom, Mercy, Diligence banished Murder, Rapine, and Treason. The Inquisition was a lean and hungry hag. The lady representing the Pacification had linked to her Catholicism and Protestantism bound lovingly together by a chain of seventeen links, the seventeen provinces of the Netherlands.[40] She presented the Prince with a heart of pure gold on which was inscribed *Sinceritas*.

No one since Motley in his *Dutch Republic*[41] seems to have paid any attention to this entry, and he regards it with amused contempt. Yet where else in all the propagandist art of the sixteenth century, in all the triumphal entries, will one find—not one *Veritas* triumphant over another and crushing it underfoot—but both *veritates* tolerated?[42] Catholicism and Protestantism bound lovingly together! It is unheard of. Yet this was the imagery with which Lucas de Heere welcomed William of Orange to Ghent in 1577.

We next hear of Lucas as the author of a Flemish translation of Philippe du Plessis-Mornay's *Traité de l'Eglise*, published in 1580 at Antwerp with a dedication to the Prince of Orange.[43] Lucas would have known the famous French Protestant theologian in London, whither he had fled from Paris after the Massacre, and he was at this time in the Netherlands in Orange's circle. The extremely liberal theology of Mornay, which was influenced by currents running from the religious syncretism of earlier humanism, is of importance for the theological background of the Pacification. Lucas had earlier shown an interest in Anglican theology, as is evident from the *Beschrijving der Britsche Eilanden*, paying particular attention to the works of Bishop John Jewel whom he greatly admired and seems to have known personally.[44] It was thus not without meditation on religious questions that Lucas arrived at the position which enabled him to support Orange's policy of toleration.

We have now reached the time when François, Duc d'Anjou, begins to loom large on the European horizon as the "politique" man of destiny. William of Orange and the Estates had for long been negotiating with him; but Catherine and Henri III had tried to prevent him from accepting the proffered position in the Netherlands which they feared might involve them in war with Spain. But now Anjou's affairs seemed to be prospering. It seemed possible that this "politique" prince might become the Catholic husband of the Protestant Queen of England; and Orange and his friends were awaiting his arrival in the Netherlands to take up the titles of Count of Flanders and Duke of Brabant in the atmosphere of the Pacification.

The ridicule which pursues Anjou in history for having been jilted by Elizabeth and the utterly contemptible character which revealed itself in the collapse of his career in the Netherlands, have caused it to be forgotten that there was a time when a good many serious thinkers and able people believed in him. William of Orange believed in him, or rather he believed in the necessity of replacing Philip II, who had been solemnly abjured by the Estates as their sovereign, by the representative of some other European power.[45] He was convinced that the hard won momentary independence of the southern provinces could not be maintained by his and their efforts alone. The Spanish Monarchy would not for long suffer the indignity of this rebuff and the Spanish forces were already reamassing under the generalship of the Duke of Parma. It was essential that the provinces should be placed under the protection of some other great European Monarchy. Whatever he was personally, dynastically Anjou was a very great man—brother of the King of France and heir to the French throne. It was François as brother of the King of France and presumably able to rely on the full support of his family that Orange wished to see installed as Count of Flanders and Duke of Brabant, and it is not too much to say that the whole project of establishing this French prince as titular sovereign in the Netherlands was the invention of William the Silent and carried through by his influence alone against considerable opposition.

Moreover, Anjou had built himself up as a "politique".[46] The edict of 1576, which allowed remarkable privileges to Protestants, owed something to his negotiation and marked a cessation of the wars of religion which was called the "Peace of Monsieur" after him. This Catholic French prince was supposed to have had nothing to do with the Paris Massacre, which had blackened the name of his brother Charles IX, and he was on good terms with Navarre and the French Protestants. Liberal Protestants, like Hubert Languet and Du Plessis-Mornay, belonged to his circle in which a very liberal religious outlook was represented by Jean Bodin.[47] All these were serious and very learned men. Thoughtful people at this hour in history—looking at what the wars of religion had done to France and the Netherlands—were wondering whether, since the extermination policy had obviously failed, there was no way of escape from these suicidal conflicts. If a prince with a great name were willing to lend that name to the liberal party, such serious people might well have been willing to turn a blind eye to defects in his character—his overweening vanity, egotism, and ambition, his tendencies to moral depravity.

Though empty and superficial as compared to his brothers—lacking both the melancholy passion of Charles IX and the profound intellectual subtlety of Henri III—François was not deficient in the Valois culture and the Valois intelligence. He maintained an academy of poets and musicians,[48] and was able, it seems—in spite of his repulsive appearance—to exercise considerable charm. His brilliant sister Marguerite adored him, nor was Elizabeth of England quite impervious. He must have been able to give the impression of having more in him than he had, and the serious-minded would tend—through wishful thinking—to see in him more than was there. How else can one explain the fact that a man like Marnix de Sainte Aldegonde could write a glowing account of Anjou's character to the Estates in 1580, telling them that in this prince "lies our deliverance, and we have in him the means at hand for escaping for ever from the insupportable Spanish yoke and restoring to our country its former bloom and prosperity." [49]

An Anjou married to the Queen of England would have been a still more desirable acquisition from the point of view of William of Orange, for such a match would join in one the two allies whom he most needed. In the winter of 1581, Anjou was in England courting the Queen and appearing to make great progress. Marnix was with him, anxiously watching the ill-assorted lovers, and hoping against hope that the match would come off. Impressed by the Queen's significant gift of a ring to her suitor, Marnix wrote a letter to the Estates prematurely announcing the engagement and suggesting that the happy event should be celebrated with public rejoicings.[50] Probably as a result of this letter, Orange, who was then in Ghent, publicly announced there, on November 26th, 1581, the betrothal of Elizabeth and Anjou and also the recognition by the Estates of Anjou as sovereign in place of Philip of Spain.[51] The rejoicings, as described by a contemporary diarist[52], seem to have consisted mainly in showing to the people a very large allegorical picture. A virgin, representing the Netherlands, turned her back on Philip and Cardinal Granvelle and their priests and monks, and gave herself to the French prince and his captains. Near the King of Spain and his army was an array of wheels and other instruments of torture used by the Inquisition. There does not seem to have been much about Queen Elizabeth in the picture, unless there was a fusion of her virgin imagery with the virgin of the Netherlands.[53]

On the good grounds that Lucas de Heere was the man for such things in Ghent, De Busscher supposed that he was the artist of this picture. This was almost certainly the case, and we begin to perceive in what capacity Lucas was of value to Orange. It was as a propagandist, an artist trained in the organisation of public shows. It was essential to persuade the people to accept the new régime. Marnix de Sainte Aldegonde had always been Orange's publicist, and the rôle of Lucas as "pensioner" to Orange and Marnix probably included the exercise of his various skills in "putting across" the new French ruler. Themes which he had seen used, or had perhaps used himself, of that anti-Spanish Virgin, Queen Elizabeth, in England, might also have been applicable to a build-up of Anjou in the Netherlands. Like her, he could be presented to the people as bringing the blessings of peace instead of the horrors of war.

At last, on February 19th, 1582, came the great day of the triumphal entry of the new Duke into Antwerp, fully described and illustrated in the handsome record of it published by Plantin.[54] The decorations of the streets of Antwerp for Anjou's entry were paid for by the city, and executed by the city artist, Peter Leys, assisted by Vredeman de Vries.[55] They harped one and all on the theme that the Spanish tyranny was now replaced by the gentle rule of the new Duke. The Maiden of Antwerp wore a laurel crown in token of victory over the King of Spain and deliverance by means of the French prince; beside her was Religion holding the open book of the Law and the Gospel. Saul and David typified the removal of the sovereignty of the Netherlands from the unworthy King of Spain and its bestowal on a new David. The Giant of Antwerp (Pl. 19, d) let fall the arms of Spain and raised those of France as the Duke passed. The monster of Tyranny was subdued by Concordia. Apollo and the Muses drove Discord, Violence, and Tyranny into a cave. An elephant (Pl. 19, c) which had formerly worshipped the moon, now turned itself towards the sun of the new ruler.

It was the sight of this elephant, which he compared to the one in the "Elephant" tapestry (VIII) where Anjou stands in the foreground, which suggested to J. Ehrmann his fruitful hypothesis that there is a connection between the Valois Tapestries and Anjou's entry into Antwerp.[56]

There is no mention of Lucas de Heere in the *Joyeuse Entrée*, but this does not preclude the possibility that he may have helped to devise the themes or to write the text. The plates in the book were almost certainly engraved by Abraham de Bruyn, who was paid by Plantin for colouring the illustrations in some copies.[57]

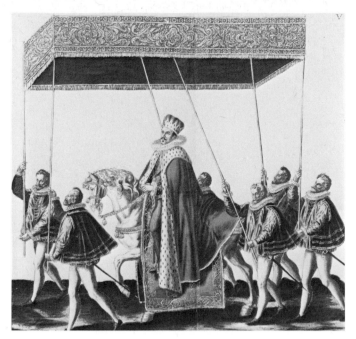

a Anjou at his Entry into Antwerp
From *La Joyeuse Entrée*, 1582 (pp. 35, 95)

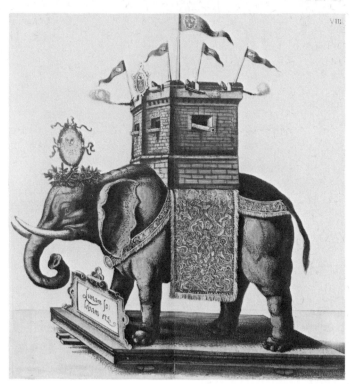

c The Elephant at the Antwerp Entry
From *La Joyeuse Entrée* (pp. 34, 36, 95)

b Lucas de Heere, Anjou at his Entry into Ghent, 1582 (p. 35)

d The Giant at the Antwerp Entry. From *La Joyeuse Entrée* (pp. 34, 95)

Six months after his entry into Antwerp, Anjou made a formal entry into Ghent, the decorations for which were designed by Lucas de Heere, as discussed in the last chapter where we used two of them (Pl. 17, b, c) as stylistic evidence for Lucas as designer of the Valois Tapestries.[58] In the dedication of the manuscript copy to Anjou (quoted in full above),[59] Lucas expresses the hope that the unillustrated text of the Ghent entry which he had already published would be followed by an illustrated edition, reproducing his designs. The splendid illustrated edition of the Antwerp entry had probably already appeared, and Lucas no doubt thought that the Ghent entry deserved similar honours. His drawing of Anjou entering Ghent (Pl. 19, b) is strongly reminiscent of the illustration in the *Joyeuse Entrée* which shows him riding into Antwerp (Pl. 19, a).

In the preface to the reader before the Ghent entry, which appears in both the manuscript and the printed copies, we are told that before leaving England, in December, 1581, Anjou had sent to say that he would visit Ghent. Preparations were then made for his entry "employant à ceste fin Lucas d'Heere & aultres pour ordonner & designer quelques patrons & projects propres." Lucas must therefore have begun to work on the entry at nearly the same time that he was celebrating with his allegorical picture the—unfortunately premature—announcement of the betrothal of Anjou to Elizabeth.

The title-page of the manuscript of the Ghent entry shows a view of low countries from which a sun is dispelling the clouds, alluding to Anjou's device of a sun dispersing clouds with the motto *Fovet et discutit*. This device and its application to Anjou as a sun chasing the clouds from the Netherlands recurs throughout the entry. The first of Lucas' sketches for the main decorations shows the virgin or "Pucelle" of Ghent seated on a dais with attendant maidens and wearing a gown covered with French fleur-de-lys in token of her new loyalty. Next comes the allusion to Anjou himself as a young man smartly dressed in French court style standing between two armies of angry combatants whom he is appeasing with the gesture of his outstretched arms (Pl. 17, c). The meaning of this picture is made quite clear by the text which explains that it alludes to how peace was made between the King of France and those of the reformed religion by Anjou, here represented as a young man standing between two armies about to fight and pronouncing these words: —

> Cesse d'ainsi combattre & soyez bons amis
> Sans faire a vos despens rire vos ennemis.

Anjou is then addressed as follows: —

> Ta prudence celeste a reuny les coeurs
> Des Francois tous bouillans en guerre paricide
> La Flandre attend de toy comme de son Alcide
> Un pareil benefice, & fin de ses malheurs.

It is an appeal to the people to cease from conflict, and to Anjou to exercise in Flanders the same pacificatory influence that he has shown in the French wars of religion. Nothing could show more clearly that it was his reputation as a French "politique" which made Anjou a suitable representative of the Ghent Pacification. The next sketch shows Concordia seated on a throne, spurning with her banner the arms and crown of Spain and attended by heralds wearing tabards with the lions of Flanders and Brabant. Then comes the picture of Gideon and the Angel (Pl. 17, b),alluding to Gideon as patriot and deliverer of the people of Israel and adjuring Anjou to follow his example with the words "Fay comme Gedeon". Gideon, as no one in Ghent was likely to have forgotten, was a patron of the Order of the Golden Fleece; he symbolised Anjou as knight and deliverer. Antique figures on prancing horses and with Roman standards who are delivering the lady Flanders expressed the same theme on another of the theatres.

It will be noticed that Lucas has applied to Anjou the themes of Biblical champion and peace-bringer from the wars of religion, which he used of Orange himself at his entry into Ghent in 1577. This transference of his own rôle to the French prince would have been warmly approved by Orange, who during all this time kept himself in the background, trying by all means in his power to induce the people to accept the ruler he had chosen for them as worthier than himself to be the focus of their affections and loyalty.

The comparison of Lucas' composition showing Anjou appeasing the fighting armies (Pl. 17, c) with the "Elephant" tapestry (VIII) is highly suggestive. If stylistically the comparison of this sketch with the tapestry is significant, it is also revealing from the point of view of content. Turning from the "politique" Anjou of Lucas' sketch, standing quietly between the fighting armies, to the "Elephant" tapestry, where he stands in front of the fighting masqueraders, one cannot but feel that the same mind is behind both these compositions. Combining this with Ehrmann's comparison with the elephant in the Antwerp entry (Pl. 19, c), who is saluting Anjou as its rising sun, the conclusion seems inescapable that the "Elephant" tapestry reflects propaganda about Anjou as the "politique" peace-bringer to the Netherlands.

In the other Anjou tapestry, the "Barriers" (VII), an ideal knight figure turns deferentially towards Anjou and seems to be handing him his helmet; we now wonder whether this scene may reflect transference to Anjou of the "knight deliverer from tyranny" theme, and again betray the mind of Lucas de Heere as designer of the Anjou propaganda.

All is not yet explained in these two tapestries.[60] Yet our policy of following whither Lucas de Heere might lead us has been a profitable one. It has led us to the point where he is found doing artistic propaganda for Anjou in the Netherlands which has both stylistic and notional correspondence with the tapestries, and that at about the time when they were probably being designed. Combined with all the other evidence amassed in the preceding chapter, this makes us feel more confident than ever that we are on right lines.

We know that Lucas de Heere was in the paid employment of William of Orange and Marnix de Sainte Aldegonde, and we have strongly suspected that an important part of his work for them consisted in helping as an artist and designer with propaganda for the new régime which they had established. Now comes a piece of direct evidence that Lucas was employed by Orange *as an artist*. The source is Carel van Mander, though not in his life of Lucas.

In his brief notice of an obscure painter called Cornelius Enghelrams, of Malines, Van Mander makes this statement:

"At Antwerp, (Enghelrams) painted for the Prince of Orange, in a room in the castle a "History of David", following the compositions of Lucas de Heere. De Vries added the architectural motifs..."[61]

Here we have evidence from an unimpeachable source that Lucas de Heere was employed by William of Orange as designer of a series of compositions.

Van Mander does not give the date at which the work was done, but it is significant that one of the artists who carried out Lucas' designs was Vredeman de Vries. At the Antwerp entry, for which De Vries worked, Anjou was twice represented in the character of David, symbolising that the rule was taken from the unworthy Saul, or Philip of Spain, and given to this new David. It is therefore not impossible that Lucas de Heere's "David" compositions were a glorification of the new régime in Biblical symbolism, perhaps made at the same time as the Antwerp entry, or soon after, and reflecting one of its themes.

Obviously, this is a conjectural interpretation of these now non-existent David compositions, but it is one worth making for the parallel which it would afford to the Valois Tapestries, which are compositions by Lucas de Heere which reflect the glorification of Anjou at his Antwerp and Ghent entries.

Leaving aside all conjecture as to the meaning of the David designs, we have in Van Mander's statement proof that it was for William of Orange that Lucas produced these compositions. We suggest that the most likely origin of the Valois Tapestries is that they also were designed by Lucas at the instigation of William of Orange. As for the David series, he may have been assisted by other artists. There is no sign of the architectural expert, Vredeman de Vries, in the Valois Tapestries, which tend to avoid Caron's architectural features and in which we saw the influence of Hoefnagel's topographical landscapes. Hoefnagel settled in Munich in 1578, but is known to have visited Antwerp in 1579 [62] and it is therefore not impossible that he could have been still in touch with Lucas de Heere in 1582.

We do not think that it is necessary to postulate other artists working with Lucas on the design of the tapestries, but it is a possibility and one which has to be borne in mind in view of Van Mander's statement that other artists executed his David compositions.

We have called this chapter "Lucas de Heere leads to William of Orange" and we have now to resume our findings. We have seen that Lucas de Heere was an enthusiast for the cause of William of Orange and the liberation of all the provinces of the Netherlands from Spanish domination. When hopes of the possibility of this arose, he went back to the Netherlands from England and entered Orange's service as his "pensioner". We have seen good reason to believe that an important part of the services which he rendered to Orange was in assisting in the propaganda for Anjou whom Orange had established as titular sovereign of the southern provinces. We have quoted proof that, on one occasion at least, Lucas de Heere was employed by William of Orange in the design of artistic compositions. There is thus good foundation for the suggestion that the person who commissioned the design of the Valois Tapestries from Lucas de Heere could have been William of Orange, though the only "document" for such a commission that we can produce is the fact that Lucas was Orange's "pensioner", in his paid employment and probably chiefly used for his services in propaganda for Anjou.

This suggestion will be supported if we can find evidence within the tapestries themselves of the influence of William of Orange. The analysis of the meaning of the tapestries, which we shall arrive at through the history of the festivals in our second part, will show, we believe, conclusively that the mind behind the Valois Tapestries is the mind of William of Orange, that they are a pathetic monument to his hopes of finding a solution to the problem of the Netherlands by putting his trust in the House of Valois.

CHAPTER VI

ANTWERP UNDER ANJOU

The weaving of the Valois Tapestries is of superlative quality. At a time when the great age of Flemish tapestry art is said to be over, damaged beyond recall by the disasters which had overtaken the Netherlands, these works emerge from some unknown atelier, woven by hands unknown, to demonstrate that the art is still capable of products equal to, or even surpassing, the finest ever made. The amazing richness in the rendering of rich stuffs, the marvellously delicate colouring of these—in particular the exquisite "changeant" effects, pink, mauve, and dove-colour of some of the women's dresses—the fineness and brilliance of the details, the alive rendering of the faces, the splendour of the crowded masquerade scenes, all combine to produce an effect which overwhelms the beholder with admiration and amazement at the consummate skill of the weaving.

The eight magnificent panels, of enormous size,[1] which form the suite are marked in the lower left hand corners (all except two of them) with the mark of Brussels, the two capital Bs, with a red shield between them, standing for Brussels in Brabant. All students of the tapestries—with one exception—have therefore supposed that they were made in Brussels.[2] Though J. Ehrmann suggested their connection with Anjou's Antwerp entry, he did not question that they were woven in Brussels. His theory is that they were put together in a Brussels atelier, from the Caron designs, from published descriptions of French festivals, from albums of fashion, and from motifs traditional in the atelier—all without any coherent or consistent overall plan[3].

On two of the tapestries, the "Whale" and the "Fontainebleau", there are, in the lower right-hand margins, the personal marks of two weavers (Pl. 20). The lower of these two marks is also found, without the other one, on the "Journey", "Quintain", and "Polish" tapestries. The remaining three ("Barriers", "Tournament" and "Elephant") have no weavers' marks. There were thus two head weavers engaged on two of the tapestries, one of whom also affixed his mark on some of the others. There was once a register in which, from 1528 onwards, all weavers were obliged to enter their names and marks, but this register has disappeared.[4] The situation as regards weavers' marks therefore is that only a very few of these have been identified. They can be identified if a tapestry is found which is signed with the weaver's name, as well as with his mark, as in the case of the Antwerp weaver, François Spiering; or if documents turn up in archives signed by weavers with their names and marks. Several remarkable documentary finds of this kind have been made in recent years, but the vast majority of these marks remain unidentified. Amongst the unknown ones are the two on the Valois Tapestries.

It would seem that one of these marks (the upper one of the two on the plate) has so far been found on no other tapestry; the lower one, however, has been found in reversed form on a few, for example on a tapestry representing a hunting scene, now at Turin, which M. and V. Viale therefore think must have emanated from the same atelier as the Valois Tapestries.[5]

The weavers' marks, therefore, leave us pretty much in the dark, and this darkness is increased by the fact that recent research has forcibly demonstrated that by no means all tapestries bearing the Brussels mark were made in Brussels.

Before bringing forward our own theory, we must spend a few moments in chasing the wild goose started by the great French expert J. J. Guiffrey, the only one of previous writers who did not accept the Brussels origin of the tapestries.

A certain Pierre Colins, native of Enghien in Hainaut, was the author of a history of Enghien, published in 1643 but based on early experiences in his long life in the course of which he travelled frequently to France. Speaking of the visit of the Polish ambassadors to the French court in 1573 he says that it occasioned much public rejoicing in Paris,

"en festins, joustes, & combats à pied & à cheual, qui ont esté naifuement representés en certaines tapisseries faictes à Enghien l'an 1585." [6]

Guiffrey, who was the first to notice that one of the tapestries represents a festival for the Poles, jumped to the conclusion that it is to them that Colins' remark refers.[7]

An old-established tapestry atelier existed at Enghien (and it is known that on one occasion its products were misleadingly marked with the Brussels mark)[8] but the Enghien style is totally unlike that of the Valois Tapestries and moreover the historical considerations now known to us render it impossible that they should have been made there. Enghien was in the Catholic province of Hainaut which, with Artois, chose not to break off allegiance to Philip of Spain, and so remained outside the state built up for Anjou by William of Orange.

There is no reason, however, to doubt Colins' statement that tapestries representing French festivals were made at Enghien in 1585, but these were not the Valois Tapestries but another set. This is in itself interesting for they might have been a set made from the Caron designs. The six Caron drawings which we know must have been made after the festivals for the Poles, since one of them refers to these, and probably soon after, since they look as though they had all been made at one time. It is possible to make a suggestion as to who had these Enghien festival tapestries made and where they went.

The situation of Enghien was extremely curious, for though, with the rest of Hainaut, it acknowledged the most Catholic majesty of Spain as its King, its feudal allegiance belonged to his Protestant enemy, Henry of Navarre, Enghien being a fief of the Bourbon family.[9] Navarre never visited this possession of his, in his enemy's dominions, and the business of the absentee landlord was transacted by Pierre Colins, who seems to have been an agent, his frequent journeys to France being in connection with Navarre-Enghien business. On one of these trips, made in the year 1598, Colins called on the Lord of Enghien (now Henri IV, King of France) at the château of Monceau, bringing with him tributes from Enghien, in the shape of portraits for the decoration of his palaces and falcons from his Enghien aviaries for his hunting.[10] Monceau was the château in which Henri had established his mistress, Gabrielle d'Estrées, and Colins saw her walking with the King in the gardens. Gabrielle died in the following year, 1599, and an inventory of her possessions at Monceau was made. Several tapestries which sound like festival tapestries, are mentioned in this inventory. The subject of one of them was "les plaisirs

Pl. 20

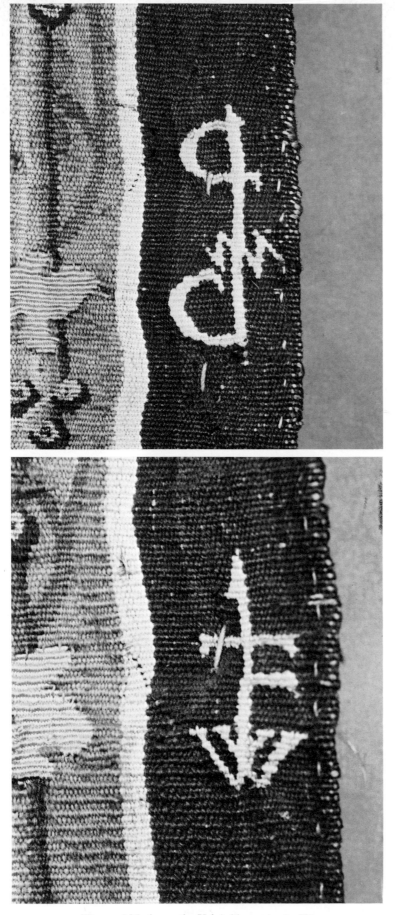

Weavers' Marks on the Valois Tapestries (p. 39)

du feu roy Henri" within a great oval; others showed, in central cartouches, a "tournoi", a "combat à la barrière", a "combat de l'ours", and other hunting scenes and games.[11] Some of these may well have been the festival tapestries made at Enghien in 1585, perhaps by order of the Lord of Enghien, brought by Colins to his Lord, who gave them to Gabrielle d'Estrées.

It is interesting to notice that one of them represented a "combat à la barrière", suggesting that a French design of this subject existed. This re-enforces the supposition that a French "barriers" design—though not among the Caron drawings known to us—may be the basis of the "Barriers" of the Valois Tapestries, though transformed and thickly overlaid with other allusions.

The most likely place for the Valois Tapestries to have been made at is Antwerp, where Anjou held his court in 1582, where his glory had been celebrated in the great Antwerp entry, and where Orange also lived during most of the year in attendance on him. Antwerp was not only the centre for the tapestry trade; it was also a weaving centre.[12] And, moreover, the Antwerp weavers were the chief offenders in infringing the regulations by which Brussels tried to enforce that only tapestries made at Brussels should be marked with the Brussels mark.

In the article in which M. Crick-Kuntziger published some of her major documentary discoveries about weavers' marks [13] she also discussed the cognate question of the Brussels mark. In 1560, complaints were made by the Brussels authorities to the Council of Brabant that the Brussels mark was being tampered with in Antwerp where weavers were putting the mark onto their tapestries. The burgomaster of Antwerp argued the question and tried to have the regulation modified, but the Council supported the Brussels weavers and demanded the republication of the regulation. Years later, in 1617, the controversy was still going on, and, once again, the Antwerp weavers were ordered to cease putting the Brussels mark on tapestries made in Antwerp.

M. Crick-Kuntziger suggests that this obstinacy of the Antwerp weavers may have been due, not to fraudulent intentions, but to a conviction that they had the right to use the Brussels mark.[14] Many of the Antwerp weavers were of Brussels origin, and had established themselves in the city, either as refugees or to be near the chief centre of the trade in tapestries. She points out that the only Antwerp weaver who can be identified as having used the Brussels mark— namely François Spiering—had connections with Brussels, and his house in Antwerp bore on it as a sign the shield of Brussels. She thinks that the fact that Spiering signed a tapestry of his, marked with the Brussels mark, with his full name as well as his personal mark, indicates that he had no intention to defraud but used the Brussels mark openly, as his right.

It would therefore be possible for the Valois Tapestries to have been made in Antwerp by a weaver—or weavers—who believed that he had the right to place the Brussels mark on them because he came from Brussels.

That weaver was not François Spiering whose mark is known and is not that of either of the two on the Valois Tapestries. Nevertheless there are certain affinities between our tapestries and those made by Spiering. The borders to tapestries made by Spiering are rather close to those of the Valois Tapestries, using similar patterns of "grotesques".[15] From this it might be deduced that the Valois Tapestries use a type of border common in Antwerp. Secondly, G. T. van Ysselsteyn has pointed to the marvellous quality of Spiering's tapestries, particularly in the rendering of stuffs, and of materials with "changeant" effects.[16] This latter is also a notable characteristic of the Valois Tapestries, which is therefore perhaps suggestive of the excellent "Antwerp style" of weaving.

A tapissier of Antwerp called Joos van Herseel is mentioned more than once in connection with preparations for the reception of the new Duke of Brabant. Documents in the Middelburg Archives, which have been published in full by G. T. van Ysselsteyn,[17] record a large payment to Joos van Herseel and Franchoys Sweerts, tapissiers of Antwerp, for two "rooms of tapestries", bought of them in January, 1582, to furnish the apartments of Anjou at Middelburg. (Anjou stayed at Middelburg, after landing at Flushing, and before going on to Antwerp). The purchase of these tapestries for the furnishing of Anjou's apartments at Middelburg was ordered by the Prince of Orange and paid for by the Estates of Zeeland. This transaction tells us something of importance, namely that William of Orange, who was a poor man at this time having spent most of his great private fortune on financing the wars, could order tapestries in connection with his installation of Anjou and get these paid for by contributions from public funds. Secondly, we learn the names of two tapissiers of Antwerp with whom Orange was having dealings, Joos van Herseel and Franchoys Sweerts. Herseel was evidently a tapestry merchant who was doing a good deal of business in Antwerp at this time, for in February, 1582, the City of Antwerp paid him for rooms of tapestries which he had supplied for furnishing the palace of Anjou in Antwerp.[18]

In these dealings, Herseel and Sweerts appear as tapestry merchants, not as weavers, for the tapestries bought for Anjou were in their stock and not made specially for the occasion. We know however that Joos van Herseel was not only a dealer but himself a weaver, with an atelier in Antwerp. This information comes from a document which was published in 1896 by F. Donnet from the *Request Boek* for 1584, that is to say from the series of Antwerp municipal archives relating to pleas and complaints.

On February 5, 1584, a number of Antwerp tapissiers lodged a complaint to a magistrate to the effect that

"Josse de Herseele, a fabricant from Brussels, came not long ago to Antwerp to work at the making of tapestries. He settled within the enclosure of the citadel. The colonels in command of the "garde bourgeoise" permitted exemption from all guard duties both to him and to seven of his employees. Now he is employing a larger number of assistants, and these are benefiting unjustly from the privilege accorded to him." [19]

The complainants go on to say that the unfair advantages allowed to Herseel damage them and other tapissiers who have orders which they cannot execute for lack of labour. They further point out that Antwerp fabricants have generously received into their ateliers refugees from Flanders and have given them work to prevent them from emigrating and carrying to foreign countries the secrets of an art which brings prosperity to the town. They therefore request the magistrate to recall Herseel to the strict observance of the privilege which he has obtained.

Joos van Herseel was thus a weaver *from Brussels*, established in Antwerp, who might therefore have felt justified in affixing the Brussels mark to his tapestries. He had been busily at work for some time before 1584, and under specially favourable conditions. He must have had very influential patrons who procured for him and his workers the exemption from guard duty in order to enable them to execute orders as speedily as possible.

It is important to notice the date at which the complaint against Van Herseel was made. It was a year after the *furie française* of 1583, which had utterly discredited Anjou who was driven from the city by the infuriated inhabitants. Orange had retired into the northern provinces, despairing of the situation. Town after town in Flanders and Brabant was yielding to the Duke of Parma, and it would not have taken much foresight to realise that Antwerp would soon follow their example. In 1584, therefore, Joos van Herseel is not so powerfully protected as he used to be and envious voices are raised against him.

We suggest that it may have been in the privileged atelier of Joos van Herseel of Brussels that the Valois Tapestries were woven. Obviously, this is an hypothesis built up from circumstantial evidence alone, and which cannot be proved unless a document is discovered connecting Van Herseel with the tapestries, or the weaver's mark used by Van Herseel is identified and turns out to be one of those on the tapestries.

Joos van Herseel possibly belonged to the same family as the weaver of the same name who was one of those who wove, about 1540, the Mantua tapestries from Raphael's cartoons.[20] According to J. Denucé, the Franchoys Sweerts who appears in partnership with him in the Middelburg deal was a relative of his.[21] Sweerts was a scholar and an author, as well as a "tapissier of Antwerp."

We have now to ask ourselves for whom and with what object were the Valois Tapestries made. We know that they belonged at one time to Catherine de'Medici, who gave them to her grand-daughter. This need not however necessarily mean that they had reached her as a gift, for when Anjou died in 1584 his mother had a legal right to his property.[22] Might they, therefore, have belonged to Anjou before they belonged to Catherine? He certainly did not leave them to her by will, for in his will there is no mention of any property whatsoever except debts.[23] We cannot however be absolutely certain, owing to the fact that Anjou died before his mother, as to whether they were originally made for him of for her.

Let us consider some possibilities. J. Ehrmann thought that the tapestries were perhaps ordered by some Flemish organisation to commemorate Anjou's entry into Antwerp.[24] No record of this has, however, as yet been found. If they were ordered by the City of Antwerp, this would be mentioned in the *Collegiaal Actenboek* for the relevant year. When the Archduke Albert entered Antwerp in 1599, the City presented him with a set of tapestries glorifying his victories, and the *Collegiaal Actenboek* for the year in question contains entries concerning payments to Otto Vaenius for their design, to Jan Snellinck for drawing the cartoons, and to Martin Reynbouts for weaving them.[25] The *Collegiaale Actenboeken* for 1581 to 1583, the years in which records of the making of tapestries for Anjou ought to appear, are among the documents in this series which have been printed.[26] They contain no mentions of payments to artists or weavers for tapestries.[27] This constitutes negative evidence that the Valois Tapestries were not commissioned by the City of Antwerp.

Another possibility is that Anjou himself might have ordered them to be made, determined to make full use of the opportunity for acquiring tapestries which his position provided. Anxious to please him and to keep him amused and contented, Orange might have put Lucas de Heere at his disposal to make the designs, and have raised the money to pay for them as best he could. We have seen him raising money to pay for the tapestries bought from Herseel and Sweerts.

Finally, we have to consider that perhaps they were not made for Anjou, either as a gift or because he ordered them, but made to be sent to France as a diplomatic present, as propaganda for the Anjou régime designed to plead with the Queen Mother and the King of France to support their son and brother, in fact to obtain that French support the hope for which was one of the main reasons why Orange put Anjou into his position. In this case, the probability is that William of Orange requested his pensioner Lucas de Heere to make the designs, and was able to procure considerable sums to pay for the making of the tapestries (works of this size and quality would be very expensive to make) from official sources on the ground of their diplomatic importance. The plan of the tapestries themselves, which are not centred on Anjou by himself, but on Anjou as part of his family, son of the Queen Mother, brother of the King of France, seems to us to indicate that this last hypothesis is the right one. Catherine and Henri needed persuading to support Anjou's venture in the Netherlands, for they had all along been nervous about it, in case it should involve them in war with Spain. It was through the pleading of Catherine that Henri at last consented to support it; in 1582, Marnix was still writing to Catherine urging her to engage the King of France to help his brother.[28] This is exactly the kind of appeal which the tapestries make; they are a plea to Catherine, and through her to Henri, to welcome Anjou and the Netherlands into the protection of the French family circle.

There is another point which has a bearing on these problems. The design of the tapestries was made, we believe, in the year 1582, certainly after Anjou's Antwerp entry of February, and perhaps not completed until after his Ghent entry of August. It seems likely that the weaving of such huge works would not have been completed before Anjou's expulsion from Antwerp in the *furie française* of January, 1583. Possibly they were still uncompleted on the looms at that time. Yet even after this event William of Orange wished to keep up the connection with Anjou and so would not have stopped the weaving of the tapestries. Further, after the deaths of both Anjou and of William of Orange the sovereignty of the Netherlands was offered to Henri III, and envoys went to Paris on this business in 1584 and in 1585 and had interviews with Catherine de' Medici. The tapestries would still have been valid as a diplomatic gift to be taken to France by these embassies, as a touching record of the deceased Anjou and a plea to his mother and brother.

Our conclusion therefore is that both the plan of the tapestries and the probability that they were not finished before Anjou's hurried departure from Antwerp make it highly unlikely that the Valois Tapestries were made for Anjou or were ever in his possession. We think that they were made at the instigation of William of Orange to be sent to Catherine in the hope of influencing her and Henri III to support Anjou in the Netherlands. Even after the collapse of Anjou's regime, and even after the deaths of Anjou and of Orange, it was still most necessary to keep in touch with the French court, and it is possible that the tapestries actually went to Paris with one of the embassies from the Netherlands in 1584 and 1585.[29]

Their design was, however, we believe, completed in 1582 and probably the weaving was begun in that year.

The world from which the Valois Tapestries emanated was a curious one. In the devastated and impoverished city of Antwerp an attempt was made to create a court and a court life around the figure of the Valois prince whom William of Orange was trying to build up as Count of Flanders and Duke of Brabant. Anjou was established in the abbey of St. Michel in as fine a style as the financial situation would permit. His household included an official painter, Frans Frank, and a historiographer.[30]

The most distinguished of the French noblemen who had followed him to the Netherlands was François de Bourbon, Duc de Montpensier, also known as the "Prince Dauphin" because of his title of Dauphin d'Auvergne.[31] This high personage had lodgings provided by the city.[32] He was a prince of the French royal blood, and also the brother of William of Orange's third wife, the ex-nun Charlotte de Bourbon-Montpensier who died during the year of Anjou's reign. He had been present at the festivals of Bayonne, where he had led the troop of Amazons;[33] he had also been present in Paris at the time of the festivals for the Polish ambassadors.[34] And as one of the commissioners sent to England to arrange the match of Anjou with Elizabeth, and who had also been with Anjou when he was personally in England,[35] he had seen festivals at the English court. This man must have been an important element in the French court life exported to Antwerp; he could also, together with Anjou himself, have been a source of information about French festivals to the designer of the tapestries.

Behind this transplanted Valois court, supporting it firmly against criticism and unpopularity, stood the Prince of Orange; his chief adviser at this time, as always, was Marnix de Sainte Aldegonde. Though his home was at Ghent, their "pensioner" Lucas de Heere must, it is to be presumed, often have been in Antwerp in connection with his work for them. We have found no evidence that Lucas held any position in Anjou's household, though the words of Carel van Mander about the princes who gave him splendid offices and whom he amused with his agreeable company probably refer to this time.

Orange is said to have called nearly every day upon Anjou to pay him his respects. We gain a fleeting glimpse of this Orange-Valois society through the accounts of the sinister event which occurred in March, 1582, when Jaureguy attempted to assassinate William the Silent.[36] It was Anjou's birthday in honour of which festivities, including a carrousel, were arranged. At the birthday banquet, Orange had been talking about the cruelties of the Spaniards, and after it he took the guests, both French and Flemish, to an antichamber where he showed them

"une tapisserie où estoient representés quelques soldats espaignols usans de leurs cruautés."[37]

Whilst they were all looking at this tapestry, the assassin wounded the Prince with a pistol shot, but not fatally. Thinking he was dying, Orange is said to have exclaimed to the Frenchmen standing by, "Oh what a faithful servant His Highness (Anjou) loses in me!"

This scene brings vividly to us, for a moment, the atmosphere which gave birth to the Valois Tapestries—a French court pursuing its customary pastimes in Antwerp, the intense loyalty of Orange to the Valois prince whom he had introduced, the murderous dangers lying in wait for him below the surface of this artificial "pacification". It even shows us Orange in the act of *using tapestries as propaganda*.

In the chapel of Anjou's palace, the Catholic cult was established. Orange, of course, was surrounded by eminent Protestant ministers. Du Plessis-Mornay, the liberal Protestant, was in favour with both Orange and Anjou. Though Protestant opinion probably predominated in this state which had defied Philip of Spain, there is some evidence that the "politique" attitude was making headway amongst Catholics. For example, the famous printer, Christopher Plantin, a most firm Catholic and official printer to Philip II, certainly compromised with the "rebels" and it was actually he who printed the sumptuous description of Anjou's entry into Antwerp. It was not, however, without much strain, dangerous incidents, and general tension that the religious "pacification" was maintained in Antwerp during this year.

We remember our puzzlement when discussing the foreground portraits in the Valois Tapestries at the curious juxtaposition of figures representing opposite sides in the French wars of religion. Antwerp in 1582, almost alone in Europe, was a place in which such a juxtaposition might have been made with deliberate purpose.

The Antwerp merchants (whom Lucas de Heere had known in London) had, many of them, returned to Antwerp, which was now hoping to revive as a great international port. The geographical group was again active, and further volumes of the *Civitates orbis terrarum* were probably in preparation. An edition in French of Ortelius' atlas, now entitled *Theatre de l'Univers* was published by Plantin in 1581. It contains prefatory verses by Plantin addressed to the senate and people of Antwerp and beginning:

> "C'est grand honneur, Messieurs, de voir tant d'estrangers
> Des quatre parts du Monde (auec mille dangers)
> Apporter ce qu'ils ont d'esprit & de puissance,
> Pour rendre vostre ville un Cornet-d'abondance." [38]

It is interesting that this connection between the geography of the four quarters of the earth and the mercantile internationalism of Antwerp is made in French at this time. In the same year, 1582, that the city of Antwerp paid for Anjou's entry, it genially rewarded Plantin with some Rhenish wine for the French edition of Ortelius' atlas.[39] Antwerp in 1582, looking out afresh to the four quarters of the earth, was thus a place conducive to that curious "re-vision" of French festival scenes in terms of costume and topography which we detected in the Valois Tapestries.

The enlarged editions of De Bruyn's costume manuals, published at about this time, may suggest that the enthusiasm for the study of international costume was connected with the

a William of Orange as a Belgian Rider (p. 47)

b François de Valois (Anjou) as a French Rider (p. 47)

c Maurice of Nassau (?) as a Belgian Rider (p. 47)

d Robert, Earl of Leicester (?) as an English Rider (p. 47)

From De Bruyn, *Diversarum gentium armatura equestris*, circa 1582

liberalism associated with the new régime in Antwerp. The new edition of his manual of 1577 was published at Antwerp in 1581. As we saw, it was enlarged to include costumes from all the four quarters of the earth, and contained many more plates of French fashions than the earlier edition.[40] Even more suggestive is the fact that the enlarged edition of De Bruyn's manual of costumes and accoutrements of riders of different nations actually contains portraits of William of Orange and of Anjou.[41] The portrait of Anjou (Pl. 21, b) introduces the section on French riders; that of William of Orange (Pl. 21, a) [42] heads the Belgian riders, amongst whom there is also a Belgian "Adolescens Princeps siue Dominus" (Pl. 21, c). This is probably intended as a crude likeness of Maurice of Nassau (Pl. 33, d), son of William of Orange, who rode into Antwerp in the train of Anjou at the Antwerp entry of 1582. And the section on English riders is headed by a "Nobilis Anglus" (Pl. 21, d), who is not unlike the portrait in the National Portrait Gallery of Robert, Earl of Leicester, the head of the English contingent sent by Queen Elizabeth to support Anjou at his Antwerp entry.

Since De Bruyn was almost certainly the engraver of the plates in the description of the Antwerp entry published by Plantin, it seems more than probable that these portrait riders of his reflect that entry, the most striking feature of which was provided by the contingents of French, Belgian, and English riders who accompanied Anjou into the city. The enlarged edition of De Bruyn's manual containing these portraits, and published, it would seem, at Cologne, should therefore be dated circa 1582. And these crude costume plates, which are also portraits of Anjou and Orange and other celebrities who entered Antwerp in Anjou's train, afford a remarkable parallel to the raising of costume types into portraits of Anjou and his circle in the Valois Tapestries.

Emanating from the brief, and as it was to turn out, disastrous experiment which Orange had attempted in making Anjou the figure-head of his effort to preserve the southern provinces of the Netherlands in independence of Spain, the Valois Tapestries are likely to have an unusual slant on the French court and its festivals. We shall now take an entirely different route into their meaning, namely the history of the festivals which they represent, and this will lead us eventually to the solution of most of the problems.

PART II

THE FESTIVALS

FOREWORD TO THE FESTIVALS

The major French festivals of the latter half of the sixteenth century took the form of a series of "magnificences" lasting over many days, a different entertainment being provided on each day. Most of these were the traditional pastimes and exercises of chivalry, tournaments, barriers, running at the quintain, running at the ring, and so on, often performed, as was also not new, in exotic masquerade costumes, or associated with romantic plots. These were varied by mythological shows and spectacles set to music which gradually developed, as the century proceeded, into *ballets de cour*. One set of such magnificences was very like another; the same exercises in the same kind of disguises were repeated again and again; so were the themes of the mythological shows. The Valois Tapestries, though based on French designs referring to festivals of different dates, show us a representative set of French magnificences. There is the "Tournament" (II) in a setting of romantic allegory; the "Quintain" (VI) in masquerade dress; the "combat à la barrière" (VII); there is a water combat in fancy-dress (I) and a land combat in fancy-dress (VIII) reflecting the dramatising of the carrousel into these more elaborate forms; there is a water fête (III) with those singing sirens and deities of the sea which formed such a constant theme in the mythological entertainments; there is a dance and a rock with ballet-dancers on it (IV) reflecting the rise of *ballet de cour* out of this type of show. To pass in front of the Valois Tapestries is to have been present at a series of magnificences at the French court.

The presiding genius in them all is the Queen Mother, Catherine de' Medici, watching from the pavilions or present somewhere in every one (the only exception being "Fontainebleau"). From the beginning of her regency, she had lavishly encouraged such spectacles. She would not allow heavy tilting of the type at which her husband had accidentally met his death; her influence was all towards rendering harmless the pastimes of chivalry and diversifying them with costumes and dramatic effects. She always herself gave and produced one or more of the shows in a series of magnificences and these were the mythological-musical shows, to which ballet was gradually added, which formed the climax and the artistic core of each series.

At the courts of the Dukes of Burgundy, of whose territories Flanders and Brabant had once formed part, the pastimes of chivalry had been produced with consummate artistry. The French court magnificences of the sixteenth century were carrying on a tradition with which a Burgundian artist would feel himself in sympathy, and the rendering of the French court festivals in the Valois Tapestries reflects such sympathy, as it translates them into the tapestry medium with marvellous richness and splendour.

The French "magnificences" of chivalry developed, fostered by the Italianate artistry of the Queen Mother and by the French musical humanist movement, until they gave birth to new art forms. Those who wish to understand the context in which the famous early *ballets de cour* appeared should look at the Valois Tapestries. They formed an event in a series such as the tapestries show.

Catherine de' Medici used her festivals with a purpose; as has been said "les fêtes faisaient partie de son programme de gouvernement". She used them to impress foreigners with the splendour of the French court; to arouse loyalty to the monarchy among Frenchmen; to draw together warring factions in pleasant and harmless recreations. The great festivals mark phases in her policy of "politique" appeasement, which was suddenly and disastrously abandoned during one of them.

In the following account of the major French festivals we have two objects in view. The tapestries and the Caron drawings on which they depend constitute a body of visual evidence for the history of French court festival. We shall study them here as such, trying to identify the festivals which they represent. We shall not discuss, or hardly at all, the poetry and music of the festivals, but dwell only on the visual side as this is illustrated in our material, endeavouring particularly to bring out how the visual evidence shows us a new side of the history of these French festivals, namely that their unit is a set of magnificences within which individual forms develop.

Secondly, we shall relate the festivals to the political circumstances under which they took place. This bears both upon the history of the festivals in themselves, and also upon the interpretation of them made by the designers of the Valois Tapestries. For the period of history which they cover is the period of the revolt of the Netherlands. If we follow the festivals, pondering on the phases of history which they represent, we shall find ourselves led to the solution of the central problem of the Valois Tapestries, which is the identity of the three unknown men in the "Journey".

CHAPTER I

FESTIVALS OF THE REIGN OF CHARLES IX

In his panegyric of Catherine de' Medici for her magnificence and liberality "tout pareil à celuy de son grand oncle le pape Leon, et du magnifique le seigneur Laurens de Medicis", Brantôme singles out three occasions on which her Medicean magnificence was most wonderfully displayed.[1] The first of these was at Fontainebleau in 1564; the second at Bayonne in 1565; and the third at the Tuileries in 1573 for the reception of the Polish ambassadors. These three major magnificences all fell within the reign of Charles IX, during the earlier part of which Catherine was regent for her young son.

The Fontainebleau Festivals, 1564

It was at Fontainebleau, in 1564,[2] that the gentle and artistic influence of the Queen Mother on the traditional chivalrous pastimes of the French court first made itself felt on a large scale. The "magnificences" went on for several days. They included "tournois et rompement de lances, combats à la barrière, bref toutes sortes de jeu d'armes". Several of these exercises were "joûtes mascarades" or jousts in fancy dress and in allegorical settings. There was a combat between twelve knights, six a side, dressed as Greeks and Trojans.[3] There was an enchanted tower, on an island, from which Charles and his brothers, as knights of romance, delivered imprisoned ladies.[4]

Instead of the chivalrous exercise in masquerade dress there was, on one of the days, a little mythological play, with verses by Ronsard set to music.[5] This was the entertainment given by Catherine.[6] It was a water-show, for Sirens swimming on the canals sang loyal songs of greeting to Charles IX; and a Neptune floated in his car drawn by sea-horses. This plot of the water-creatures doing obeisance to the Monarchy was to be utilised again and again. At Fontainebleau in 1564 it was enacted on the artificial waters in the grounds of the château.

It is certainly Fontainebleau and its waters which we see in the Caron design (IX, a) on which the "Fontainebleau" tapestry (I) is based. Comparison with Du Cerceau's drawing of Fontainebleau[7] proves this, though Caron seems to have moved the tiny island, which Du Cerceau shows connected by a jetty with the shore, out into the centre of the lake. We know that the island was used at the festivals of 1564, which included an attack on an enchanted tower on an island. There is also a cartel by Ronsard headed "fait pour le combat que fist le Roy en l'Isle du Palais"[8] which undoubtedly refers to a water-masquerade using the island at Fontainebleau, though not necessarily to the one in 1564. In the descriptions of the Fontainebleau fêtes of 1564 there is nothing quite corresponding to the scene in Caron's drawing in which attackers and defenders of the island are in vaguely classical costumes. We cannot therefore be certain as to what fête at Fontainebleau this drawing refers. It was, however, certainly on these waters, and on the adjoining canals, that the Sirens and the Neptune swam in 1564 to the music of Ronsard's verses. To visualise this, we should transfer the Sirens and the Neptune of Bayonne (III; X, a) to this Fontainebleau setting.

For the tapestry, Lucas de Heere turned the classical water-masquerade of Caron's drawing into one in which the combatants are attired in costumes of peoples from many quarters of the earth; he puts American Indian savages on the island and Turks into one of the boats (I; IX, a). This was his own exuberant invention as costume expert, and is not a record of any real fête at Fontainebleau using such costumes.

The brief reign of François II had been overshadowed by the death of his father, and by the plot of the Huguenots to seize the person of the young king in an attempt to break the power and influence of the extreme Catholic party, led by the Guises. The first of the wars of religion broke out in the early part of the reign of Charles IX, but now, in 1564, there was an interval of peace, and Catherine brought together the opposite religious parties in festivals. Both Catholic and Huguenot leaders took part in the mock combats of the "joûtes mascarades" at Fontainebleau. This was the first prominent occasion on which Catherine used the court festival as a mollifying influence on the opposed factions, turning the real conflict into a chivalrous pastime. Though the word "politique" was perhaps hardly yet in general circulation in the sense in which it was to be used later,[9] it describes this policy of mingling Catholics and Protestants together in peaceful masquerades. The theme of Catherine's "Sirens" entertainment was also peace, announced by the reappearance of the gentle deities of nature whose cosmic powers support the power of the French monarchy and whose magic songs are to unite all hearts in loyalty to it. Mauvissière, who took part in the Fontainebleau shows, recognised their object and its failure, for he concludes his account of them with the words "nevertheless the hatred of those of the Guise against the Admiral (Coligny) remained in their hearts."[10]

The Fontainebleau fêtes are the immediate prelude of those of Bayonne, for the court was assembling there in preparation for the long journey to the south. The new Spanish ambassador to the French court was present at Fontainebleau; he had been commissioned by Philip II to sound Catherine about the enforcement in France of the decrees of the Council of Trent.[11] She, however, was still hoping that the French religious problems might be solved through a council. The divergence between the religious policy of the French Monarchy, as represented by Catherine, and that of the Spanish Monarchy, as interpreted by Philip II, was profound. Catherine's methods of temporising with the Huguenots, and attempting to bring together the members of opposite religious parties in preparation for some new religious settlement, were diametrically opposed to the rigidity now beginning to formulate its plans at Madrid. It was not through new councils, and most certainly not through mollifying festivals, that Philip II of Spain intended to deal with the religious situation in Europe.

As the themes of the Fontainebleau festivals foreshadow those of Bayonne, and are almost like a rehearsal for them, so the situation behind them forecasts that of the Franco-Spanish Interview of Bayonne.

The Bayonne Festivals, 1565

Family history was inextricably mingled with the festivals. From Fontainebleau, the court travelled to Lorraine to attend the christening at Bar-le-Duc of the son of Catherine's second daughter Claude, married to Duke Charles III of Lorraine (whose portrait at a much later age we see in the "Whale" tapestry). A series of rejoicings including tournaments and a little verse drama by Ronsard marked this event.[12] Catherine, with the King and her younger children, then started on the "grand voyage de France",[13] the lengthy royal progress down to Bayonne to another family meeting. Elizabeth her eldest daughter, wife of Philip II, came out from Spain to meet her mother at the famous Bayonne Interview.

One of the chief objects of the festivals was as propaganda witnessing to the wealth and power of the court which financed them. At this dangerous turning-point in history, Catherine wished to impress the Spaniards as to the resources of the French Monarchy, and in this, according to Brantôme, she was successful, for he says that at Bayonne "la magnificence fut telle en toutes choses que les Espaignols qui sont fort desdaigneux de toutes autres, fors des leurs, jurarent n'avoir rien veu de plus beau."[14] We have several printed accounts of the entertainments at Bayonne,[15] the most important of which is the *Recueil des choses notables faites à Bayonne*, published in 1566.

The majority of these shows were based on the normal pastimes of the court, held to the accompaniment of verse recitations set to music, and in splendid costumes. There was a "course" (whether a running at the ring or at the quintain is not specified) in which the participants wore costumes of many nations; there was a tournament between "Knights of Great Britain and Ireland"; an attack and defence of a magic castle; a "disenchantment" of knights and maidens who had been turned into rocks. All these shows were developments of the romantic dramatisation of knightly sports such as had taken place at Fontainebleau, though now much more sumptuously produced. And here, as at Fontainebleau, Catherine gave her own entertainment, a mythological water-festival in which she further developed the plot which she had tried out in her "Sirens" show at Fontainebleau. Upon designs by Caron representing two of the Bayonne shows, Lucas de Heere based two of the Valois Tapestries.

On June 25th, the tournament between the Knights of Great Britain and Ireland[16] took place, with Charles IX leading the British Knights and his brother Henri those of Ireland. Cartels were recited to music, and the subject of their debate, which was on "Virtue and Love", was made visible by two chariots. Representing the side of the British Knights, there entered a chariot drawn by four white horses; in it were ladies symbolising five virtues, "Vertue heroique, Prudence, Vaillance, Justice, Temperance". The views supported by the Irish knights were represented by a chariot carrying Venus and Cupid and accompanied by many little cupids. Ladies distributed pendants inscribed with devices, and these devices were the same as those carried by the knights on their shields. The pendant-devices are illustrated in the *Recueil*. To Charles IX as head knight of Great Britain was given a pendant showing the "Temples of Honour and Virtue" (Pl. 22 c). The climax of the show came towards the end, when the knights crossed between one another without touching, and were separated by little balls of fire thrown in among the horses.[17] The whole event took place in a specially prepared enclosure[18] to the accompaniment of much music and musical recitation. The tournament of chivalry was, in this spectacle, so refined away into a semi-musical entertainment that we can already see in it an ancestor of *ballet de cour*. The horses were no doubt carefully trained to perform the various movements, the balls of fire being in the nature of the cracking of whips, giving the horses their signal for abrupt turns.

Caron's design (IX, b) shows the dance-like finale of the tournament of the Knights of Great Britain and Ireland. The knights are crossing between one another without touching, to musical accompaniment, and the horses are turning at the signal of the balls of fire. In the background are the allegorical chariots. In the corresponding "Tournament" tapestry (II), Lucas de Heere followed the French design but enriched it from the printed description of this festival in the *Recueil*, which he was certainly able to consult. Indubitable proof of this is provided by his adding the devices to the knights' shields, which Caron does not show; he has taken these devices from the illustrated pendants in the *Recueil*. (Pl. 22, a, b, c.) The device of the "Temples of Honour and Virtue" can be clearly seen on the shield of the foremost knight; other of the pendant devices in the *Recueil* can also be recognised on the shields in the tapestry. Lucas also added details to the chariots and their occupants, enriching Caron's representation of these by consultation with the description in the *Recueil*. For example, he shows clearly Venus and Cupid in the left-hand chariot, and the attendant small Cupids, which are not in Caron's design; and he makes much more of the scene of the ladies distributing pendants from the central daïs. The dwarf whom he puts in the foreground, standing in front of Catherine, also comes out of the *Recueil* which describes how an elegantly dressed dwarf entered in front of the king's troop.[19]

The "Tournament" tapestry is thus a representation of the Bayonne tournament which the Flemish artist has taken pains to make richer and more accurate than Caron's sketch of it by consulting the printed description.

Lucas de Heere evidently enjoyed this scene, and he added to the tournament a tiny detail which is neither in Caron's design nor in the *Recueil*. He put on one of the shields, as the knight's device, the lion of Flanders; this shield can be seen in the top centre of the detail from the "Tournament" (Pl. 22, a). The lion could also stand for that of Brabant which is of exactly the same shape but light on a dark ground; both lions appear on the tabards of the heralds at Anjou's Antwerp entry (see Pl. 31, b). The lion shield in the tapestry is an allusion to the presence, somewhere in the mêlée, of François, future Count of Flanders and Duke of Brabant. This detail reveals the heraldically trained artist, and also how congenial was the scene of the tournament of chivalry to his Burgundian temperament.

On June 24th, the Queen Mother gave her own especial entertainment.[20] She caused to be erected on an island in the river Ladour "une grande salle octogone" which was to serve as a banqueting-hall and which was placed in a clearing in a wood on the island. On the appointed day, the royal party was transported in a barge to the island. During the crossing they saw, and heard, a musical water-spectacle; people in boats, whose costume is not described, attacked an artificial whale; and when this was over, six Tritons playing cornets approached on a sea-tortoise. Then Neptune floated by, drawn in his chariot over the water by sea-horses; he addres-

a   Knights with Devices in the "Tournament" (p. 56)

b, c   Pendant-Devices from the *Recueil des choses faites à Bayonne* (p. 55)

The Festival on the Island in the "Whale" (pp. 57–8)

sed the occupants of the barge in verses recited to music supplied by the Tritons. After this, they were greeted by Arion singing on his dolphin to the accompaniment of six violins who were concealed on the shore. Finally, three Sirens swam up, singing most beautifully. The theme of all the songs was peace, peace between France and Spain, universal peace announced by the reappearance of the deities of nature around the French King, and the overthrow of the monster of war, represented by the whale. It was Catherine's plot of Fontainebleau, expanded and improved.

When the party landed on the island, they saw dances of shepherds and shepherdesses to the music of bagpipes. They then walked up a specially prepared and turfed avenue to the banqueting hall in the wood. After the banquet, six violin players entered and nine nymphs, and the nymphs danced a ballet.

Caron's drawing (X, a) shows the crossing in the barge, the attack on the whale, the Tritons, Neptune, Sirens and other creatures of the water-festival. It shows the banqueting house in the clearing of the wood, and vaguely some round dances taking place near it.

For the "Whale" tapestry (III), the Caron design was followed to some extent. The Sirens, the Tritons, the Neptune are similarly placed and the barge crosses the water, though its position is shifted. In several respects, however, the tapestry disagrees with the Caron design. The most marked divergence is in the attempt at topographical accuracy in the depiction of the island and its surroundings which was probably arrived at by consulting the topographical description in the *Recueil* to which the tapestry conforms much more closely. We have already discussed this redrawing of the scene with an eye to greater topographical accuracy.[21] Apart from this, there are other divergencies between the Caron design and the tapestry. The latter does not show the banqueting house, but indicates a banquet taking place *al fresco* under the trees on the island (Pl. 23). Also the round dances of shepherdesses, so vaguely indicated by Caron, have taken on a much more precise form and now look like peasant dances in local costumes, for which the bag-pipe players are merrily playing. The strong "costume" interest of the tapestry artist manifests itself here, as he shows peasant costume in the dances, carrying on the costume interest of his foreground, with its noble and bourgeois differentiations. Nevertheless the peasant dances in the tapestry also conform more closely to what actually took place at Bayonne than does the Caron design.

Marguerite de Valois, who was present as a very young girl at Bayonne, gives her impressions in her memoirs of the dances and the banquet on the island. She says that the dancers whom they saw on landing from the barge were in troops who danced after the manner of the province of France to which they belonged, "les Poitevines avec la cornemuse, les Provençales la volte avec les timballes, les Bourguignones et Champenoises avec le petit hautbois, le dessus de violon, et tabourins de village; les Bretonnes dansants les passepieds et branlesgais; et ainsi de toutes les autres provinces."[22] The printed *Recueil* and the other early printed sources do not tell us that the dances were those of the provinces of France, and Marguerite's memoirs were not published until 1648 and so not accessible to the ordinary reader at the time that the tapestries were made. Yet the tapestry agrees with Marguerite in making the dances provincial dances, for we can see that the dancers are in peasant costumes. Further, Marguerite, though she mentions the banqueting-hall, emphasises its semi-*al fresco* character. Speaking of "le festin superbe de la Royne ma mere en l'isle" she says of the banqueting-hall that it seemed formed by nature, for there was in the centre of the island an oval meadow surrounded by trees "où la Royne ma mere disposa tout à l'entour de grandes niches, et dans chacune une table ronde à douze personnes."[23] We seem to see this oval meadow and one of the "niches" with its table in the tapestry (Pl. 23).

Lucas de Heere and his friends have thus been careful to make the "Whale" tapestry correspond as closely as possible to what actually took place at Bayonne. Not only has the *Recueil* been used, as for the "Tournament" tapestry, to supplement the Caron design; it is also possible that personal memories of eye-witnesses, who had seen what Marguerite saw, were used. Who can such persons have been, in Antwerp in 1582? Anjou himself, of course, had been at Bayonne as a boy, the youngest of the family. And an older person who had been there, and had taken an active part in some of the masquerades, and who was also in Antwerp in 1582, was François de Bourbon-Montpensier, the "Prince Dauphin".[24] We may therefore fancy that the tapestry may have benefited from the advice of some who remembered the glories of the Bayonne water-festival and who, dissatisfied with Caron's vagueness, might say, "It was the dances of the provinces of France which we saw when we landed from the barge" or, "You must show more clearly the prepared avenue up which we walked to the banquet" or, "The banqueting tables were laid in niches in the oval meadow." The tapestry may therefore be a more accurate record of the festival than the Caron design, though the latter seizes the classical spirit of French court festival, some of which has been lost in the Flemish exuberance of the tapestry.

If we could walk up the avenue on the island we might find ourselves witnessing perhaps the earliest example of a new art form, the *ballet de cour*. Marguerite tells us that the musicians who entered after the banquet were attired as Satyrs, and that the nymphs who danced to their music entered on a luminous rock from which they descended to perform the ballet. Just so did the nymphs representing the Provinces of France enter to perform the famous ballet of 1573; and, in 1581, the *Ballet comique de la reine* was based on entries of Sirens and other water-creatures, with water-nymphs, and Satyrs and wood-nymphs who combined to dance the most superlative ballet yet seen. These future artistic triumphs are present in embryo in the Queen Mother's entertainment at Bayonne, and it is one of the chief fascinations of the marvellous "Whale" tapestry that it shows us in a natural setting of woods and waters the creatures of one of Catherine de' Medici's festivals. We should listen to this tapestry as though it were set to music. The horns of the Tritons are sounding. Near them is the orchestra of stringed instruments concealed on the bank, and on the island dance the provinces of France. We are here present almost at the birth of what was to be the most distinctive art of the French court in the centuries to come.

On June 29th, at Bayonne, knights and ladies of different nations made their appearance[25] and asked to be allowed to give proof of themselves. The two queens, Catherine and her daughter Elizabeth, Queen of Spain, watched from échafauds. The knights and ladies were Charles IX and his brother and various noblemen in masquerade costume; the leaders were followed by groups attired similarly to themselves. After all had assembled, each troop ran the course; this was either a running at the ring or at the quintain. This show, unlike the elaborate dramas staged by the Queen Mother at the water-festival, was simply one of the normal knightly exercises of the court turned into a masquerade through the costumes.

The costumes are described in great detail in the *Recueil*. The King (Charles IX) was attired as an antique Trojan, with a short cuirass and kirtle, high boots, and a mantle on his shoulders; the colour-scheme was predominantly blue and silver. His brother (Henri) followed him as an Amazon, and he was followed (also as members of the King's troop) by a French knight and lady, a Moorish knight and lady, and other couples in different costumes. The women were men, dressed as women. Next followed the troop of the Prince Dauphin, all dressed, like himself, as "femmes à l'antique"; the Duc de Guise and his troop were "Escossois sauvages"; Longueville and his men were star-demons; Nevers and his followers were à la Moresque, with decorations formed of silver leaves hanging round them.

The Caron design (XI, b) which was used in the "Quintain" tapestry shows a festival of the same type as this one, but it is not taking place at Bayonne, but in Paris at the Tuileries. The architecture at the back is based on the garden front of the Tuileries, as it can be seen in Du Cerceau's drawing.[26] The troops in their various exotic costumes are waiting to take their turn at running at the dragon "quintain"; it has a weight attached to its tail, and the object of this exercise was to hit it with the lance and get away without being touched by the swinging weight. Some of the riders are in the act of running the course, one of these having leafy decorations depending from his horse. A queen (Catherine)[27] is watching.

Lucas de Heere, perceiving that the Caron "quintain" design illustrates a show of the same type as the one at Bayonne described in the *Recueil*, used it as the foundation of his "Quintain" tapestry (VI). He swept away the foreground of this design, substituting for it groups in costumes of many nations assembling to take their turn at the running. These groups he probably built up from the description in the *Recueil* of the Bayonne show of this type. His Henri III wears a costume like the one described as worn by Charles IX at Bayonne; there are knights and ladies of many nations in the group, including a Moorish knight. And there are Amazons and "femmes à l'antique" about whose costume the Prince Dauphin, now in Antwerp, might have had memories.

The "Quintain" tapestry thus represents a masquerade running at the quintain built up from two separate occasions on which this type of festival was enacted. For the foreground masquerade of many nations, the description in the *Recueil* of this show at Bayonne was utilised; the actual scene of the running, behind it, was taken from a Caron design depicting the same kind of exercise at the Tuileries, of unknown date but almost certainly within the reign of Charles IX.

There is yet another complication about the "Quintain" tapestry. We believe that Lucas de Heere did not mean it to refer primarily, either to the Bayonne show, or to the undated show at the Tuileries which Caron depicts. He intended it to allude, we believe, to shows *of the same type*, at various dates, and particularly in the reign of Henri III. This matter will be discussed further at a later stage.[28]

Philip II did not come himself to Bayonne for the Interview; his beautiful wife came without her husband to greet her mother, accompanied by no less a person than the terrible Duke of Alva as the emissary entrusted to impart the views and wishes of the King of Spain to the Queen Regent of France. The Interview is well documented from the Spanish side by the letters of Alva to his master,[29] and those of De Alava, the Spanish ambassador, who had also been at Fontainebleau. What Philip wanted was that Catherine should publish the decrees of the Council of Trent in France and enforce them by the setting up of the Inquisition, thus bringing France into line with the Spanish policy in the Netherlands, where the Inquisition was already introduced and working at full pressure, and whither, in two years time, the Duke of Alva would be despatched to impose Philip's idea of Catholic order. The letters of Alva show very clearly that Catherine's reactions were highly displeasing to him; she talked of arranging marriages, which Alva dismissed as not to the point; the point was religion. She talked of herself summoning doctors and theologians to a council which Alva reports with contempt. She would not admit that her chancellor, the tolerant Michel de l'Hôpital, was a Huguenot, nor consent to dismiss him. The young Queen of Spain supported Alva's arguments, earning from her mother the remark "vous êtes devenue bien espagnole".[30] Catherine fenced and hedged and juggled, with a skill which the Spaniards acknowledge, but they could get nothing out of her; and when it was discovered that she was actually at that very moment, and nearby, treating with emissaries from the Grand Turk, their reactions may be imagined. She was also angling for the marriage of Charles IX to that arch-heretic, Elizabeth of England, to whom Ronsard dedicated his collection of verses for masquerades.[31] It was therefore probably not with great satisfaction that Alva watched such a show as that of the costumes of many nations, which, under the circumstances, and to his Spanish pride, may have seemed a piece of frivolous impudence; nor is it likely that he was at all mollified by the effects of poetry and music, or ensnared by the songs of the Sirens of Bayonne. In fact, he only once mentions the festivals in his letters, and that with some irritation, because on one of the occasions when he was pressing on Catherine the necessity for taking strong measures against heretics, to which she was replying with "very weak and cold arguments", there were crowds of courtiers in the next rooms preparing to go to a festival, and who (Alva feared) might overhear their conversation.[32]

Rumours gathered about the Interview of Bayonne. The Huguenots feared that some terrible thing against them was planned there.[33] It was known that a project for the mass extermination of the Reform party had for long been in the air. As was mentioned earlier, William of Orange tells in his apology that when out hunting with Catherine's husband, Henri II of France, that King revealed to him such a plot, information which "William the Silent" received with horror but in silence. Such fears were therefore not groundless. Nevertheless, historians are agreed that the Spanish correspondence proves that no engagement for the adoption of forcible measures against French Protestants, in concert with Spain, was in fact given by Catherine, or by Charles IX, at Bayonne.

Festivals at the Wedding of Marguerite de Valois
and Henry of Navarre, 1572

Henry of Navarre was at Bayonne, as a young boy, with his Calvinist mother; seven years later, he married Marguerite de Valois from whose memories of the "festin" on the island we have quoted. The marriage of Catherine's daughter with the leader of the French Protestants, which looked as though it were intended as a culmination of the conciliatory policy towards Reform which the French court had been pursuing for several years previously, was actually the occasion of the Massacre of St. Bartholomew's Night when most of the Huguenots assembled in Paris for the wedding were exterminated. Some people said that this act of treachery was the trap which had been set at Bayonne. The attack on Admiral Coligny happened whilst the sequence of "magnificences" for the wedding were in progress, and put a sudden stop to them. The history of Catherine's festivals, and Catherine's whole reputation in history, is darkened, or reddened, by those "noces vermeilles", red with blood.

Naturally no "livret" or "recueil" was published describing the magnificences for that disastrous wedding,[34] and nearly all we know about them has to be gleaned from two Protestant authors, who view them with the gravest suspicion. The fullest account is that in the *Mémoires de l'Estat de France sous Charles Neuviesme*, published at Middelburg in 1578, with which various scattered remarks in the works of Agrippa d'Aubigné are roughly in agreement. Both writers view the festivals as sinister portents of the coming massacre. Yet reading between the lines of their notes on the festivals, which are both fragmentary and strongly coloured by their horror of what happened after them, we gain the impression that the magnificences for the Navarre-Valois wedding were a set of the usual type, like those which had gone before at Fontainebleau and Bayonne, and like those which were to follow in later years.

It appears that one of the entertainments was planned to be based on a "fort" which was to be attacked, as though in play, by Coligny and his co-religionists, and defended by the King and the Catholics, who were to be dangerously armed and to kill the unsuspecting attackers. The "fort" plan, however, was cancelled because Coligny was not in sufficiently good health to take part in the supposed game.[35]

An entertainment which did take place consisted in a procession of chariots, formed like rocks, on which were figures representing marine gods and sea-creatures, amongst them Neptune and his seahorses. This was evidently a musical show, since on one of the chariots was Etienne Le Roy, the famous singer.[36]

On another day, the show held was called the "Paradis d'Amour" (according to D'Aubigné, this took place behind closed doors, without an audience). The setting represented Hell and Paradise, and the heavens with the revolving spheres of the stars. In the "Paradise" were twelve nymphs. It was defended by the King and his brothers, and the attacking rebels whom they sent to Hell were Navarre and his Huguenot companions. The attacking and defending knights were attired in "diverses livrées." In the second act, the imprisoned rebel knights were delivered from Hell by a descending Mercury, represented by Le Roy singing divinely, and a Cupid. The nymphs celebrated the rescue of the rebels by dancing a long and complicated ballet.

After the ballet, there was a combat between the knights of both sides, and the hall was alarmingly filled with fire and smoke from exploding "trainées de poudre." [37]

On another day, the Louvre was prepared for the exercise of running at the ring ("courir la bague") with a stand for the watching ladies. Several troops presented themselves, amongst others the King and his brother attired as Amazons; the King of Navarre and his troop, dressed as Turks in long golden robes and with turbans on their heads; the Prince de Condé and others "à l'estradiotte"; the Duc de Guise and his friends, dressed, like the King, as Amazons.[38] It was on the day following that on which this festival was held that the unsuccesful attempt to assassinate Coligny was made. It was therefore the last of an interrupted series, for there were naturally no other festivals after this. An atmosphere of gloom and suspicion was generated and eventually the terrible massacre broke out.

It is quite certain that none of the Caron designs refer to these dreadful wedding festivals, about which the less said the better, and which could not be published nor recorded in art. Nevertheless, since they were clearly on the usual pattern we may look at the Caron drawings and the tapestries to gain an impression of the kind of things they were doing in Paris just before the Massacre of St. Bartholomew. Consider, for example, the Caron "Quintain" drawing (XI, b), where the masqueraders are "running the course" at the Tuileries; Turks in long robes and turbans are drawn up on the left awaiting their turn. Just so would Navarre and his men as Turks have awaited their turn to "courir la bague" at the last festival of the interrupted wedding series. The show on that day was evidently of the same type as the one at Bayonne and the one in the Caron design which were combined to form the "Quintain" tapestry (VI) In that fatal August, 1572, Protestant-Turks were taking part in such a show with Catholic-Amazons.

The sinister "fort" plan in which, according to Huguenot rumour after the massacre, a mock attack and defence of a fort was to have turned into murder, would have been like those attacks and defences of magic castles in which, at Fontainebleau, Catholics and Protestants had taken part on opposite sides, *without* a following massacre. The attack and defence of the island (I; IX, a), the attack and defence of the elephant (VIII, XII) are festival mock combats of this type.

The combat between the knights "en diverses livrées" which took place after the ballet of the "Paradis d'Amour" when the hall was alarmingly filled with smoke and fire from the "trainées de poudre", presaging horrors to come, would have been like the finale of the "Knights of Great Britain and Ireland" tournament at Bayonne, when the combatants passed between one another without touching and were separated by the fireballs which can be seen exploding quite harmlessly in the Caron drawing of this event (IX, b) and in the "Tournament" tapestry (II). In the "Elephant" tapestry (VIII), they are exploding under the Turkish attackers of the elephant-fort. These fireballs were evidently a normal firework accompaniment to such shows.

The rocks entering bearing the mythological creatures of the waters to musical accompaniment sounds like an entertainment specially contributed by the Queen Mother to the series, with a theme similar to that of her water-shows at Fontainebleau and Bayonne.

The "Paradis d'Amour" must have been structurally a very interesting and significant performance, and the understandable absence of a "livret" describing it is an unfortunate gap in the history of French court entertainment. It evidently used fairly elaborate stage machinery and its plot seems to have combined the masquerade attack and defence, the tournament, and the mythological drama with ballet. The complicated dance of the nymphs lasted for over an hour, and was perhaps directed by the Savoyard ballet expert, Baltasar de Beaujoyeulx, who was to produce the famous later ballets of 1573 and 1581. There is a payment in the royal accounts, dated on the last day of August 1572, to Baltasar de Beaujoyeulx of five hundred livres tournois, [39] probably indicating that he had been employed for the ballets at the ill-fated wedding festivals of August, 1572. A manuscript by Jean Passerat contains descriptions of devices probably to be distributed at these festivals.[40] They are mostly on the theme of peace and union through the wedding.

From the rumours which we hear of them—rumours distorted by the horror of the subsequent massacre—the magnificences for the Navarre-Valois wedding sound like a series of "conciliatory" festivals, bringing together the opposite religious parties in the normal chivalrous pastimes of the court, diversified, as usual, by special efforts of the Queen Mother which were probably of considerable artistic importance.

The general similarity of such shows to those which had taken place at Bayonne may have helped to foster the belief that the wedding festivals deliberately lured the Protestants to Paris to be massacred and that this trap had been plotted at Bayonne.[41] But we know that there was no anti-Protestant extermination plot at Bayonne.

The striking feature about the political and religious situation of the year 1572 is that the Protestant-Catholic wedding looks like a continuation of the policy of resistance to Spanish pressure which Catherine and Charles IX—and particularly Charles—had been pursuing in the preceding years; yet the massacre totally reversed that policy, with a suddenness which astounded the world, and played right into the hands of Philip II, who is said to have laughed aloud at the news of it.

The Peace of St. Germain of 1570 had given more favourable terms to the Huguenots than any previous treaty. A policy of toleration seemed about to be inaugurated. It was in this hopeful year that Charles IX founded his *Académie de Poésie et Musique* in which Protestant and Catholic musicians collaborated in the effort to recover the music of the ancients and its effects upon the souls of men.[42] In the following year, 1571, Charles married the daughter of the Emperor Maximilian II whose influence was all in the direction of religious toleration and who was working to that end with German Protestant princes.[43] The marriage of the Catholic princess, Catherine's daughter Marguerite, to Navarre, the Protestant, must have seemed like a further step in the conciliatory direction.

Such a policy was, almost of necessity, anti-Spanish. The moving spirits in a plan for active French intervention in the Netherlands against Spain were the Huguenot leader, Admiral Coligny, and Count Louis of Nassau, the brother of William of Orange. Charles IX, who was very much under the influence of Coligny at this time, seemed enthusiastically in favour of the plan.

The terrible Duke of Alva had gone to the Netherlands with his armies in 1567, there to enforce the iron will of Philip II. The standard of revolt against his impossible government was raised by William of Orange in 1568, and his brother Louis came to the fore as a military leader, though this first campaign of the "rebels" ended in defeat. Orange and his brothers went to France to strengthen their contacts with the French Protestant leaders, whilst the wretched Netherlands were subjected to ever more rigid measures of repression by the triumphant Alva.

In September, 1571, Charles IX and his mother were at Blois, holding conferences with Coligny and with Louis of Nassau, who had earlier met Charles secretly in Paris.[44] Louis of Nassau was very active in the mysterious negotiations going on at this time around Charles IX. It was planned to send an expedition to the Netherlands against Spain; Coligny and his Huguenot troops would take part and it would be sanctioned and aided by Charles IX. Louis seems to have held out the possibility that Charles might be elected Emperor, through his influence with the German princes, and become the centre of a European grouping counterbalancing the power of Spain. Louis was much in favour of the marriage of Marguerite with Navarre which, according to some, he helped to arrange through his friendship with Navarre's mother, the devout Jeanne d'Albret. Obviously such a match, from the Orange point of view, would be of value in cementing the alliance of the French King with their Huguenot allies. Walsingham, then in Paris, knew of Charles' alliance with Louis of Nassau and favoured it; these plans were partially linked with a project, very dear to Catherine, for the marriage of one of her sons to Elizabeth of England.

In the spring of 1572, Louis of Nassau, believing himself sure of the support of Charles IX, invaded the Netherlands, together with some Huguenot troops under La Noue, and took the town of Mons. Siege was laid to the town by the Spaniards, but William of Orange was also moving, and prospects were looking brighter for the "rebels" than ever before. Philip II was seriously alarmed. Through the capture of some papers, he gained certain information of what he had already suspected, namely that Charles IX was in correspondence with Louis of Nassau and that France was supporting the "rebels". Fortunately, a miracle happened to save him, and that miracle was the Massacre of St. Bartholomew, which destroyed the French Protestant leaders and all hope of French help for the revolt of the Netherlands; it made inevitable the fall of Mons, and wrecked all Orange's chances, for the present, of breaking the power of Alva. The Huguenots shut themselves up defensively in La Rochelle and Mons surrendered. Not only were the French Protestant leaders invited to the wedding betrayed to their deaths by the massacre; it was also an utter betrayal of Louis of Nassau.

Other results of the massacre were that it made impossible (or so it then seemed) one of Catherine's most cherished projects, the marriage of a son to the Queen of England; and it very nearly ruined another, namely the election of Henri to the throne of Poland.

Fortunately, it is not necessary for us here to attempt the task of finding out who was responsible for the attack on Coligny which led to this appalling disaster. The alacrity with which the massacre was carried out, not only in Paris but in other French towns, shows that there was fanatical opposition in France to the policies which Charles IX had recently been pursuing and a dangerous tendency to mob violence on which the extremist Catholic and pro-Spanish party, of which the Guises afterwards became the acknowledged heads, could count.

The deed was lauded to the skies in Rome and Philip's satisfaction knew no bounds. Many in France publicly praised the massacre "which in their hearts they detested, because they thought that the good of the state demanded that they should stand by a deed done". [45] Medals were struck in its honour, including one showing Charles IX enthroned with the sword of justice in his hand and many corpses under his feet; the motto is *Virtus in rebelles*. [46] More terrible still is the hunting metaphor used of the massacre. Charles' violent and almost pathological passion for hunting was well-known, and he was the author of a treatise on his favourite sport, *La Chasse Royale*. Now, said admirers of the massacre, he had shown himself a hunter of other game. Rumoured plots for the extermination of Huguenots had been spoken of as "La Chasse Royale" even before the massacre, [47] and the mind of Agrippa d'Aubigné was so deeply imbued with this metaphor that the name "Camillo Capilupi" of the author of the work in praise of the French King's pious "stratagem" in luring so many heretics into the trap with the bait of the wedding suggests to him "Taker of Wolves", although it was his real name and not a pseudonym. [48] The simile of the hunter's trap is used of the festivals by the author of the *Mémoires de l'Estat de France sous Charles Neuviesme* when he says that

"il (Charles) faisoit comme le chasseur qui chante & loue fort la beste qu'il detestoit & maudissoit en chassant." [49]

It has been essential to discuss the "noces vermeilles" in the sequence of the festivals because no one in the sixteenth century, and particularly no Protestant, could ever forget them. The Valois Tapestries, as we know, were designed by a Protestant. Lucas de Heere's English patron had led the delegation to Paris to confirm the alliance with Charles IX, which witnessed the wedding festivals and their ghastly sequel. Lucas noted the awful "feeste" in his diary of current events. Du Plessis-Mornay, representative of French liberal Protestantism at Antwerp in 1582, had barely escaped from the massacre with his life. It was bound up with the history of the revolt of the Netherlands, for the sudden treachery of the French king ruined the first Orange liberation campaign. The *Mémoires de l'Estat de France sous Charles Neuviesme* which are the chief source for the festivals at the Navarre-Valois wedding, tell the whole story from the Protestant point of view (the book it will be remembered was published at Middelburg) and with horror at the treachery of the French court. This work is very likely to have been known to Lucas de Heere and he might have read in it of the festivals (about which he would also have known from eye-witnesses) in the violently anti-Charles IX light in which its author sees them.

It would be safe to conjecture that the attitude of Lucas de Heere to Charles IX would be highly unfavourable, but this does not rest on conjecture for among the papers by Lucas in the Rotarius album at Ghent there is a poem by him about Charles IX, which is as follows:

Charles de Valois
Tu as autrefois

Donné cest indice
Nous faisant vanter
Que deuois planter
PIETE ET IUSTICE

Lon disoit de toy
Ce ieune bon Roy
L'Eglise console:
Et tout reuestu
D'honneur et vertu
VA CHASSER L'IDOLE.

Mais veu ton forfait
Si enorme et laid,
De droit on te nomme,
Un boreau papal,
CHASSEUR DELOIAL
De Dieu et de l'homme. [50]

The first verse alludes to Charles' device of *Pietas et Justitia;* the second speaks of the trust which the Protestants placed in him, summed up in "va chasser l'idole", which is an anagram of Charles de Valois; the third finds another anagram of that name in "chasseur deloial", the treacherous hunter turned papal executioner.

It was the man who wrote this who turned the Caron designs, all of festivals in the reign of Charles IX, into the Valois Tapestries, *in which every allusion to Charles IX has been obliterated.* We would not expect to find him in the foreground portraits for these, as was explained earlier, depict only members of the family of Catherine de' Medici who were alive in 1582. But he has also been obliterated within the festivals, in which he should have been the leading participant. In the Caron drawings he can be faintly seen in the barge at Bayonne (X, a), as the leading knight in the Bayonne tournament (IX, b), dancing at the reception for the Poles (X, b). In the corresponding tapestries there either is no sign of him or the leading rôles are given to someone else, who looks like his brother Henri. This substitution becomes flagrantly obvious in the "Quintain" (VI), where the foreground group is built up from the description of the Bayonne masquerade in which Charles was in the leading rôle as an antique Trojan captain; in the tapestry this rôle is assigned to Henri III.

This obliteration of the scapegoat for the massacre is perhaps negative evidence that the St. Bartholomew neurosis haunted the Protestant designer of the tapestries.

That the Protestants were Turks on that last day of the fatal wedding festivals throws a kind of tragic illumination over the masquerades. The costumes of many countries become in themselves a kind of "politique" symbol, the masks under which foes could for a while disguise their sectarian personalities for the purposes of conciliatory fraternisation in the festivals—

festivals which on one occasion most signally failed to achieve such an object. We have seen how close the "Elephant" tapestry is to Lucas' drawing for the Ghent entry of Anjou standing as the "politique" peacemaker between the warring religious parties. Is the masquerade war behind him, between Turks and others, in itself an expression of the same theme?

The Festivals for the Polish Ambassadors, 1573

Exactly one year after the wedding festivals which had been so disastrously interrupted, Paris was again *en fête* for the reception of the ambassadors from Poland who arrived in the capital in August, 1573, to offer the crown of their country to Catherine's son, Henri. The French campaign for the election of Henri had at last succeeded, and the ambassadors brought with them the decree of election. The Polish ambassadors and their suite made a great impression during their state appearances in the streets of Paris "dressed in long robes of cloth of gold.. the bridles of their horses trimmed with silver and brilliant with precious stones." [51] They must have looked like De Bruyn's noble Polish rider (Pl. 7, b).

The Poles were treated to a whole set of magnificences of the usual pattern. We have already learned this from Pierre Colins who speaks of the "festins", "joustes", "combats à pied & à cheual" which took place in their honour.[52] This implies tournaments, and mock combats, barriers and running at the ring or at the quintain, as well as the "festin" on a splendid scale at the Tuileries which was the Queen Mother's special contribution to the series and of which a printed description was published, soon after the event, by Jean Dorat. [53]

Dorat's *Magnificentissimi spectaculi* is in Latin verse, includes French verses by Ronsard and Amadis Jamyn, and describes the ballet, with some illustrations. Sixteen nymphs representing the provinces of France came in on a moving rock from which they descended to dance the long and intricate ballet designed by Beaujoyeulx. They presented devices to the spectators on which were designs symbolic of the provinces they represented; these devices are illustrated in Dorat's booklet, which also has a picture of the rock with the sixteen nymphs disposed in niches on it (Pl. 24, c) and of a moment in their dance (Pl. 24, b).

Brantôme calls this "le plus beau ballet qui fust jamais faict au monde" [54] and makes his description of it an occasion for the defence of the Queen Mother for her expenditure on such shows which added so greatly to the prestige of France. D'Aubigné tells of the astonishment of the Poles at the spectacle and how they exclaimed with one accord that "le bal de France estoit chose impossible à contrefaire à tous les rois de la terre". [55] The famous French *ballet de cour* was now fully fledged.

We have watched its gradual growth in the entertainments contributed by the Queen Mother. Brantôme recalls Bayonne in connection with the ballet for the Poles, not to compare it with the island show, but in connection with the devices. Speaking of the devices symbolic of the provinces of France which the nymphs presented, he reminds that at Bayonne "quasi semblables presens se firent en un combat qui s'y fist." [56] He is thinking, of course, of the "Knights of Great Britain and Ireland" tournament in which the devices on the shields of the knights were repeated on the pendants presented by nymphs. This is a valuable reminder that the ballet for the Poles, which has always been studied as an early example of *ballet de cour* in total isolation from its context as one of a set of magnificences, is the offshoot of the allegorical tournament, such as we see in the "Tournament" tapestry. The devices presented at ballets are a vestige of this connection.

After his comparison of the devices at Bayonne with those at the ballet for the Poles, Brantôme continues in the following words:

> "Et nottez que toutes ces inventions ne venoient d'autre boutique ny d'autre esprit que de la royne; car elle y estoit maistresse et fort inventive en toutes choses. Elle avoit cela que, quelques magnificences qui se fissent à la court, la sienne passoit toutes les autres. Aussy disoit on qu'il n'y avoit que la royne mere pour faire quelque chose de beau. Et si telles despenses coustoient, aussy donnoient elles du plaisir: disant en cela souvent qu'elle vouloit imiter les empereurs romains qui s'estudioient d'exhiber des jeux au peuple et luy donner plaisir, et l'amuser autant en cela sans luy donner loysir à mal faire." [57]

Here we have Brantôme's confirmation that the best shows in a series of magnificences were always those given by the Queen Mother, and that they were of her own invention. It is her shows which lead to *ballet de cour*, now emerging in the entertainment for the Poles. The question of Italian influence on French *ballet de cour* seems solved. It was invented, in the context of the chivalrous pastimes of the court, by an Italian, and a Medici, the Queen Mother. Many poets, artists, musicians, choreographers, contributed to the result, but it was she who was the inventor, one might perhaps say, the producer; she who had the ladies of her court trained to perform these ballets in settings of her devising.

Note, too, the purpose which Brantôme had often heard the Queen Mother say was behind her expenditure of money in this way. Like a Roman Emperor, she entertained the people with games and pleasing shows so that they might not have "loysir à mal faire." What universal honour would have been accorded to her for using her artistic genius with this civilised purpose, had it not been for the mischief which broke out during the festivals at the marriage of her daughter! The Massacre of St. Bartholomew not only blackened the name of Catherine de'Medici in history; it obscured her life-work as a great creative artist in festivals.

The Caron design (X, b) on which the "Polish" tapestry (IV) is based, shows three couples dancing; the music for the dance appears to be coming from the figures of Apollo and the ladies seated on a rock and holding musical instruments. A wall of courtiers divides the dancers from the formal garden in the background; near the rock is a seated woman, recognisable as Catherine de' Medici as Caron elsewhere depicts her. On the parterres of the garden are two coats-of-arms; one, the arms of France; the other probably those of the Queen Mother. The Poles, distributed on and between the platforms in the foreground, watch the marvels of the French court ball with gestures of admiration. The scene really takes place in a ball-room, [58] and not out of doors; the line of spectators behind the dancers follows the position of the wall which has been removed to show the gardens which have been identified as those of the Tui-

a   The Rock in the "Polish Ambassadors" (p. 69)

b   The Ballet

c   The Rock

b, c   Engravings from J. Dorat's Account of the Entertainment for the
Polish Ambassadors, 1573 (p. 67)

leries.[59] Some of the statues may be temporary ones of plaster, such as we know were designed by Germain Pilon for the Polish festivals.[60]

It is not the famous ballet of the nymphs of the provinces of France which is going on, but an ordinary court ball, with three couples in court dress. We know that it was customary after the presentation of some elaborately prepared symbolic ballet for the evening to end with a general court ball; and we know from d'Aubigné that such a ball certainly took place after the ballet of the sixteen provinces and went on far into the night.[61] It is this ball, after the ballet, which the dance in the drawing shows us; one of the dancers has a vague resemblance to Charles IX.

The rock (Pl. 24, a) alludes to the famous ballet which has just taken place. At first sight one would take the figures playing musical instruments on it to be Apollo and the Muses, but, though the topmost figure with the lyre is certainly Apollo, the female figures are not character-ised as Muses and bear some resemblance to the provinces of France as shown on the rock (Pl. 24, c) illustrating Dorat's account of the ballet. Apollo does not appear on that rock, but the illustrated title-page to Dorat's book shows a "Gallic Pallas" and a "Gallic Apollo" on either side of a Jupiter, alluding to the Queen Mother as the Gallic Pallas, and to Henri as the Gallic Apollo, both serving the King as Jupiter. It may therefore be conjectured that the Apollo on the rock is a "Gallic Apollo" uniting with his music, not the Muses, but the provinces of France, in harmony under the King. The "Gallic Pallas" who invented the show sits beside the rock.

We are also inclined to associate Caron's "Quintain" drawing (XI, b) with the festivals for the Polish ambassadors. The masquerade "quintain", or masquerade running at the ring, was, as we have seen, a common feature in a series of magnificences, and this one is taking place at the Tuileries.[62] Catherine in the pavilion here, with her coat-of-arms above her,[63] is rather closely parallel to the Catherine with the Tuileries gardens behind her in the other drawing. It is also not impossible that some of the watching figures in the pavillon, particularly the man leaning out excitedly, may be dressed in Caron's somewhat vague idea of Polish costume. This drawing may therefore, we suggest, refer to one of those "combats à pied & à cheval" which Pierre Colins tells us took place in honour of the Poles. [64]

It is even possible that Caron's "Fontainebleau" drawing (IX, a), with its crowds of spectators along the banks, may be a spectacle given for the Poles in 1573. They went to Fontainebleau, together with the whole court, before leaving for Poland with Henri. [65]

Colins' statement that tapestries were made at Enghien representing a whole set of festivals for the Polish ambassadors rather supports the hypothesis that more than one of the Caron drawings may refer to these festivals for—as we suggested earlier—it seems possible that the Enghien tapestries may have been made from Caron designs. Caron was working for the French court at the time of the Polish festivals, for he painted the decorations on the triumphal arches for Henri's entry into Paris as King of Poland,[66] which took place on the same day as Catherine's evening festival at the Tuileries.

From the point of view of the Valois Tapestries, however, there is only one of the Caron designs which we can be sure that the author of the tapestries *recognised* as belonging to the festivals for the Poles, and that is the ball at the Tuileries with the rock of the ballet of the provinces of France. There are no corrections or expansions of the festival scene introduced into the "Polish" tapestry from Dorat's printed account, such as were made in the "Bayonne" tapestries from the printed *Recueil*. The tapestry accepts the rock of the ballet, reversed, and the three dancing couples of Caron's design, without adding anything to the festival from printed sources (X, b; IV).

The tapestry, however, makes several alterations from the drawing. Catherine has been moved to the centre, and the empty chair beside her emphasises that a king has risen to dance; but the dancing king, in the couple nearest to the rock, no longer resembles Charles ix but is dark and agile and wears the "bonnet Henri iii".

Great weight is thrown in the tapestry on the Polish spectators, and their wonderful costumes. The figure on the left, with his back to us, is a "nobilis Polonus"[67] wearing a long robe of rich reddish cloth of gold. On it is a brilliant pattern composed of birds, crowns, and couchant lions surrounded by sun-rays. It has been pointed out by M. Crick-Kuntziger that this pattern occurs on stuffs in two well-known Brussels tapestries of the early sixteenth century, whence J. Ehrmann concluded that this pattern was added in the atelier by the weavers.[68] There are other "nobiles" amongst the Polish spectators, in reddish gold robes and caps; the one in the centre is in darker clothes and wears a round hat. The Poles seem to penetrate into the festival itself; the bewhiskered figure leaning on Catherine's chair looks like one of them.

The head Polish ambassador was Prince Albertus Laski,[69] for whom the figure in the gorgeously patterned robe is perhaps intended. Though the Duc de Joyeuse appears to be involved with him, his presence here is an anachronistic insertion, belonging to the time of the other foreground portraits and not to that of the festivals for the Poles, some of whom, however, seem to wear velvet hats of his pattern.

Caron's Polish spectators gave Lucas de Heere an opportunity to revel in his love of costume of which he took full advantage. Perhaps he also wished to stress that here were people of a foreign nation admiring the festivals of the French court and choosing a ruler from the French royal family—as the people of Flanders and Brabant had now chosen Anjou as their Duke and were raising an admiring monument to French festivals in tapestry. [70]

Poland was remarkable in sixteenth-century Europe for its tolerance in matters of religion. The country had early been infiltrated with the influences of the Reformation, and was the home and place of refuge of sectaries of the most diverse kinds; but Catholicism had maintained a strong hold and was being reinvigorated with Counter Reformation enthusiasm. All the ingredients, therefore, which in other countries were leading to wars or to the enforcement of religious conformity by forcible methods, were present in Poland, yet Poles of all classes were unanimous in deploring the resort to violence for the settlement of religious differences.[71] A zealously Catholic Polish nobleman is reported to have said that he would give half his life to see heretics return to the true religion, but his whole life to prevent them from being forced to do so.[72] Religious toleration was an established fact in Poland, and there only in Europe.

The Poles were therefore, it might be said, symbols of those "politique" aspirations which in other countries failed to materialise.

The campaign for the election of Henri de Valois to the throne of Poland was very ably conducted by Monluc, Bishop of Valence—well-known as a liberal and conciliatory Catholic— and was going well when news reached the country of the Massacre of St. Bartholomew. [73] Pictures of its cruel scenes were circulated and aroused great indignation, and things began to look black for Henri's candidature. In a despairing letter, Monluc complains that the unhappy wind from France has sunk the ship which he had almost brought into port. A propaganda campaign had to be instituted to defend and explain the part played by Charles IX and his brother in the shocking business; Pibrac's famous apology was a part of this effort. Monluc eventually did bring his ship into port and obtained the election of Henri. Amongst the conditions to which he agreed in Henri's name was a promise to "maintenir la paix entre les dissidents de la religion."

Of the twelve ambassadors who brought the decree of election to Paris, some were Catholics and some were Protestants. [74] They were not only firm in demanding adherence to the promise to maintain religious peace in Poland; they also intervened on behalf of French Protestants in France, [75] demanding, amongst other things, that the property of the relatives of the victims of the massacres of the preceding year should be restored to them. Murmurs were raised by some in Paris against the attitude of the Polish ambassadors, nevertheless they were received, as we have seen, with the utmost honour by the court. In the context of this situation the festivals for the Poles begin to look like a celebration of return to pre-massacre policies, a negation or abolition of the massacre as an unfortunate mistake, a rehabilitation of the Protestant-Catholic marriage whose festivals it had darkened.

The bride and bridegroom of the former year, Marguerite and Henry of Navarre, seem to have been very much on show during the visit of the Poles, although Navarre had been kept more or less a prisoner since the fatal events which followed his marriage. When the ambassadors, shortly after their arrival, made formal calls on the members of the royal family, these included a visit to the King and Queen of Navarre. This was the occasion on which, according to Brantôme, Marguerite scored a double triumph for her beauty and her learning. She appeared "si belle et si superbement et richement parée et accoustrée, avecq' si grande majesté et grace, que tous demeurarent perdus d'une telle beauté." [76] Albertus Laski was so deeply impressed that he felt that he desired to see nothing more after such a vision and would willingly have his eyes put out, like a Turkish pilgrim after seeing the tomb of Mahomet. [77] She also astounded all present by her learning and culture when she replied herself in Latin to the Bishop of Cracow's address. [78] At the Queen Mother's "festin" for the Poles at the Tuileries, Marguerite wore what Brantôme considers the most becoming of all her gowns, "une robe de velours incarnadin d'Espaigne, fort chargée de clinquant". [79] Always a star turn at the French court, Marguerite was evidently particularly carefully "produced" to impress the Poles.

At the two most important ceremonies of their visit, the swearing of the oath by their new king, Henri, in Notre Dame, and the presentation to him of the decree of election in the "grande salle" at the Louvre, Marguerite and her husband were prominently seated as members of the royal family. [80] For the presentation of the decree, a platform was specially erected: on it, in the centre, sat Charles IX between the two Queens, his mother and his wife; next to Catherine was Henri, the King of Poland; on Charles' other side, next to his wife, sat his youngest brother, François; and next to Francois, the King and Queen of Navarre. The Prince Dauphin was also there (there were thus two people in Antwerp in 1582 who would well remember all this, Anjou and the Prince Dauphin). It was in the "grande salle" at the Louvre that, exactly a year previously, Navarre and Marguerite had been betrothed. [81] Through this grouping, their marriage must have seemed, in a manner, publicly reaffirmed to the Poles and to all those present.

The whole of French policy was, in fact, veering back to what it had been before the massacre. Hopes were again raised of marrying Henri to the Queen of England; this was referred to in one of the paintings by Caron decorating the triumphal arches for Henri's entry as King of Poland. [82] In the spring of the year, negotiations had been reopened between the French court, the princes of Germany, and William of Orange for some united effort to check the power of Spain by supporting the revolt in the Netherlands. [83] The moment when the massacre seemed to have taken France right into the Spanish camp had passed. Now policies are almost back at what they were just before the massacre; friendship with England with renewed hope of the English match; the election of Henri as King of Poland achieved; renewed contacts with Louis of Nassau and William of Orange; the marriage of Marguerite and Navarre re-emphasised.

In this situation, the magnificences for the Polish ambassadors begin to appear almost as the continuation of the interrupted magnificences of the Navarre wedding festivals at the French court but this time *without* a massacre of invited Protestant Poles.

In the *Mémoires de l'Estat de France sous Charles Neuviesme*, the whole story of the important visit of the Polish ambassadors to Paris is told, with emphasis on their intervention in favour of French Protestants. The author also quotes from Dorat's book some description of the festival at the Tuileries.[84] From these memoirs, therefore, as well as from his friends, Lucas de Heere could have been fully informed of the situation around the Polish festivals. Looking at the Polish ambassadors in the tapestry, we wonder whether an attempt has been made to indicate through their costumes that they are both Catholics and Protestants, whether, in fact, varied Polish costume may also be a "politique" symbol.

Great weight is placed, in the tapestry foregrounds on the brilliant figure of Marguerite who appears three times. The Protestant-Catholic wedding is reaffirmed when she and her husband stand in front of the Bayonne festival, and it is through her appearance with her brother Anjou in the "Elephant" that the Anjou tapestries are linked with the family groups in the others.

CHAPTER II

HENRI'S JOURNEY

Late in 1573, after considerable delays, Henri started on the journey to his new kingdom.[1] He would pass, first through Lorraine, the domain of his brother-in-law, Duke Charles, and afterwards through the territories of the Empire. Charles IX had been taken gravely ill and was unable to escort his brother on his way, but his other royal relations went with him on the first part of his journey, through Lorraine. Catherine herself fondly accompanied her favourite son; his brother François and his sister Marguerite came too; and his brother-in-law, Charles of Lorraine. The Polish ambassadors, of course, attended their new monarch; a concourse of French noblemen and dignitaries were in his train; and many troops for his protection, including large numbers of German mercenaries, or "reîtres". It was a vast concourse of people travelling over the roads to the north, with the members of the French court at its centre, a journey which, for its importance, might be compared to the journey to Bayonne of former days. Then, as now, the first stage of the journey was to Lorraine; then, the christening of the first child of Charles of Lorraine and Catherine's daughter, Claude, had been attended at Bar-le-Duc; there was a christening of a later child of the couple on this occasion, at Nancy, and two of the ecclesiastical Polish ambassadors stood as godfathers to the infant. Duke Charles gave the new King of Poland a royal welcome at Nancy, and it was there that Henri first saw Louise de Lorraine, whom he afterwards married.

At Blamont, a town in Lorraine on the borders of the Empire, Henri said farewell to his mother, brother, and sister, who then returned homeward. But not before a very important interview had taken place between the members of the French court and certain personages who had come to Blamont to meet them. Count Louis of Nassau came to Blamont, empowered by his brother the Prince of Orange to renew negotiations with Catherine and her sons. He was accompanied by Count Christopher, son of the Elector Palatine Frederick III, the most important of the Protestant princes of Germany. The Interview of Blamont between the French court and the Orange and German Protestant representatives was held more or less in secret,[2] and is much less well-known to history than the immensely publicised Interview of Bayonne between France and Spain. The two Interviews were both preceded by a long state journey of the French court, such as we see in the "Journey" tapestry, and it has been suggested that the tapestry represents the journey to Bayonne.[3] This is, however, not the case though an understandable guess; the tapestry represents the journey to Blamont and alludes unmistakeably to the Valois-Nassau Interview of Blamont.

Foreign alliances, and especially the French alliance, were forever a necessity for William of of Orange as he battled alone, and with limited resources, against the Spanish tyranny in the Netherlands, and the recent "revirement" of French policy towards the pre-massacre alignment made possible the reopening of contacts with the French court. Louis of Nassau, the agent for these negotiations in pre-massacre days, had already been at work on a rapprochement. In a remarkable letter which he wrote to Charles IX in June, 1573, he pointed out the good position in which the King had been placed before the massacre. The Queen of England had been well disposed towards him and perhaps willing for a closer connection with his family; the German princes were desirous of electing him King of the Romans; the Netherlands, driven to desperation by the tyranny of their own sovereign, were eager to throw themselves into his arms. All this had been owing to his edict of pacification (the Peace of St. Germain of 1570). How changed was everything now! "Your Majesty to-day", said Louis bluntly, "is near to ruin", whilst the Spaniard, his mortal enemy, had gained by the massacre. He reminded the King of his treachery towards Coligny, and warned him that he was surrounded by men who desired to work his ruin, and who, for their own purposes, would cause him "to bathe still deeper than he had done before in the blood of his subjects." In conclusion, Louis spoke a few solemn words concerning religion, and the religious sentiment which is "deeply rooted in the souls of men and not to be plucked out by force of arms." [4]

At the Interview of Blamont, Catherine and Henri renewed the earlier understandings with Orange and with the German princes. They undertook to aid the revolt of the Netherlands against Spain. Catherine envisaged Henri as a leader in this, but the importance of François as a candidate for the rôle was already emerging. He had been friendly with Coligny, and was believed by the Protestants to have been less implicated in the massacre than the rest of the family. His legend as the Catholic "politique" or tolerant prince was already forming, and already Orange had his eye on this French prince whom he was in later years to place in the position of titular sovereign of the Netherlands.

Louis of Nassau wrote a letter to his brother William reporting to him what had transpired at Blamont.[5] He tells him that the King of France has promised to espouse the cause of the Netherlands in the same way that the Protestant princes of Germany espouse it. Money has been given to Louis for this purpose; in fact large quantities of gold were taken on the journey to be handed over to those whom it was expected to meet. He reports also that François has shown himself to be especially friendly.

> "I had an interview with the Duc d'Alençon (afterwards Anjou) who whispered to me as he pressed my hand that if he had the government there (i.e. in the Netherlands) as his brother that of Poland, he would second you to the utmost. I know how to use his fidelity, which would be of no slight service to us. If God grant that France and Poland work together, as I think they promise to do, I believe our affairs will be marvellously furthered." [6]

Thus the future position of Anjou in the Netherlands was adumbrated between him and Louis at Blamont in 1573, and a parallel was drawn between such a position and that which Henri was going to Poland to take up. We may here pause to reflect that only two people in 1582 would know of this conversation. One was Anjou who privately whispered the words to Louis; the other was William of Orange to whom his dead brother had reported them in a confidential letter.

We may also reflect that it was at a secret meeting, in the wilds of Lorraine, that the French royal family seem to have reaffirmed the policy which had been urged upon them by Coligny and other victims of the massacre. The historical documents upon which we depend for the reconstruction of what passed at Blamont in 1573 had not been published in 1582. Who, amongst those living in 1582, would have had inner knowledge of what passed at Blamont? None but those who had been there, namely Catherine de' Medici, Henri, now King of France, and Anjou; and William of Orange who had received the reports of it from his brother.

After parting with his family at Blamont, Henri and his train crossed the frontier into the territories of the Empire.[7] For a considerable part of his transit through these lands, Count Louis of Nassau and the German Count Christopher remained with him, assuaging by their influence the difficulties and dangers of the way. Henri visited Christopher's father, the Elector Palatine, at Heidelberg, and d'Aubigné says that he was there shown a portrait of Coligny and pictures of the horrors of the massacre, with which his Protestant host reproached him.[8] Eventually he reached Poland, and was received at Cracow by vast concourses of people.

Encouraged by the renewed French support and by French financial assistance, Louis of Nassau immediately busied himself in raising troops for a new attempt at a liberating invasion of the Netherlands. It is said that when he ceased his escort of Henri through the Empire, he actually engaged for his own purposes a large number of the German mercenary troops who had been employed to accompany Henri.[9] Early in 1574 he and Count Christopher crossed the Rhine with an army. A new campaign for the liberation of the Netherlands had begun, and was noted in large letters by the Flemish refugee in London, Lucas de Heere, in his diary of current events; "Count Lodovic and Count Christopher, the Palsgrave's son, with other German noblemen, came over the Rhine.." [10]

The eyes of all Europe, indeed, were upon this sequence of events. Philip Sidney and Hubert Languet, who had both witnessed the Massacre of St. Bartholomew, follow them with close attention as they anxiously correspond with one another about European affairs. Languet urges Sidney, who had once been talked of as a possible candidate for the Polish throne, to go to Cracow in time to see the wonderful shows which will take place there on Henri's arrival. They note the stages of Henri's journey. Languet writes that the King of Poland "has at last bidden a long farewell to his family at Blamont in Lorraine. His mother, his brother Alençon, the Duke of Lorraine and other nobles attended him so far...On the 12th of this month he passed the Rhine at Spires and went to Heidelberg to the Elector Palatine who is out of health. He had sent his son Christopher...and Lewis of Nassau as far as Blamont to meet the King." Later, the news is that "Christopher the Palatine and Count Lewis of Nassau" are encamped near Maestricht.[11] This was the news of the beginning of a new liberation campaign which also reached Lucas de Heere in London.

Unfortunately it was to end even more disastrously than the one of two years previously which had been ruined by the massacre. Louis of Nassau and his hastily assembled troops fought the Spanish army at Mook, near Nijmegen. The battle resulted in a total victory for the Spaniards. Louis of Nassau, his younger brother Henry, and Christopher of the Palatinate were never seen again; it was supposed that they perished in making a last stand together. [12]

William of Orange did not give up his long struggle but this was one of the darkest moments in it, when he lost his best captain and dearly loved brother Louis, "le bon chevalier." [13]

In the "Journey" tapestry (V), an important French royal personage is going on a journey. We know that he is royal because the cavalcade is led by a detachment of Swiss guards. They are followed by three men on horseback the nearest of whom can be seen to be using a stirrup much shorter than those of the other riders (Pl. 12, e). Details like this in the tapestries are always used with accurate costume reference; the short stirrup here shows that these riders are Polish riders using the shorter stirrup customary in their country (Pl. 7, b); the round hats worn by two of them are also not unlike hats worn by some of the Poles in the "Polish" tapestry (IV). These riders are, we believe, the Polish ambassadors accompanying Henri to Poland. The King on the white horse is not like Henri as we see him in the "Fontainebleau" and "Quintain", but he is here at a younger age, for this is a scene of past history, not of the present. He is dark, as Henri was, and has no resemblance to Charles or François. He is not unlike the Henri subsituted for Charles as the dancing figure in the "Polish" tapestry, which would fit very well, for this is Henri as he was at the time of the Polish festivals, and as King of Poland, not yet as King of France. Some of the riders who follow the king could be German "reîtres" (compare Lucas de Heere's "reître", Pl. 12, d) by whom, as we know, Henri was accompanied on the journey to Poland. It is a "riders of different nations" cavalcade, but referring to a real journey in which riders of different nations took part, the journey of Henri to Poland in 1573.

On the stretch of road in the middle distance, Catherine de' Medici travels in her litter, accompanied by a cavalcade in which are several ladies. This was the retinue with which the Queen Mother was accustomed to travel, as described by Brantôme; "il faisoit beau veoir aussy quand la royne alloit par pays en sa litière...vous eussiez veu quarante à cinquante dames ou demoiselles la suivre, montées sur de belles haquenées." [14] Amongst these ladies must be Marguerite, who went with her mother and brothers to Blamont. Coming down the hilly road on the right is a state-coach with some distinguished personage in it; the King of Poland's brother, François, future ruler of Flanders and Brabant, travelled to Blamont with the family; the occupant of the coach is, however, too small a figure to be identifiable.

Now that we understand whither the winding roads of this journey are leading, we can at last solve the central mystery of the Valois Tapestries and identify the three unknown men who stand beside the road. No wonder that unremitting search for them amongst portraits of French courtiers has been useless, for these men are not Frenchmen; to meet them we must go whither the King of Poland with his family and train is going, to the Interview of Blamont.

The figure who stands in the forefront with his right hand on his sword is a portrait of *Louis of Nassau* (Pl. 25, b). The likeness of the face in the tapestry (Pl. 25, a) to the portrait of Louis at Amsterdam is unmistakable; there is the same high forehead on which the straight hair grows to a point; the same rather heavy-lidded eyes; the same long nose and well-shaped lips; the same moustache and pointed beard; the same expression, rather weary and sad, yet calm. These resemblances are so striking that the conviction grows upon one that the artist of

a Louis of Nassau in the "Journey" (p. 76)

b Louis of Nassau (p. 76)

The Group of Three in the "Journey" (p. 77)

the tapestry was using a portrait of Louis of Nassau of the same type as the Amsterdam portrait. The face in the tapestry is, beyond a doubt, the face of "le bon chevalier", Louis of Nassau, brother of William of Orange, who came to Blamont to meet Catherine de' Medici and her two sons and to renew the Orange alliance with France.

Who then, are the other two in the group of three (Pl. 26)? We suggest that the man beside Louis, or rather, a little behind him, with the upraised hand, must be Christopher, the son of the Elector Palatine, who came with Louis to the Interview of Blamont representing the Protestant princes of Germany. Unfortunately, it has proved impossible to trace any existing portrait of Count Christopher for comparison with the long, grave face in the tapestry.

The third person in the group stands directly behind Louis, so that we only see his head. We believe that this is probably Henry of Nassau, another brother of William of Orange. There is a portrait of Henry in the Rijksmuseum which has some resemblance, particularly about the eye, to the face immediately behind that of Louis in the tapestry, but this comparison would not be in itself convincing. Circumstantial evidence, however, suggests that the central face in the group of three may be that of Henry of Nassau. Henry was not, so far as we know, at the Interview of Blamont, but in the following year he was killed, together with his brother Louis and Christopher the Palatine, at the Battle of Mook. It would fit with the grave significance of the group of three in the tapestry if the allusion were, not only to the meeting at Blamont, but to the death of these three together in battle.

Louis of Nassau wears a long, heavy cloak which is not of the French cut, nor is the small hat worn on the back of the head, with brim upturned in front, a French style. In some costume manuals, the "Burgundus" wears a small hat on the back of the head. The upturned brim of the one which Louis wears is of a striking colour which stands out amongst the colours of this tapestry; it is of a strong orange-brown. The young man behind him who we think may be his brother also wears a hat with the brim turned up in front. The third man in the group has no hat, and wears a garment, rather like an academic gown, with the arm protruding from the loosely hanging sleeve. Comparison with costume manual Germans suggests that this is a German style. The evidence from the costume, therefore, tends rather to confirm that the two wearing hats are Burgundians, namely the brothers, Louis and Henry of Nassau, whilst the third is the German Count Christopher.

In Louis of Nassau we meet, for the first time in the tapestries, with a dead man, that is to say, with one who was not living at the time the tapestries were designed. Louis has returned from the grave to speak to the living recipients of the tapestries. Is it not, therefore, probable, that the two who are with him are also dead men? And if so, who should they be but the two who died with him?

We are therefore of the opinion for these various reasons that the identification of Louis of Nassau as the chief personage of the group of three also identifies the other two, although in their case we cannot present the convincing portrait evidence which we have in the case of Louis.

These three figures are set further back into the scene behind them than are the other foreground portraits of the tapestries. They are cloaked for a journey, and they seem to belong into the journey.

And so they should, for they are people of the past, not of the present; their time is the past time of that journey. That journey is the journey of the French court to Blamont in 1573 to meet Louis of Nassau and Christopher of the Palatinate, and to hand over to them the French money which made possible the abortive liberation campaign in which Louis, Henry, and Christopher met their deaths. No wonder that the three seem to stand in sad, grave, and intimate communion with one another.

And now we remember that we earlier looked at a view of Blamont by Hoefnagel (Pl. 14, b) which Lucas de Heere had almost certainly seen. Are not those country roads, winding up and down hill, rather like the hilly, tree-shaded roads of the tapestry?

Thus the most baffling cipher of the Valois Tapestries is at last broken. But how astounding the solution is! Who would have dreamed of finding amongst the portraits of the French royal family, the portrait of Louis of Nassau? Who could have imagined that amidst the gay and brilliant festival scenes of the court of Catherine de' Medici we should come upon three Protestants who died in the revolt of the Netherlands against Spain?

The "Journey" tapestry (V) is a most strange transformation of Caron's "Anet" design (XI, a) of which the most prominent feature is the famous château itself; we can see the stag over the entrance and the Diana fountain in the court on the left. Out of the main gateway is coming an important party of people following a royal coach. This is preceded by a curious procession which winds along the road and over the bridge, passing out of the picture in the right foreground. It includes a horse-litter, the usual mode of conveyance for royal ladies. There is a pack of hunting dogs in the middle distance, and several pairs of fierce looking hounds are being led on leashes in the procession. Drummers, a man with birds, a strange jester-like figure on a horse, follow the most notable animal in this medley of men and beasts, the muzzled bear which is being led out into the woods.

The Château d'Anet, set in the midst of vast forests, was a centre for the royal hunt. The goddess Diana and Henri II's mistress were both mighty huntresses, and it was as a kind of super hunting-box that Henri II built Anet for his Diana. After her death, in 1566, it became the property of the Duc D'Aumale, and Anet's hunting traditions were carried on; for D'Aumale, and his son who succeeded him, held the title of "Grand Veneur de France". [15] Here, at Anet, lived the Head Huntsman of France; some of the King's dogs were permanently kept here; and we suggest that the Anet of the Caron drawing is not so much the château of Diane de Poitiers as the home of the Grand Veneur de France, the place where the royal hunting dogs are kept, the embodiment of the idea of the chase. The reference is to the hunting tastes of Charles IX, rather than to his father's mistress.

Charles' treatise on hunting, *La Chasse Royale*, [16] is a detailed discussion of his favourite sport. Several chapters of it are about different kinds of hunting dogs; black dogs, long and not very strong; grey dogs, very swift; the "chiens blancs greffiers", the true royal dogs, dogs of St. Louis and St. Hubert; various kinds of little dogs. In the drawing, care is taken to distinguish between different kinds of dogs. In the left foreground, two huge beasts with short ears and curly tails are being led. Coming over the bridge is a powerful dog with drooping ears; then three greyhound-like creatures; further back is a little dog, and a pair of spaniels. Charles also devotes a chapter in his book to the subject of how to train "valets de chiens". We note how the dogs in the drawing are carefully led by their "valets". The drawing, in fact, forms an admirable illustration to the precise, scientific discussion of dogs and their valets in *La Chasse Royale*. It does not show the usual type of hunting scene, with the dogs actually attacking an animal, but the mechanics of the royal hunt, with the business-like valets in charge of their various dogs. The unfortunate, unsuspecting bear is being led off the scene to some spot where the dogs will be set upon it.

Hunting goes normally with festivals in tapestry sequences, and a set of designs showing festivals of the reign of Charles IX would have been incomplete without a reference to his favourite pursuit. The drawing no doubt refers to some specific hunting party and bear-baiting at Anet in the reign of Charles IX. A very large party has assembled at the château and bivouacs have been set up in the grounds. Charles and his mother stayed at Anet, with the Duc d'Aumale, in May, 1571. [17] Possibly the Grand Veneur arranged some great hunt to amuse the young King during this visit. At any rate it can be said with certainty that this design was made before the death of Charles IX in 1574; his successor was not interested in hunting, whereas this drawing seems to reflect Charles' passion for every detail connected with the royal hunting-packs.

The "Journey" (V) and the "Quintain" (VI) tapestries are the two which differ most radically from the relevant Caron drawings (XI, a, b). In both, the whole forefront of the French design has been swept away and an entirely new scene put in its place. But whereas in the "Quintain" tapestry the new scene has the same subject as the French design, being a festival of the same type as the one Caron is depicting, in the "Journey" the new scene is of an entirely different subject, having nothing to do with hunting. What should have been a "hunting" tapestry, a perfectly normal subject in a sequence of festivals and one of the commonest subjects for tapestries, is turned into a state journey, which is an unusual subject. The reader is here asked to compare most carefully Caron's "hunting" drawing with the "Journey" tapestry.

It is with growing amazement that we study the details of the transformation. The tapestry keeps Anet, shifted to the left, the crowds coming out of it, the bivouacs, the winding road, and the bridge. It transforms features in the hunting procession to suit its new purpose. The horse-litter and the running figure beside it are used in the tapestry, reversed, and with Catherine now visible in the litter. The royal coach in the centre of the hunting procession comes downhill on the right in the tapestry. The little bridge is crossed, not now by the huntsmen and their dogs, but by the relay horses for the journey in their royal liveries. Finally, with what seems almost cynical carelessness, some vestigial recollections of the hunt are kept in the journey. A pair of hunting dogs and their valet can be discerned just behind the relay horses, and just in front of them a small bear is being led, offspring of the hunted bear towards which the now obliterated hunting procession was converging. The presence of this bear, trotting after Catherine's litter, was one of the many features which made the "Journey" tapestry a totally insoluble mystery, before the discovery of the Caron drawing. It is now seen to be a curious survival from the earlier design.

Strange thoughts and questions arise as we watch these very peculiar alterations being made. Was there someone looking over the artist's shoulder who was reminded by Anet of hunting in Silence with Henri II? Was the artist himself reminded of the "chasseur déloyal"? Is it with deliberate sense of detestation that they are blotting out the "chasse royale" of Charles IX by painting it over with his brother's journey to Blamont to meet Louis of Nassau? Did they notice that the three Protestants now stand in the place of the hunted bear? We leave these thoughts in the form of unanswerable questions. Perhaps there was no such deep purpose in the alteration. Yet when we remember how Charles IX has been systematically deleted from his own festivals in other tapestries we wonder whether it was horrified avoidance of his hunting which prompted the total change of subject in this one.

The "Journey" is a kind of pendant, or pair, of the "Quintain", the other tapestry into which an entirely new group has been introduced. In the latter, Henri III as King of France mounts his horse as the centre of the masquerade of riders of many nations; in the former, a younger Henri, as King of Poland, rides his horse in the centre of the journey to Blamont, accompanied by Polish, German, and other riders. Glancing from the one to the other, the thought occurs that in the "Journey" we have the real political background of the masquerade of many nations, that it implies the alliance of liberals, an orientation towards the Orange policy for the Netherlands—such as we actually see in the "Journey" where the riders are not a masquerade, but accompanying Henri to liberal Poland, and to his meeting with a Burgundian and a German, Louis of Nassau and Christopher of the Palatinate. It is as though the costume artist's interest in riders of many nations transforms before our eyes into a real "politique" journey.

However we may interpret them, these two tapestries, in which the French designs were most radically altered, belong together. They should hang next to one another, so that the festival and the journey, the journey and the festival, may be constantly compared.

When we meet Louis of Nassau and his friends in the "Journey" we are at last penetrating to the heart of the Valois Tapestries. The three unknown men in the "Journey" are indeed the clue to the whole. They are unique among the foreground portrait groups, not only because there is no member of the French royal family among them, but also because they are dead men, missing believed killed at the Battle of Mook in 1574. When we look round the foreground portraits as a whole, the living family group of the members of Catherine de' Medici's family as they were in 1582, these three men are seen to be set apart. They belong to past history, not to the present. They are set there to remind the present of the tragedies of the past, ghosts of the dead standing beside the Blamont road.

They have, however, a connection with the present, for they recall a past moment in French relations with the Netherlands which the present installation of Anjou as sovereign is continuing and affirming. And it is now that we seem to perceive the mind, and feel the heart, of William

Pl. 27

Adriaan Key, William of Orange (p. 81)

of Orange (Pl. 27) behind the tapestries. Surely this infinitely pathetic presentation of his dead brother, sadly and wearily gazing towards us as he leans on his heavy sword, must have been his choice, reminding that the life of Louis was laid down in the darkest hour of the struggle of the Netherlands. The "Journey" tapestry, as now understood, seems to us to indicate that the tapestries were not made for Anjou, for what would that selfish egoist have cared for this delicate and allusive reminder of what passed at the Interview of Blamont. They were made to be sent to Catherine de' Medici to remind her of what she knew, to appeal to her and to her son Henri III to support in the present the liberal policies, the "politique" alliances, such as Louis of Nassau had urged upon them in the past, by supporting Anjou in his position in the Netherlands.

William the Silent is sending his brother Louis once again on a mission to the French court.

CHAPTER III

FESTIVALS OF THE REIGN OF HENRI III:
THE MAGNIFICENCES FOR THE LORRAINE-JOYEUSE
WEDDING OF 1581

Henri was King of Poland for only one year. On the death of his brother Charles in 1574 he hurriedly and secretly left the Polish capital and returned to France to ascend the throne as Henri III. Seven years later, the most splendid of all the French court festivals of the sixteenth century were produced.

In September, 1581, Henri III's favourite, Anne, Duc de Joyeuse, married Marguerite de Lorraine, sister of Henri's wife, Louise de Lorraine. A series of magnificences on an unparalleled scale marked this wedding, which was attended by all the members of the house of Lorraine, including Duke Charles III, the head of the house. In these festivals, the evolution of court festival under the last Valois kings reached its climax. It was a set of magnificences of the usual type, but more and better than ever before, with more spectacular production, richer and more varied costumes, and above all, accompanied by music the like of which had never been heard. The court of Henri III stood revealed as the most refined, the most artistic, the most musical court in Europe. One of the entertainments in the series, which went on for over a fortnight, was the ballet given for the bride by her sister Louise de Lorraine in which they both danced together. This was the famous *Ballet comique de la reine*,[1] in which the new art form, *ballet de cour*, announces its full arrival.

With the festivals for the Joyeuse wedding we arrive at the present day—the present day of the makers of the Valois Tapestries. This was what was going on *now*, or very recently, at the Valois court. The tapestries wish to glorify the King of France, the brother of the new Count of Flanders and Duke of Brabant, as he is *now*, that is at about the same time that Anjou entered upon his position in the Netherlands. Since it is through its festivals that the French court is glorified in the tapestries, these will wish, above all, to celebrate those of the present day and those of the present king, the super-magnificences of 1581. How glorious a King the ruler of Flanders and Brabant has for his brother! How surpassingly marvellous are the present-day festivals of Henri III!

The allusions to the festivals of the present are made in the foregrounds. With the one exception of the group in the "Journey", which belongs to past history, all the foreground people are people of the present. As we discussed in the chapter on the French portraits, most of them represent Catherine de' Medici's family as it was around 1582, when the tapestries were designed. More than this, they represent her family at recent festivals. As we shall suggest in the next chapter, the people in the foregrounds of the two "Anjou" tapestries, the "Barriers" and the "Elephant", allude to the displays in honour of Anjou at Antwerp in 1582. The other five festival tapestries allude in their foregrounds to those taking part in his brother's festivals of 1581, the stupendous magnificences for the Joyeuse wedding.

In the forefront of the "Polish" festival (IV), with which he had nothing to do, stands the super-elegant Duc de Joyeuse, the most fashionable of bridegrooms. In the "Tournament" (II) his wife, with her back to us, treads a solemn measure with her sister Louise, as she did at the *Ballet comique de la reine*. One of the illustrations to the *Ballet comique* (Pl. 28, b) shows the scene set for the great entertainment and for the ballets in which Louise danced with her sister, the bride of the Joyeuse wedding; beside it we have placed (Pl. 28,a) Louise and her sister as they are seen in the Valois Tapestries. Louise wears the necklace which she wore in 1581 both here, and when she stands with her husband, the King, in the "Fontainebleau" tapestry (I). Here we see the present King and Queen of France in full glory, arrayed for the supreme festivals of their court. Henri in the "Quintain" (VI) is taking part in a masquerade of a type used in every festival from Bayonne onwards, but this one belongs to the "now", to the most recent of all magnificences, as is shown by the young exquisites who gaze adoringly at him as he mounts his horse and who can only be "mignons" of the court of Henri III. Even the sober figure of the Duke of Lorraine in the "Whale" (III) carries on the allusion, for he graced the Lorraine-Joyeuse wedding as head of the house, and took part in the magnificences. He was certainly present at the *Ballet comique* for he is named as the recipient of one of the devices which were presented after it.

Only Marguerite and Navarre, of the French court foreground figures, were not present at the Joyeuse wedding. They were not there, but in the tapestries they are brought in to complete the family.

If it is objected that they could not have known much in Antwerp in 1582 about the magnificences for the Lorraine-Joyeuse wedding of the preceding year, the answer is that they could have consulted the printed description, the *Balet comique de la royne faict aux nopces de Monsieur le Duc de Ioyeuse*, published in 1582. There they could have read the full and illustrated description of the great ballet, seen the illustration of its opening scene (Pl. 28 b), in which Catherine, Henri III and Joyeuse sit in the front row of the audience, and noted the likeness of its plot to the old plot of the water-festival at Bayonne. They could also have known from the printed book, if from no other source, that Louise de Lorraine's ballet was only one item in a grand series of festivals of the usual pattern. The opening sentences of the preface to the ballet are as follows:

"Le Roy ayant conclu & arresté le mariage d'entre monsieur le Duc de Ioyeuse Pair de France, & madamoyselle de Vaudemont soeur de la Royne, delibera solenniser les nopces, de toute espece de triomphe & magnificence, à fin d'honorer une si belle couple, selon sa valeur & merite. Pour cest effect oultre l'appareil des riches habits, delicieux festins, & somptueuses mascarades, sa maiesté ordonna encore diuerses sortes de courses, & superbes combats en armes, tant a la barrière comme en lice, à pied & à cheual, auec de balets aussi à pied & à cheual, prattiquez à la mode des anciens Grecs, & des nations qui sont auiourdhuy les plus esloignees de nous: le tout accompagné de concerts de musiques excellentes & non encores iamais ouyes: saditte maiesté ne voulant rien omettre de ce qui pouuoit entretenir de plus agreable varieté, la grande & illustre compagnie qu'elle auoit faict conuier à ces nopces." [2]

It is probable that this is a crucial text for the understanding of the treatment of the festivals
in the Valois Tapestries. The makers of the tapestries wish to honour the present King of
France and his recent festivals, with their "sumptuous masquerades", different kinds of "courses"
(that is running at the ring or at the quintain), combats both on foot (barriers) and "en lice"
(tournaments), and wonderful ballets, both on foot and on horse-back (horse-ballets). They
possess a set of French designs of earlier festivals *of the same type*, for all the magnificences
repeat one another. They therefore put the chief personages of the Joyeuse wedding-festivals—
Henri and Louise, Joyeuse and his bride—in front of these earlier designs which they then
assimilate to these more recent festivals.

They possess a view of ballet dancers on a rock at a famous ballet, with the court dancing
after the ballet (X, b); they put Joyeuse, the fashionable bridegroom, into the foreground,
and make two of the dancers behind him look like Henri and Louise dancing at his wedding
("Polish", IV). They have a tournament design, with the riders passing between one another
after the manner of a horse-ballet (IX, b); they place Louise about to dance a ballet with the
bride of Joyeuse in front of it, making the whole suggestive of ballets and tournaments at the
Joyeuse wedding ("Tournament", II). They have a masquerade combat at Fontainebleau (IX, a);
in front of it they stand Henri and Louise arrayed for the Joyeuse magnificences, with
possibly an allusion to the Joyeuse couple in the pair just behind them ("Fontainebleau", I).

Above all, they have a "course", a French design of a running at the quintain in masquerade
costumes (XI, b). They wish to make this more sumptuous and more exotic, like the festivals
for the Joyeuse wedding. They therefore use their other printed source, the Bayonne *Recueil*,
and make up from the description in that of a sumptuous masquerade, a many-coloured, exotic
group with Henri III as its central figure, attended by exquisite "mignons" of his court ("Quintain", VI).

Finally, they could consult the full illustrated text of the supreme event in the series, the
Ballet comique itself, noting how it opens with an entry of singing Sirens, followed by a fountain
drawn by a sea-god and his horses, and an entry of singing Tritons. Though held in a hall and
now developed into a complete ballet, how like this was in plot to the supreme event at Bayonne,
when the Tritons, Sirens and Neptune greeted the occupants of the barge with songs! They
could also have noted the devices presented at the end of the performance by the nymphs of
waters and woods who danced the ballet, for these are illustrated in the printed livret of the
Ballet comique. The Duke of Lorraine received a Neptune; it is perhaps accidental that Lorraine
in the "Whale" tapestry happens to have the Neptune of the Bayonne festival just above his
head. The bride, the Duchesse de Joyeuse, presented a Siren (Pl. 29, b); other water-devices
were a whale; an Arion; a Triton; an oyster (Pl. 29, c); a lobster (Pl. 29, d). These devices
might have suggested the idea (not in the Caron drawing of this festival, X, a) of showing fishy
and shell devices on the shields beside the rowers of the barge (Pl. 29, a). These devices are
not so close to those in the *Ballet comique* as are the shield-devices of the "Tournament" to
those in the Bayonne *Recueil;* but they include some shells and a lobster.

But when Lucas de Heere drew the Siren on the barge he was thinking of his own device
(Pl. 18, b), not of the French Sirens of the Bayonne festival and of the *Ballet comique*.

a   Louise de Lorraine and her sister in the "Tournament" (p. 83)

b   The opening of Louise de Lorraine's Ballet.
From the *Ballet comique* (p. 83)

Pl. 29

a   The Barge in the "Whale" (p. 84)

b, c, d   Siren, Oyster and Lobster Devices. From the *Ballet comique* (p. 84)

It has been a part of our purpose in all this discussion of the festivals to try to elucidate how far the Valois Tapestries are of value as evidence for the history of French festivals. In so far as they were made up at a distance, and not by eye-witnesses, they are not direct records. Yet in two ways they give visual evidence of two most important and overlooked facts about the history of these festivals.

The first of these we have already emphasised, that the development of *ballet de cour* occurs within the context of sets of chivalrous magnificences. Looking round the tapestries, we can *see* this, see the island festival at Bayonne, the ballet of the provinces for the reception of the Poles, in the context of tournaments, mock combats, barriers, running at the quintain, and so on.

The second way in which the tapestries give visual evidence is perhaps even more important. Standing in their present, at the festivals for the Joyeuse wedding, we see the past festivals receding away from that present, as the memory of the past behind the present, and so hold their whole history in one all embracing, poetic view. This was all one long story, told in serial episodes from 1564 to 1581, in which the same themes were repeated again and again, so that one "course" in masquerade costume can stand for them all, one allegorical tournament for them all, one watery drama with the singing sirens, Neptunes and so on, for them all. The change is that they grow progressively better, artistically, musically, and in the technique of the dance, until, in 1581, there pour out upon the world those spectacles of supreme brilliance, accompanied by music of a kind unheard until now. These were the last great magnificences of the Valois court which was soon to go down into utter ruin and disappear from the world. But not before it had perfected its festival art, the influence of which upon the subsequent development of European theatrical spectacle can hardly be overestimated.

Though the makers of the tapestries may be relying only on the printed book of the *Ballet comique*, we know from other sources how right they were in seeing the festivals of 1581 as the past in the present. There were many echoes of earlier shows in the series, particularly of those of Bayonne. There was a combat "for and against love", with cartels by Ronsard and Desportes and music by the Huguenot musician, Claude Le Jeune. [3] This sounds very much like the Bayonne tournament, though greatly developed as regards musical accompaniment. There was a water fête planned on the Seine; the royal party was to cross in a barge to the Cardinal de Bourbon's entertainment at St. Germain-des-Prés. During the crossing boats in the form of seahorses, tritons, whales, sirens, tortoises and other marine monsters were to provide musical entertainment, musicians being concealed in the boats. [4] This would evidently have been almost an exact replica of the crossing to the island at Bayonne, but it failed to come off.

In the programme of the Joyeuse Magnificences, the *Ballet comique* is planned to come on the day before this water-show, [5] a sequence which would have brought out the fact that the plot of the *Ballet comique* was really one of Catherine's old plots and particularly reminiscent of her show at Bayonne. Sirens and Satyrs were leading characters. They and other water and wood deities entered, singing to the accompaniment of music from the "voute dorée", which represented the harmony of heaven, songs which were to deliver the French Monarchy from the evil enchantment of Circe. Jupiter and Mercury descended from heaven to render divine aid in the struggle. Towards the end of the performance, all the characters rushed across the hall to the assault of Circe in her garden. They broke her power and delivered a band of nymphs whom she was keeping in imprisonment. The rescued nymphs then danced the ballet, produced by Beaujoyeulx, and afterwards presented the devices.

To recognise the ingredients in this epoch-making performance, look at the Valois Tapestries. The deities of nature, so wonderfully shown in their natural setting in the "Whale", have come within doors. The rush on Circe's garden is like a mock combat (see "Fontainebleau" or the "Elephant"). The connection with the tournament (see the "Tournament") is indicated by the presentation of devices. For the insinuation of ballet into a festival sequence see the dancers in the "Whale" and those on the rock in the "Polish" tapestry.

Though the printed text of the *Ballet comique* ascribes its authorship to Beaujoyeulx and La Chesnaye, and though the Queen who gave this entertainment was Louise de Lorraine, it bears unmistakeably upon it the stamp of its true origin. It was evolved out of the entertainments which Catherine de' Medici gave as her personal contribution to a series of chivalrous pastimes at the French court.[6]

Interest in the book describing the *Ballet comique* and the Joyeuse wedding festivals might well have been considerable in Antwerp in Anjou's circle, for Anjou was a music-lover and several of the musicians who worked for these festivals had belonged to his circle when he was in France. Beaujoyeulx had been his *valet de chambre;* Estienne le Roy, who sang the part of one of the Satyrs in the ballet, had been his almoner; whilst Claude Le Jeune who composed music, not for the ballet, but for other entertainments in the series, had been his *maître de la musique*.[7] Anjou was also a patron of Baïf, and of the *Académie de Poésie et Musique*[8]. The fact that the tapestries were made in the circle of Anjou adds to their validity as a document on French festivals, for Anjou, like all his family, though he might be guilty of moral errors, is not likely to have been guilty of errors in artistic taste. If it were artistically wrong to place participants in the Joyeuse festivals in front of scenes referring to earlier festivals, he would have felt this. Moreover there was at least one other person in Antwerp who had first-hand knowledge of French festivals, namely the Prince Dauphin. We have seen that some features in the "Whale" tapestry, which correspond to Marguerite's descriptions in her memoirs, may have been described to the artist by persons who had been present at Bayonne. Thus, though the Valois Tapestries were composed at a distance from the French court, and with second-hand materials, they were composed in a milieu in which there was considerable knowledge of French festivals. Their telescopic presentation of festivals of the past behind festivals of the present can therefore be relied upon as a view of French festival history satisfactory to knowledgeable contemporaries.

Where the tapestries are not altogether reliable as a presentation of French festivals is in the matter of costume. It is possible that Lucas de Heere may have had some advice from French courtiers in Antwerp when he was composing some of the masquerade costumes, but in general, as we have seen, he is drawing for these on his own repertoire of costume studies, and these belong into the Flemish rather than into the French tradition. Also, in the matter of the French court fashions worn by his foreground figures, he is reproducing French fashions as known in Antwerp and as depicted in the manuals of De Bruyn, rather than the latest fashions as actually worn at the French court. The styles in vogue at the time of the Joyeuse wedding can be seen in the two well known paintings at Versailles and at the Louvre, both usually called "Le Bal du Duc de Joyeuse". The dresses of the women in these pictures have enormous balloon-like sleeves and very full skirts, such as we do not see in the gowns worn by Louise and her sister in the tapestries. The men wear a species of low top-hat, with a mass of feathers in front, which is not like the velvet hat worn by Joyeuse in the tapestry, though this is a French style. In their presentation of French fashions the Valois Tapestries are, as in all other respects, a view of the French court taken from afar.

In 1581, Henri III appeared to be drawing closer to the extreme Catholic party amongst his subjects, the party which was soon to form the pro-Spanish League.[9] The House of Lorraine, the members of whom he was particularly honouring in the Joyeuse wedding festivals, was to be identified with this party. Duke Charles was the head of the house, but the chief movers of the League were its cadet branch, the Guises. The turbulent and ambitious Guises had always been one of the chief problems confronting Catherine and her sons. They had risen to power under François II, through their relationship to his queen, Mary Stuart; and now a second generation of them was proving even more troublesome. The Joyeuse wedding, which was a predominantly Lorraine affair, was attended by all the leading members of the house, including the Duke and Cardinal of Guise who gave some of the entertainments in the series of magnificences.

Henri III was at this time genuinely seized with Counter Reformation Catholic fervour and was deeply involved with his many religious confréries and their processions. The musicians and singers who took part in these processions were, for the most part, the same as those employed for the court entertainments, and these processions are, as it were, the sacred or religious manifestations of the mood of which the Joyeuse Magnificences were the expression in profane art.[10] Henri III's religious movement has not been taken sufficiently seriously, nor has it been sufficiently emphasised that it was explicitly a *non-violent* Counter Reformation, a religious revival which should appeal to heretics through works of charity and exhibitions of penitence, without forcing their consciences by war or the methods of the Spanish Inquisition.[11]

Just after the wedding festivals, Antoine de Baïf dedicated his *Les Mimes* to the Duc de Joyeuse, admiringly referring in the preface to the wonderful magnificences which have just taken place.[12] Baïf was, of course, the moving spirit of the *Académie de Poésie et Musique*, in which Catholic and Protestant musicians had worked together, one of the Protestant members being Claude Le Jeune who wrote some of the music for the Joyeuse wedding and whose researches in musical humanism had profoundly influenced the artistic development of French court festival.[13] *Les Mimes* is a collection of proverbial teaching in verse in which Baïf bitterly deplores religious wars, the Inquisition, and all use of violence in religious matters, and calls for a moral reformation and more charity throughout the world. He warns the Papacy not to stir up civil war in France nor to think to extirpate heresy with the "sword of the powerful". He implores that "noble and valiant blood" (the House of Lorraine) to remain loyal to the crown and not to stir up war against it in the name of religion.

Such was the state of mind of one who had just witnessed the festivals and was addressing their hero, Joyeuse. Baïf's verses reveal very clearly the loyalist, non-violent, Catholic movement of which Joyeuse is taken as typical, which fears the disloyal, pro-Spanish movement using Catholic orthodoxy as its cloak, to which it yet appeals and hopes still to be able to disarm by peaceful methods. These were the tensions underlying the Joyeuse-Lorraine wedding festivals.

Henri III's recently founded Order of the Holy Spirit seems to have had, as one of its objects, the binding together of Catholic and Protestant noblemen in loyalty to the crown.[14] Joyeuse seems to have been very much in Henri's confidence concerning this Order. In 1583, he was sent on an important secret mission to Rome about the Order and about other business which remains unknown, though the general scope would seem to have been to try to counteract Spanish influence in Rome.[15]

The enigmatic Henri III, though flattering the House of Lorraine in the Joyeuse festivals, was thus by way of being a Catholic "politique", a believer in non-violence and tolerant methods. We can learn from the League propaganda against him after his death how deeply he was suspected by that side. One of the many League cartoons satirising the King is called "The Portrait of a Politique". It shows Henri in front of a Siren, probably alluding to the sirens of the festivals, with a number of Turkish turbans lying on the ground. The meaning of the turbans, so the accompanying verses explain, is that the "politique Siren" will believe anything.[16] We have perhaps here an indication that the exotic masquerade costumes of festivals were suspected of having a "politique" meaning, of concealing an indulgent attitude towards heretics.

When the authors of the Valois Tapestries put Joyeuse, and allusions to the Joyeuse festivals, in the foregrounds, they may be giving proof of a good deal of political penetration. Those festivals, which seemed like a rapprochement with the Lorraine and extreme Catholic party, in reality concealed beneath their exoticism a "politique" attitude and a deep fear of Spanish intrigue. Perhaps this is why the "Quintain" tapestry stresses the costumes of many nations in relation to Henri III. Enigmatic he looks as he mounts his horse in the midst of the masquerade, with the little man in the mask beside him. Are we to solve the enigma by looking from the "Quintain" with the King of France in the masquerade surrounded by his favourites, to the "Journey" where the King of Poland rides to meet the Protestants? As then Henri was supporting Louis of Nassau, so now he will support his "politique" brother Anjou in the Netherlands. Is that the moral, or the meaning, or the appeal of the costumes of many nations?

CHAPTER IV

FESTIVALS FOR ANJOU IN ENGLAND AND THE NETHERLANDS, 1581-2

French Designs behind the two Anjou Tapestries

In the "Barriers" and "Elephant" tapestries (VII, VIII), Anjou reigns supreme. He has appeared in none of the other foregrounds, but in these two scenes the beholder's attention is immediately focussed on his presence. With them, therefore, we reach the *fons et origo* of the series, the personage in connection with whom the whole elaborate design came into being, namely François, Duc d'Anjou.

These two tapestries are not separated off from the other six; on the contrary, they are organically connected with the main subject, the Valois court and its festivals. In the "Elephant", Anjou stands lovingly with his sister Marguerite, and this relates him to his family in the other tapestries, where Marguerite appears twice again, with her mother and her husband. In the context of the other foreground groups, the Anjou of the "Barriers" and the "Elephant" is recognised as son of Catherine, brother of Henri III, brother of Marguerite. On the other hand, he has other people with him in these tapestries, people who are not his relatives and whom we do not yet know. These unknown persons are the young man who stands between him and Marguerite in the "Elephant", the significant-looking knight who gazes deferentially at him in the "Barriers", and the young man who is with this knight. Unsolved mystery thus confronts us here. Who is this important knight and who are these two young men?

The festival scenes in these two tapestries are linked with the others by the presence of Catherine de' Medici in both of them. In the "Barriers" she is unmistakable as the central figure in the central pavilion; in the "Elephant" she is recognisable on the balcony in the left background. The "reine mère" is here, watching over the triumphs of her youngest son, just as she watches the festivals in the other tapestries.

We are, however, in a different position for the interpretation of these two tapestries in one important respect. We have no Caron drawings for them. It seems a reasonable hypothesis that the makers of the tapestries possessed eight Caron designs of festivals of the French court, two of which have not survived, or have not yet been discovered. The missing two, it may be surmised, were a "barriers", about which we know nothing, and a "carrousel with an elephant" which was probably rather like the existing painting of this subject by Caron (XII) but which need not have been identical with it.

The evidence in respect of the two Anjou tapestries is therefore less secure than for the others. In the absence of the hypothetical, but probable, Caron designs on which these two were based, we cannot feel any certainty as to what French festivals these referred. And, moreover, we cannot observe the alterations in them made by the designer of the Valois Tapestries, the study of which proved so fruitful in the case of the other tapestries.

In what follows, we shall proceed on the hypothesis that Lucas de Heere had before him
"barriers" and "elephant" designs by Caron which he altered in a manner similar to his alterations of the Caron designs which he used for the other tapestries. That is to say, he imposed
on them foreground portraits and also changed them in other ways, so as to make them allusions
to *contemporary festivals in honour of Anjou*. We are assuming that these two tapestries are also
a palimpsest, like the others, in which a new contemporary writing has been imposed on an
underlying French manuscript. We shall suggest that the contemporary references are to
festivals for Anjou in England in 1581, at the time of his courtship of Elizabeth I, and to his
reception by William of Orange in Antwerp in 1582.

It would be, we suggest, in the spirit of the tapestries as a whole that they should glorify
Anjou through allusions to famous festivals, or great ceremonial occasions, in which he had
recently taken part, and we believe that in following Anjou's festival history for the years
1581 and 1582 we shall be right in principle as to the route by which the "Barriers" and the
"Elephant" should be approached, though we do not claim any absolute certainty for our
interpretations.

The "combat à la barrière", like the "course" at the ring or at the quintain, was an inevitable
item in any series of French festivals. It was an old-established knightly exercise, the essence
of which was that the combatants were separated by a bar to prevent them from doing serious
harm to themselves. They fought with rebated spears, sometimes also with swords, across this
bar, and, when the spears broke, hurled the fragments at one another.[1] This is exactly what
we see in the "Barriers" (VII), where the two men fight with spears across a bar, and there are
a number of bits and pieces lying on the ground. Since no strokes were given below the bar,
it was unnecessary to wear armour on the lower part of the body, and we see that the two
fighting men wear helmets, and armour on the upper part of their bodies, but none on their
legs. On either side of the enclosure stand other combatants, similarly armed, and holding
tall spears; they are waiting to take their turn at the barrier.

Amongst the points suggestive of a Caron design behind this tapestry are the thin line of
spectators, marking the place where a wall has been removed to show a distant scene (compare
the line of people on the site of the missing wall in his Polish festival drawing, X, b), and the
statues. One of these is of Diana, or Pallas; the subject of the other cannot be clearly seen,
since only a part of it is shown, but it would be fairly safe to assume that it is an Apollo, to
pair with the Diana. Caron was much given to placing statues in tapestry designs, as can be seen
in his "Arthémise" series of drawings. Those in his Polish festival drawing (X, b) may refer
to plaster statues designed by Germain Pilon for that festival, as was suggested above.

Since a "combat à la barrière" could belong to any festival, and since we do not possess
the Caron design behind this tapestry, it is impossible to say to what French festival the French
basis of the tapestry referred. If a guess is to be hazarded, we would guess that it might have
belonged to the "Polish" series, in which there were allusions to the Queen Mother as a Gallic
Pallas, and to Henri as the Gallic Apollo.[2]

No description of an attack and defence of an elephant is known in accounts of French festivals which have so far come to light; such a scene is obviously related to the common type of mock combat, to the attack and defence of forts, enchanted castles, islands, and so on, with the opposite sides in fancy dress. That the "elephant" type of this kind of show was used at the French court is, however, proved by Caron's painting (XII)[3] which is certainly of a festival.

An elephant was available at the Joyeuse Magnificences, for one of the entertainments projected in its programme was for a running at the ring, in which each of the participants

"was to have his lance carried by a king of a distant country, chained, and was to be accompanied by a recital in some strange incomprehensible language, with "musique extravagante" chanted by six Moors carried in paniers on a camel, or in a tower on an elephant." [4]

We do not know whether this exotic plan was carried out, but it testifies to the existence of an elephant, and it is therefore possible that this elephant was used for a mock combat at night, such as we see in Caron's "Elephant Carrousel" painting. The arcades in this picture might be those which were erected near the Louvre for the elaborate shows, some of which took place at night, in the course of the magnificences for the Joyeuse wedding.[5] The "Louise de Lorraine" hair-styles of the ladies watching the show also suggest the Henri III period.

The Caron elephant design possessed by the makers of the tapestry need not, however, have been identical with the "Elephant Carrousel". We may feel pretty certain that there are more masquerade costumes in the tapestry than there were in the original Caron design. Lucas de Heere had once more consulted the Bayonne *Recueil* where he learned that "wild Scotsmen" took part in the "costumes of many countries" show there.[6] He has added his own version of the costume of "wild Scotsmen" (Pl. 11, b) and has made of the "Elephant" tapestry a display of costume comparable to that of the "Quintain" for richness. The influence of the normal subject-divisions of a costume collection, such as Lucas' Ghent "Theatre", can be perceived in this scene. A group of knights of some semi-ecclesiastical military order advance in the background; they may be compared with Lucas' "Chevalier de Rhodes" (Pl. 16, d). On the right is a group in antique costumes with Roman standards; there is a section on the antique in Lucas' "Theatre". The oriental costume of the Turks predominates in the foreground attackers, and may be compared with Lucas' "Turkish Rider" (Pl. 12, b). And Lucas' special taste for "wild" types is evident in the Scotsmen.

In fact it might almost be said that the masqueraders in the "Elephant" are the figures of the costume gallery which Lucas de Heere painted in England animated into a dramatic spectacle, rather than a reflection of masquerade attire as worn at the French court.

The Barriers at Whitehall on New Year's Day, 1582

The marriage of François d'Anjou with Elizabeth of England was a project which had been on, and off, the tapis for many years. In 1581 it reached a climax. In that year it seemed to many, not only a probability, but a certainty that Elizabeth and François would marry.

In April, 1581, French commissioners, one of whom was the Prince Dauphin, went to England to discuss the match.[7] They were royally entertained, a banqueting-hall having been specially erected at Westminster for the purpose. Together with the Queen, they witnessed a show which was staged in their honour in the tilt-yard adjoining the palace of Whitehall. This was the famous entertainment known as the "The Four Foster Children of Desire." [8] The place where the Queen was seated was called the "Castle or Fortress of Perfect Beauty"; it was assaulted by a construction described as a "rolling trench", which was on wheels and covered with canvas painted to resemble a mound of earth. On it were gunners with cannons, which at crucial moments shot off sweet powders. Within it were musicians. This object symbolised the attack on the Fortress of Perfect Beauty, or the suit of the Queen, a theme which was further carried on by the Four Foster Children of Desire who entered in splendid armour and with brilliantly clad retinues, to tilt and fight at the barriers. One of the Foster Children was Sir Philip Sidney, who wore blue armour engraved with gold. Fantastic speeches accompanied these exercises, and it is not easy to gather what was the general drift of the show, unless it was to impress on the French ambassadors how difficult of access was the Fortress. "The Four Foster Children of Desire" was an entertainment distinctly in the French taste, an example of those modern evolutions of the exercises of chivalry into court masques which had also been developing in England.[9]

In November, 1581, Anjou himself went to England to continue his courtship in person. He seemed to make very great progress; the Queen gave him a ring, and the rumour spread throughout Europe that the match was about to take place. This was the moment at which Marnix de Sainte Aldegonde wrote the letter to the Estates urging that the betrothal should be celebrated in the Netherlands, with the result that William of Orange announced it at Ghent where an allegorical picture by Lucas de Heere on the subject was publicly displayed.[10]

On New Year's Day, 1582, the two royal lovers exchanged presents, and on the same day, in the evening, the exercise of barriers was held in the presence of Elizabeth in which Anjou took part, together with the Prince Dauphin, the Earls of Leicester and of Sussex, and other English and French gentlemen. They were splendidly attired and challenged all comers to the combat.[11] Before the barriers began, Anjou made a dramatic entry on a rock, which was drawn by golden chains towards the Queen. The chains were held by Love and Destiny, who sang, very gracefully, a song in four stanzas. The Duc de Nevers, from whose memoirs we are quoting this account, gives this song in French in which language it was presumably sung. It tells, of course, how Love and Destiny have brought this prince to the feet of this princess. One of Destiny's verses warns the loved one rather firmly that she is not to trifle with her lover:

Le Destin

Reine dont le bel oeil tient l'empire des coeurs,
Triomphant auiourd'huy du Vainqueur des Vainqueurs,
Voyez combien le Ciel vous donne de puissance!
Mais qu'un si bel honneur n'enfle tant vostre coeur,
Qu'un si braue Vainqueur soit traité de rigueur:
Les Dieux, l'Amour & moy en ferions la vengeance.[12]

After this auspicious opening, the barriers began and went on until an hour after midnight, each of the defendants having fought half a dozen times. Then the Queen in the presence of the whole company of two or three thousand persons, thanked Monsieur for the honour he had done her, kissed him several times and led him to his chamber (he was lodged in the palace at Whitehall). Who could doubt, after all this, that the brother of the King of France, and prospective ruler of the Netherlands, would round off his glorious destiny by becoming the consort of the Queen of England?

In the "Barriers" tapestry (VII), Anjou is himself taking part in the barriers, for he wears half-armour (as does the knight opposite to him) and the page is taking his helmet from the knight, whose own helmet is on the ground. In his right hand he holds the knotted shaft of a long spear, so long that its tip disappears into outer space above the pavilion where the royal ladies are sitting. It is tempting to wonder whether this may not be Anjou as he was at the English barriers, and even to fancy that we can discern, on the right of Catherine in the pavilion, the stiff form of his lady-love, to whom the statue of Diana, with the palm of victory behind her, might also now allude. The opposite statue has at its feet a helmet adorned with bright orange-coloured plumes. Anjou had recently adopted the colours of William of Orange.[13]

When we remember how important Anjou's hoped-for match with the Queen of England was to William of Orange, how Marnix wrote from England a letter announcing the supposed betrothal, and how Lucas de Heere celebrated this good news in an allegorical picture at Ghent, it begins to seem almost inevitable that those triumphant barriers in England, when the lover had appeared to be so near to his goal, would be the allusion which Lucas would impose on a "combat à la barrière" design.

If we follow the line of Anjou's spear, we see behind it, in the landscape background, what looks like some large palace in a town with a great church nearby. Park-like meadows extend behind the pavilion on the other side, and, far away, the country recedes into what might be the cliffs of some distant coast-line. Is it possible that we are looking into Lucas de Heere's memories, formalised by the hand of the practised tapestry cartoonist, of the England which he knew so well? And has the line of spectators something of the look of a row of English costume figures? We remember how Hoefnagel's view of an English palace (Pl. 14, a) has the costume row in front of it. Of course we shall not find peasants and bourgeoises watching barriers at court, but some of the tiny figures of the spectators in the "Barriers" remind one of Lucas' English ladies (Pl. 10, b), and the man near the pavilion on the right, in a high-crowned hat and holding a knobbed stick, might well be some Burleigh-like English officer of state.

Though there is a speculative element in our suggestion that the "Barriers" may allude to Anjou's barriers in England, and all that they were hoped to signify, yet such an allusion would belong very naturally into the world whence the Valois Tapestries emanated, as we have come to understand it. And it can certainly be said that Anjou as we see him here, (Pl. 30) resplendent at a barriers, is a flattered portrait of Anjou as he was at a time when he had recently been in England courting Queen Elizabeth. The "Barriers" tapestry almost belongs into the gallery of English royal portraits, as that of a Prince Consort *manqué*.

Anjou's Entry into Antwerp in February, 1582,

Though the expected marriage did not take place, it was with great apparent reluctance that Elizabeth parted with Anjou when he left England in February, 1582, to take up his position in the Netherlands. She accompanied him personally on his journey to the coast as far as Canterbury; she commanded Lord Howard to choose suitable vessels to transport him and his train across the sea; and she ordered Leicester, Howard, and Hunsdon to attend him and to get together as many other lords and gentlemen to accompany him as could be assembled at short notice.[14] Anjou had not a very large French suite with him, and the notable gathering of English knights which Elizabeth sent with him, so that he should have a "traine meet for his greatnesse" [15] was a prominent feature of his entry into Antwerp. Amongst them was Sir Philip Sidney.[16]

The Prince of Orange, who had long been anxiously awaiting Anjou's arrival, greeted him on his landing at Flushing. He was at first entertained at Middelburg, where he was welcomed by the Estates of Zeeland, and then came the great day of his triumphal entry into Antwerp, of which we have a full description in Plantin's publication.[17] Nichols rightly saw this entry as an overseas extension of Elizabethan festivals, for he included an English translation of the *Joyeuse Entrée* in the second volume of his *Progresses of Queen Elizabeth.* [18]

In the opinion of the author of the *Joyeuse Entrée,* the most striking feature of the day was the wonderful sight of many men in very fine armour. The streets, it is true, were graced with triumphal arches and other shows full of witty and apt inventions, yet the like have been seen in other places equal to them. There were crowds of people, yet not so many as would be seen in Paris. Yet it would be difficult to match anywhere in Christendom such a great assemblage of men in fairest armour as were seen in Antwerp on that day.[19]

One of the illustrations (Pl. 31, a) to the *Joyeuse Entrée* brings out this side of the spectacle. The English ships from which Anjou and his suite have landed are seen on the left. Anjou is being greeted with a deferential bow by the Prince of Orange. Near them is a splendid group of noble riders in rich armour and with their horses draped in brilliantly coloured cloths; these are the nobility of France, England and Burgundy, a gathering of international chivalry.

Outside the gate of the city at which the Duke was to enter a stage had been set up (Pl. 31, b) and there the Estates of Brabant were waiting. The Prince of Orange, as one of the chief lords of the Duchy of Brabant, took his place among them. Anjou seated himself upon the platform, with the lords of France and England on either side of him, and an oration was addressed to him on behalf of the Estates. This oration is, in places, singularly moving, and, as we read it, suddenly the significance of the whole scene dawns upon us. It is an attempted Burgundian revival. The reign of the new Duke is to revive for these people who have suffered so much, the good old times when the Duchy of Brabant was in the hands of the Dukes of Burgundy.

So long as the Dukes of Brabant, said the orator, governed their subjects themselves, making it appear that they loved them and were not careless of them—as was especially the case when the duchy belonged to the Dukes of Burgundy—they reaped great advantages from the people; but when they began to leave them and to forget them, abandoning them to the will of their

Pl. 30

Anjou in the "Barriers" (p. 93)

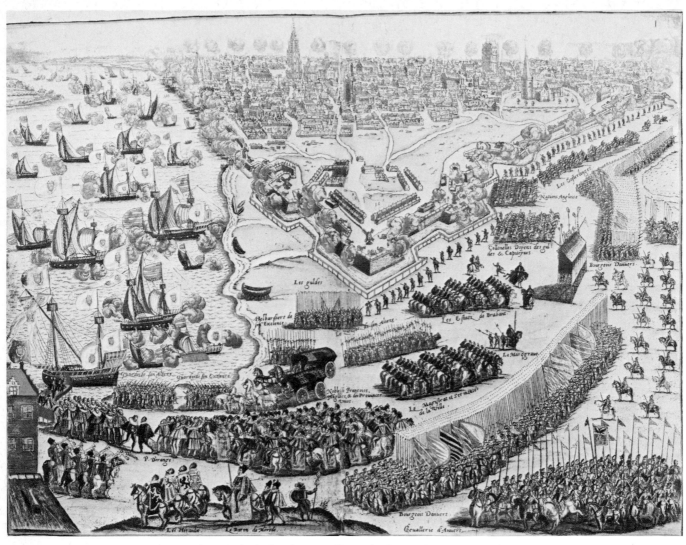

a   Anjou's Arrival at Antwerp. From the *Joyeuse Entrée*, 1582 (p. 94)

b   William of Orange crowning Anjou as Duke of Brabant.
From the *Joyeuse Entrée* (pp. 94–6)

c   Anjou and his Three Attendants.
From the *Joyeuse Entrée* (pp. 96, 99)

under officers, then all fell into ruin. The King of Spain has left them, disdainfully, utterly destitute of his presence for the space of twenty years. He has altered and changed almost the whole state of the country, and committed the offices to such as by the laws and privileges were not capable of them. Yet the insatiable covetousness, malice, and exceeding tyrannical lordliness of the Spaniards was not contented therewith: in the end, when they had abused the whole commonwealth after their lust, they grew into so great pride, that they fell to snatching the private goods and substance of the inhabitants, to living upon the labour and sweat of the poor, to ravishing the chastity of men's wives and daughters, and (to fill up the measure of all abomination and cruelty) to taking away the lives and sucking the blood of those who sought by all means to please them.

"Whereupon in the end the great and righteous God (who hath a care of his servants) being offended thereat, made that people (who had aforetimes been of great valour) to call to mind their former state and libertie; and gave them both will and courage to mainteine the same, in such sort as they had received from their forefathers. Which thing they said could not better be done than by the election which the said States of Brabant, united with the other Provinces, had made of his Highnesse person to be their Prince and Lord, of purpose to bringe all things backe to their former order."

In former times they had had princes gentle, mild, gracious and familiar, favourable to their subjects; his Highness has already given proofs of his gentleness, truth, and soundness, so that it seems, says the orator, as though "some ancient Duke of Burgognie was raised up againe unto them." [20]

The Dukes of Burgundy had, of course, held the Duchy of Brabant as one of their possessions and titles. It is infinitely pathetic to realise from the orator's speech that the installation of Anjou as Duke of Brabant was intended to encourage and rally the victims of Spanish rule by presenting him as one of their old Dukes of Burgundy come back to them.

After the speech, Anjou swore to respect the constitutional liberties of the people, that constitution of which the traditional title was the "Joyeuse Entrée"; and then the mantle and bonnet of the Duchy were brought, of crimson velvet trimmed with ermine. These robes were ceremonially placed upon him by the Prince of Orange,[21] and in them he rode through the city (Pl. 19, a). The Frenchmen marvelled to see their master in that apparel, and it was explained to them that it was "the Duklie apparell, and that he wore it as a representation of antiquitie", or, as the writer of the *Joyeuse Entrée* elsewhere expresses it, the Duke of Brabant as he rode through the city seemed to revive before men's eyes "the statelinesse of old Time". [22]

Everywhere in the streets of Antwerp floated the flag of Brabant, the golden lion, and all the decorations celebrated the removal of the duchy from the tyrannical King of Spain and its transference to the new Duke. Of these decorations, two only need concern us; one is the "Elephant" (Pl. 19, c) which turned away from the moon of Spain to worship the rising sun of Anjou's rule;[23] the other is the Giant of Antwerp (Pl. 19, d) who let fall the arms of Spain and raised those of France as the Duke passed.[24]

The significance of the whole day was summed up when William of Orange placed the mantle and crown of the Duchy of Brabant upon Anjou. This moment is depicted in the illustration in the *Joyeuse Entrée* (Pl. 31, b) showing the ceremony on the platform outside the gates of the city. Anjou has already been invested with the mantle, and Orange is in the act of placing the ducal crown on his head. Heralds stand on the right and left, wearing tabards with the lions of Brabant and Flanders and other insignia; on the roof of the platform are the arms of Antwerp as a marquisate of the Empire and, again, the lion of Brabant.

William of Orange was the heart and soul of all this spectacle; it is he who is trying to build up Anjou into a symbol, a rallying point for national revival. The French prince, as Duke of Brabant, is to awaken memories of the old Burgundian world, of the splendour of chivalrous spectacle under the Dukes of Burgundy. The affection of the people is to be transferred from himself (Orange) towards this symbol of the old better times which he is giving them. The Prince of Orange had begun his chequered life as an immensely wealthy nobleman at the court of Charles V in Brussels where the magnificent traditions of Burgundian life were enjoying a last flowering. He tries to make his French puppet represent, in the land which the Spanish rule had ruined, a Burgundian renaissance.

Orange led this representative of the "statelinesse of old time" into Antwerp; and Orange's son and Orange's nephew followed him. Another of the illustrations to the *Entrée* (Pl. 31, c) shows the Duke riding up to the gate of the city; the Prince of Orange has passed ahead of him, over the draw-bridge. The Duke, in his newly acquired ducal robes and crown, is followed by three figures riding abreast. The account tells us who they are.[25] One was an Englishman, Lord Sheffield. The other two were young princes of the House of Nassau, namely the Prince of Orange's son, Count Maurice, then a boy; and his nephew, Count Philip, the son of his brother John, a young man several years older than Maurice.

Anjou was also accompanied through the city by the splendid cortège of knights in fairest armour—knights of France, of England, of the Netherlands—which we see drawn up in the picture of his landing (Pl. 31, a). The entry was the expression of an attempted revival of international chivalry, around the revived Duchy of Brabant.

The Knight who stands on the left in the "Barriers" tapestry (Pl. 32, a) gazes deferentially towards Anjou, and it appears to be Anjou's helmet which he and the page are holding, for Anjou wears no helmet and the Knight's own helmet is on the ground. Attention is drawn to the helmet held by the Knight and the page by the gaze of the man immediately in the line of vision behind it who wears a helmet adorned with brilliant orange plumes and crested with a winged dragon (Pl. 32, c). This winged dragon crest in the tapestry may be compared with the creature on the helmet of the Giant of Antwerp (Pl. 32, d) at the entry. What did that Giant do? He raised the arms of France as Anjou passed, and lowered those of Spain. The figure in the tapestry with a helmet crested like that of the Giant is thus perhaps an allusion to the Giant; he too is saluting the raising of the arms of France, for he gazes fixedly at the helmet which the Knight is about to hand to the French prince.

Who was it who raised the French prince into the position in the Netherlands which the abjuration of Spain had left vacant? It was William of Orange. Is it therefore possible that

Pl. 32

b   Orange in a tapestry at Middleburg
(p. 97)

a   The Knight in the "Barriers" (p. 96)

c, d   Helmet in the "Barriers" and
Giant's Helmet at the Entry (p. 96)

Pl. 33

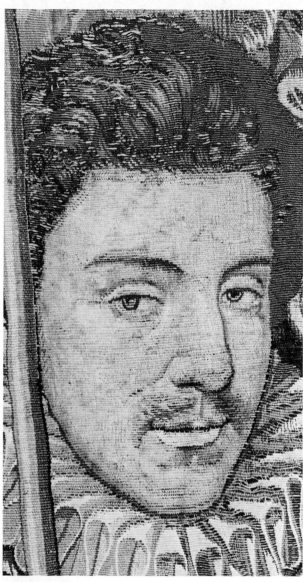

a   Youth in the
    "Barriers"
    (pp. 98, 101)

b   Philip of Nassau, Nephew of
    William of Orange (p. 98)

c   Maurice of Nassau, Son of
    William of Orange (p. 98)

d   Page in the "Barriers" (pp. 97–8)

the Knight in the tapestry represents—not a portrait of William of Orange—but Orange in the rôle of abstract knight-champion against Spanish tyranny, handing over this rôle to Anjou, a reflection of Orange's investiture of Anjou with the crown and mantle of the Duchy of Brabant at the entry?

Clearly, the dark large-eyed young knight of the "Barriers" is not like William of Orange as he was in later life (Pl. 27). Orange, however, was frequently portrayed in abstract knightly roles. We have seen that Lucas de Heere alluded to him as Judas Maccabaeus, the warrior-deliverer of Israel, at his entry into Ghent in 1577. [26] An engraving by Marcus Gheeraerts depicts him as St. George, in full armour on horseback attacking the dragon of Tyranny as deliverer of the Netherlands. [27] Another engraving shows him as a Knight-Perseus, flying to rescue the Andromeda of the Netherlands from the Spanish monster. [28]

Moreover, and this is more significant, the dark vague Knight of the "Barriers" is actually very like indeed to the presentation of Orange as a Knight in a tapestry woven at Middelburg (Pl. 32, b). This tapestry, which is a rather confused mass of emblems, allegories and coats-of-arms, shows within a wreath in the top centre a knightly figure, dark-haired, large-eyed, who is the very image of the Knight in the "Barriers". There can be no possible doubt that the Knight in the Middelburg tapestry is meant to be Orange, for the Latin inscription speaks of the "Dux Auriacus", that is, the Prince of Orange, and the figure is flanked by Orange's arms and mottoes. A vague, idealised, dark type like this could therefore be a type of Orange as a Knight.

The designer of the Middelburg tapestry was none other than Lucas de Heere's pupil, friend, and biographer, Carel van Mander the Elder. It is known from a document that this tapestry was woven at Middelburg in 1600 from a design by Van Mander. [29] Van Mander might well have had access to drawings or designs by Lucas and might, therefore, actually be using in this tapestry a type of Orange which Lucas had created. We therefore think that our hypothesis that the Knight in the "Barriers" represents Orange in deferential relation to Anjou, as his chosen overlord and successor in the rôle of knight-champion, receives some iconographical corroboration from the comparison with the Middelburg tapestry.

The ideal Orange-Knight in the Middelburg tapestry has below him a ducal crown and a lion which is emerging from the waves, with the motto "I struggle and I emerge" (*Luctor et emergo*). The Orange-Knight is therefore here identified with the struggles of the heraldic lion against tyranny. Might it not be in some such sense as this that the old pattern of crowns and lions in sun-rays is used on the breeches of the Knight in the "Barriers"? It is the same pattern as the one on the robe of the head Polish ambassador in the "Polish" tapestry, [30] where it would parallel Henri's election to the crown of Poland with that of his brother to the ducal crown of Brabant.

If the Knight in the "Barriers" represents Orange himself, this gives us a clue to the two who are with him, the young man who stands behind him, and the page-boy who is taking the helmet. Two representatives of the younger generation of the Nassau family rode behind Anjou as he entered into Antwerp. One was Orange's son, Maurice of Nassau, then a boy though later to become almost as famous as his father. If we compare the long nose and sharp features of the page in the tapestry (Pl. 33 d) with the charming portrait of Maurice of Nassau as a child (Pl. 33, c), or with the rough engraving of the "Adolescens Princeps" (Pl. 21, c) in De Bruyn's "Riders", it seems quite possible that there may be a reference to Maurice in the page. The other was Orange's nephew, Philip, then a very young man, the son of his only surviving brother, John. A portrait of this Philip (Pl. 33, b) suggests that this might well be the same face as that of the youth in the tapestry (Pl. 33a), grown older. It is a similarly broadly oval face, with heavy chin, deeply indented under the lower lip, small moustache, rather long nose, and with the placid Nassau expression. The likeness of the young Philip in the tapestry, if we are right in thinking that this is he, would, of course, have been taken from the life in Antwerp, not from a portrait.

Thus, if we are right, this group of three is a Nassau family group, showing the head of the family, Orange, with two members of the younger generation. It would link with the other Nassau family group in the tapestries, namely the one in the "Journey" (Pl. 26) where the two dead brothers of William of Orange, Louis and Henry of Nassau, stand together.

All the Nassau foreground figures in the "Barriers" would allude to Anjou's entry into Antwerp, and to his investiture by Orange with the insignia of the Duchy of Brabant. The bright orange plumes of the helmet at the feet of the statue on the right, of the winged dragon helmet, and of other details, impart to this tapestry a predominantly Orange tone. It is the most vitally important tapestry of the whole series; the foreground figures in it are larger than in any of the others. The destiny of Anjou, foretold by Louis of Nassau at Blamont, is here achieved, and the Orange colouring of the Valois Tapestries comes to the surface.

It would, however, be in accordance with the double time-vision, so characteristic of the tapestries, if the scene behind the foreground figures, and their dress in half-armour, were to allude to an earlier festival event, namely the barriers in England. The tapestry as a whole would thus represent both of Anjou's destinies—prospective husband of Elizabeth of England and ruler of the Netherlands. It would be, so to speak, an Orange view of Anjou and of Orange's hopes for him.

The "Elephant" tapestry (VIII) again has Anjou as its most prominent figure. He is now one of a foreground group of three (Pl. 34) and is no longer in armour but arrayed in a rich court suit, with an elegant lined cloak over one shoulder. With him stands his sister Marguerite, and between them there looks out the face of an unknown man.

If the background view of the "Barriers" alludes to England, so the setting of the "Elephant" might allude to Antwerp. It transports us to a large open space outside a walled city. The platform on which Anjou was installed as Duke of Brabant was outside the city, set up "towards a corner of the Castell..so as his Highnesse being there, might at one time view both the Citie and the Castell, and behold the counterscaifes; the deep ditches..the great and faier buildings, the goodlie walles..the broad rampires garnished with trees." [31] This view sounds not unlike the one we see in the tapestry, which is very different from the background of Caron's "Elephant Carrousel" picture (XII). The elephant, too, has been turned round from its position in Caron's picture, perhaps to salute Anjou as the rising sun, like the elephant at his entry.

Pl. 34

Anjou, Marguerite, and Another in the "Elephant" (p. 98)

Pl. 35

a   Edmund Sheffield in the Armada
Tapestries (p. 100)

b   Edmund Sheffield, Earl of Mulgrave
about 1626 (p. 100)

c   Youth in the "Elephant" (pp. 100, 101)

With the "Elephant" tapestry, we should also look at Lucas de Heere's drawing for Anjou's entry into Ghent (Pl. 17, c) six months after his Antwerp entry. Warring crowds advance to attack one another whilst the peaceful figure of Anjou, in court dress, stands between them. So in the "Elephant", the warring masqueraders advance towards one another behind the brilliant figure of Anjou. In the Ghent entry drawing, the combatants are the opposite religious parties in France whom Anjou is appeasing with his gesture, bringing the blessings of peace with her cornucopia of abundance. [32] Perhaps a similar meaning underlies the combat in costume of many nations of the "Elephant", assimilating this to the politique tradition in French festivals, and making of this tapestry a pendant to the "Quintain" in which Anjou's brother of France presides over the riders of different nations.

The chief problem of the "Elephant" tapestry is the identity of the young man who stands between Anjou and his sister (Pl. 34). He is clearly a distinct portrait. Can any member of the family of Catherine de' Medici be made to fit him? The only possibility would be her eldest grandson, Henri (son of the Duke of Lorraine), then a youth of about eighteen, but portraits of him show no likeness whatever to the character in the "Elephant". Can he be yet another member of the Nassau family? There is none who seems suitable.

Since the families, both Valois and Nassau, seem ruled out, we fall back on another line of enquiry, but one which is typical of the preoccupations of the designer of the tapestries, namely nationality, and we ask ourselves the following question. Where is the Englishman in the Valois Tapestries? Surely there should be an Englishman somewhere, for the English backing for Anjou was one of the reasons which made him of value as sovereign of the Netherlands. Moreover, the strong English contingent, led by the Earl of Leicester, which Queen Elizabeth sent with him was one of the most striking features of his entry into Antwerp. Gazing at the unknown young man in the "Elephant" in his plain ruff (a marked contrast to the frilly affair worn by Anjou) we wonder whether the secret which he seems to be withholding from us is merely the natural reserve of an Englishman on finding himself in strange surroundings.

Looking once again at the three small figures who ride after Anjou as he approaches the gates of Antwerp (Pl. 31, c), we remember that two of them were the two Nassau boys whom we fancy that we have seen in the "Barriers", whilst the third was a young Englishman, Edmund Sheffield. It would be a satisfactory arrangement, and a symmetrical linking of the "Elephant" tapestry with the "Barriers", if the youth in the "Elephant" were to be the third of Anjou's young attendants.

Edmund Sheffield,[33] a youth of about twenty-two in 1582, was the step-son and ward of the Earl of Leicester. His mother, whom Leicester had secretly married in 1573, was the sister of Lord Charles Howard of Effingham. Step-son of Leicester, nephew of Howard, the two most eminent members of the English contingent at Antwerp, Sheffield was a suitable choice as the English youth to accompany the two young Nassau princes as they followed Anjou into Antwerp.

The earliest known portrait of Sheffield [34] is to be found (and this may sound rather significant) in the borders of a set of tapestries woven in the Netherlands. After the victory over the

Spanish Armada, that is, after 1588, Howard of Effingham ordered tapestries commemorating it to be made; they were designed by Cornelius Vroom and woven by François Spiering at Haarlem. In the borders were medallion portraits of the commanders of the victorious English fleet, one of them being Edmund Sheffield, whose ship was called "The Bear". The Armada Tapestries used, of course, to hang in the House of Lords and perished in the fire of 1834, but not before John Pine had recorded them in engravings.[35] The medallion portrait of Sheffield here reproduced (Pl. 35 a) is taken from Pine's engraving. This characterless, bearded face is obviously too poor a likeness to be used as evidence, either for or against, the identification of the youth in the "Elephant" (Pl. 35 c) as Sheffield. The only other authentic portraits of Sheffield so far discovered show him in much later life; one is a portrait at Welbeck, in Garter Robes;[36] the other is the engraving by Elstrack (Pl. 35 b).[37] The nose and eyes of the youth in the "Elephant" might possibly have become, in late middle age, rather like those of the man in the engraving, but this is much too remote in age to be used as valid evidence for identification. Our conclusion must therefore be that, though the historical circumstances point to the probability that the youth in the "Elephant" is Edmund Sheffield, the portrait evidence at present available is too weak to give adequate iconographical support to this suggestion.

There was another relative of Leicester's present at Antwerp, namely his nephew, Sir Philip Sidney. Sidney was one of the English knights sent by Elizabeth with Anjou so that he might have a train "meet for his greatnesse" when he entered the city. Sidney was probably on the platform, with his uncle Leicester, when Orange invested Anjou with the insignia of the Duchy of Brabant. Sidney had taken a strong and public stand against the marriage of Elizabeth with Anjou, but he was no opponent of Orange's plans for Anjou in the Netherlands. He was a most warm admirer of William the Silent and all that he stood for, and the admiration was reciprocated. Languet tells how Orange, on receiving one of Sidney's letters, exclaimed that there was nothing that he would not do for him.[38]

Some of the features of the Englishman in the "Elephant" are not unlike those of Sidney in the portrait of him in the National Portrait Gallery, but our youth in the tapestry is both too young and insufficiently forceful to be Sidney. One cannot help regretting, however, that Lucas de Heere did not put Sidney into the "Elephant". Many trains of thought arise which all tend to suggest how curiously "right" it would have been to have found Sidney in the Valois Tapestries. In four years time, Sidney was to die in the Netherlands fighting against Spain, like another Louis of Nassau. Sidney was the English Protestant knight *par excellence*, as Louis of Nassau was "le bon chevalier" of the Netherlands. And what is Sidney's *Arcadia* but a long allegory of chivalrous festivals in which political meanings are concealed? The mind behind the Valois Tapestries works rather like the mind of Philip Sidney in his *Arcadia*, not because it is Sidney's mind but because it also uses courtly and chivalrous formulae to express an Orange point of view.

To sum up, now, our impressions of the "Barriers" and the "Elephant", these two tapestries, which are probably (though not absolutely certainly) based on French festival designs, carry on the festival subjects of the whole series. As on the other festival designs were superimposed portraits alluding to present day festivals at the court of Henri III, so here are superimposed figures alluding to his brother's contemporary triumphs in the Netherlands. Our suggestion that the Unknown Knight of the "Barriers" could be Orange himself in deferential relationship to Anjou might be considered fanciful were it not for the curious corroboration afforded by the figure of Orange as Knight in the Middelburg tapestry. The suggestion that the unknown young men in the two Anjou tapestries might refer to attendants who followed the French prince into Antwerp is not contradicted, but rather receives some confirmation, from the resemblance between the faces of the young man and the page in the "Barriers" to portraits of Philip and Maurice of Nassau. It seems highly probable that the English support for Anjou would be represented somewhere in the foregrounds, and if, as we think, the young man in the "Elephant" is the missing Englishman, the best candidate for him is Sheffield, he being the English youth who attended Anjou into Antwerp with the two Nassau princes.

Marguerite, who stands in the "Elephant" with Anjou (Pl. 34) was, of course, not at Antwerp. This brother and sister were deeply attached to one another, and it might have been Anjou's own choice to have her placed beside him in his hour of triumph. Politically, Marguerite's function here is to connect Anjou with his family. Through the presence of his sister, his importance as a member of the French royal family is emphasised. Through that sister's husband, Navarre, he is connected with the French Protestants. And he has England behind him. This group expresses very compactly the various affiliations of Anjou which made him politically valuable.

We are aware that some of the notions which we have put forward in connection with these two tapestries do not carry with them the same weight of certainty as does the recognition of well-known French royal personages, or the identification of the man in the "Whale" with the Duke of Lorraine, or the man in the "Journey" with Louis of Nassau. Those identifications were so certain because the artist of the tapestries was drawing those faces, not from the life, but from portraits of a similar type to those with which we compared them. But for the people in the "Barriers" and the "Elephant" (with the exception of Marguerite) the artist may have been drawing his figures and faces from the life in Antwerp. As we pointed out earlier, Anjou is the only one of the French royal personages of whom a full length, original portrait could have been taken in the Netherlands. The Anjou of the "Barriers" and of the "Elephant" can therefore perhaps give us some idea of Lucas de Heere's work as an original artist, when he is taking a portrait from the life and not working with portrait heads and costume studies. Similarly the "Philip of Nassau" (if it is indeed he) of the "Barriers" and the Englishman of the "Elephant" may also both be based on original portraits by Lucas de Heere.

Since so much is in doubt concerning Lucas de Heere as a portrait painter, these faces in the tapestry medium become of great interest. They can give us some idea of Lucas' skill in portraiture, of which Van Mander speaks. The Englishman (Pl. 35 c) is perhaps the finest and the most sensitive head in the whole gallery of portraits in the Valois Tapestries; it is probably based on an original study of a visiting Englishman made by Lucas de Heere in Antwerp in 1582.

CHAPTER V

A LOST MOMENT IN HISTORY: ITS RECORD IN THE TAPESTRIES

The Valois Tapestries are a document written in the language of festivals, and it is by following festival history from 1564 to 1582 that we have been led to the deciphering of their meaning. We must now stand back and try to view them as a whole.

One of the dominant themes is the presentation of the Two Brothers, Henri and François, as they are to-day, in the splendour of their contemporary festivals. Though the two brothers are never shown together, the tapestries fall into groups in relation to them. Henri reigns in the "Fontainebleau"; François reigns in the "Barriers"; Henri dominates a masquerade of many nations in the "Quintain"; François dominates such a masquerade in the "Elephant"; as Henri received the crown of Poland, alluded to in the "Polish" festival, so François receives the sovereignty of the Netherlands, alluded to in the "Barriers" and the "Elephant". The reason why the tapestries came into existence is to affirm, or to plead for, solidarity between the King of France and his brother the Count of Flanders and Duke of Brabant.

Catherine de' Medici also dominates the tapestries, being present in all save one. She is acknowledged as both the genius of the festivals and the mother uniting the family. The festivals for Anjou in England and in the Netherlands are an extension of the festivals of the Valois Court; in the spirit of festival, the family is integrated.

The central importance of the "Journey" tapestry in the argument is that it states the historical antecedents of the present situation, showing it as the fruit of a long previous history of relationships between France and the revolt of the Netherlands from Spain. In the "Journey" the French court goes to meet Louis of Nassau and to renew the alliance with William of Orange. William completes the work of his brother Louis when he instals Anjou in the Netherlands. Louis is the architect in the past of the work now accomplished. The only tapestry which does not represent a festival is the one which states clearly the underlying historical and political direction of the whole. As once the French court journeyed towards the support of the Netherlands, so now it is urged to journey in the same direction and to accept the Netherlands, in the person of Anjou, into the circle of its family and festivals.

Though the allusions to the present situation are imposed on designs representing past festivals, a deep understanding of the meaning and historical background of the earlier festivals can be discerned. The suppression of Charles IX suggests revulsion from the Massacre which marred one of the festivals in the great sequence. The "Polish" festival tapestry leads on to the journey to Poland in the "Journey" and to the reconciliation with Louis of Nassau, and this sequence reflects, as we have seen, the true state of affairs, the return of the French court to the liberal policy after its interruption in the Massacre.

The mind behind the tapestries is, we believe, the mind of William of Orange which his "pensioner" Lucas de Heere is interpreting with enthusiasm. William the Silent alone could have fully understood the meaning of the presence of Louis of Nassau in the "Journey". It is in keeping with his character that Louis should be acknowledged as the precursor upon whose work and sacrifice the present position of Anjou in a Netherlands liberated from Spain is being built.

The tapestries seem designed to appeal to Catherine and to Henri III, to remind them of that past meeting at Blamont and to urge them to continue in the present, by supporting Anjou, the policy there laid down. They appeal particularly to Catherine, by glorifying her festivals and her family. We therefore think that they were made as a diplomatic gift to be sent to France, a delicate appeal to the Queen Mother and to Henri III on behalf of their son and brother. They reflect Orange's determination to link the fortunes of the Netherlands with the French Monarchy and his pathetic attempt to believe in Anjou as a worthy figurehead.

In the year of Anjou's rule in Antwerp, when he was doing nothing to stem the advance of Parma, whilst the clouds of menace were gathering more and more alarmingly over Orange's experiment in raising the French prince as sovereign instead of Philip of Spain—in that year the Valois Tapestries were planned. They are, in a manner, the only solid and lasting result of that experiment. The Valois rule in the Netherlands produced a work of art, if it produced nothing else. And we may reflect, with a certain sympathy, that this is in keeping with the whole ethos of the Valois court. Just as Catherine de' Medici went on with her festivals, whatever happened, just as Henri III resorted to festivals when the menacing clouds threatened ever more gravely, so during Anjou's rule in Antwerp they record the festivals, raising a monument—the greatest and most comprehensive which we have—to the festival art of that court which was about to vanish from history.

We can also reflect from another point of view on the choice of this subject of festivals. It is clear from speeches made at Anjou's entry into Antwerp and from some of the decorations that his rule was expected to revive learning and culture in the desolated provinces. After his entry, he was addressed by deputies of the Reformed Churches with a speech which alluded to his grandfather, François I, and to the name of "Father of Learning" by which he had been known. The speaker hoped that the new Duke would imitate his grandfather's example by encouraging learning and reviving universities and scholarship. For both chivalry and learning, arms and letters, are necessary for the commonweal. [1] One of the decorations at the entry showed Anjou as Apollo on a rock with the Nine Muses; their music is banishing the evil forms of war and tyranny which are being driven into a cave.[2] Anjou is here the bearer of a revival of all civilised pursuits, following in the footsteps of his grandfather.

Combined with this hopeful presentation of the Duke was the reminder that the good old dukes of Burgundy also belonged to the race of the Valois. Amongst the opening words of the deputy's speech at the entry were the following:

"Sir, we hope, that as the great honour and felicitie which these Countries have atteined unto...have beene purchased under the Sovereigntie and Government of the right renowned

Princes, the Dukes of Burgognie, which issued out of the most noble House of France; so, under your guiding and government, being of the same house, the ancient renowne of the same dignitie shall be recovered by your prowesse and maintained by your wisdome."

Anjou in his reply said that he would fashion himself after the pattern of his "predecessors and Great Uncles", the Dukes of Burgundy,[3] thus accepting the Valois-Burgundian tradition which had been found for him and which as it were naturalised this French prince as the "natural" lord of the provinces in place of the seigneur of Spain whom they had disowned.

If one were to choose the manifestation of the French culture of the contemporary Valois court which had most in common with the courts of the Valois Dukes of Burgundy, surely the choice would fall on the marvellous artistic development of the pastimes and exercises of chivalry. A possible further reason for the choice of the festival subject, apart from its appeal to the tastes of Catherine de' Medici, might therefore be that it expressed that Franco-Burgundian revival which was being built up around Anjou.

It has been entirely forgotten even that the attempt was made to present Anjou as a symbol of Burgundian revival, and here again the Valois Tapestries may be regarded as a monument to something which never materialised. For these tapestries are the record of festivals of the Valois court made by a Burgundian artist in the atmosphere of the attempted neo-Burgundian-ism around Anjou. There is a profound historical rightness in this—from the point of view of festival history— for it was at the courts of the Valois-descended Dukes of Burgundy that the festivals of chivalry had reached a very high point of perfection, and it was out of that tradition that the great sixteenth-century court festivals arose and continued the shaping of chivalrous festival towards new art forms.

Anjou, as we have seen, was also the symbol of the "politique" attitude. Lucas de Heere had shown him, at the Ghent entry, as the pacifier of the warring religious parties. It was the supposedly tolerant attitude of this Catholic prince which made him suitable as prince of the Catholic and Protestant populations of the Netherlands, a suitable representative of the Pacific-ation of Ghent.

We have already dwelt on the possible "politique" significance of the fact that representative figures from opposite sides in the wars of religion appear in the foregrounds of the tapestries.[4] The family of Catherine de' Medici seems "catholic" in the sense of all-embracing, including in its members various shades of religious opinion, from the right-wing orthodoxy of the Duke of Lorraine, through the "politique" Catholic, Anjou, to the Protestant Navarre. Henri III's Counter Reformation Catholic movement was non-violent in purpose, disbelieving in perse-cution and advocating penitence and charity as opposed to the Inquisition and the sword.[5] The presence of Louis of Nassau and his Protestant companions amongst the members of the House of Valois, and the possible presence of other members of the Nassau family, shows the French Monarchy in a liberal light, likely to further and approve a liberal solution of religious problems for the Netherlands.

In the history of Catherine de' Medici's festivals, as we have seen, the conciliatory policy of the earlier time had been resumed after the Massacre in the festivals for the Polish ambassadors. There was a tradition for including both Catholics and Protestants in these festivities and masquerades, as a peaceful means of bringing them together and subjecting them to the pacifying influences of poetry and music. Henri III's festivals for the Lorraine-Joyeuse wedding coincide with his non-violent religious movement with which they were closely connected. It is therefore not impossible that the authors of the tapestries, with their keen insight into contemporary history, had yet another reason for choosing festivals as their subject, because they knew that festivals at the French court could mean conciliatory mingling together of opposite sides in a festival spirit.

We have already suggested that the masquerade riders of the "Quintain" with Henri at their centre form a pendant to the riders in the "Journey", with Henri at their centre, going to meet the Protestants. We have noted the suggestive similarity between the Ghent entry drawing of Anjou standing as the pacificatory "politique" between the warring religious parties, and the "Elephant" where Anjou stands in front of the masquerade combat. The possibility therefore arises that the tapestries plead through festivals for toleration; they ask that massacres should be suppressed, with the memory of Charles IX, and that the nations and the religious parties should join in international chivalrous festival.

Or could one put it on more personal grounds and fancy that William of Orange is putting the best interpretation upon the festival policy of the French court and pleading with its members to be true to their best selves? That the Silent one reads the true meaning of Catherine de' Medici's life work as the same as what he himself is now trying to put into practice in the Netherlands, through Anjou? Does one great liberal speak to another in the tapestries in the language of "magnificences"? Let all this misery of religious war and persecution be done away with; let Burgundian magnificence reawaken and join hands with French magnificence; let cosmopolitan tolerance replace the tyrannical gloom of narrow fanaticism; let international chivalry unite the nations in harmless pastimes; let the peoples of the earth wear their infinitely varied costumes, knowing that they are all masks behind which mankind is one.

As a costume artist, Lucas de Heere, as we pointed out, seems connected with the costume manuals, and these in turn belong within the sphere of those geographical and topographical studies of which the great Antwerp cartographer, Ortelius, was a moving spirit. Was this cosmopolitanism of outlook over the four quarters of the earth and the infinitely varied costume of their inhabitants in any way connected with the "politique" attitude, with tolerance concerning the varieties of religious belief to be found amongst mankind? We have found no direct evidence of this though the second attitude might be the logical result of the first. It is curious that William of Orange and Anjou both appear in person in De Bruyn's manual of riders of many countries in their various costumes, though it would not be safe to deduce from such a source that costume cosmopolitanism was symbolic of the liberalism of the Orange-Anjou combination.

"We live in a very disordered time, which we have very little hope of seeing very soon improved, as I fear that it will receive a greater shock, so that the patient will soon be entirely prostrate, being threatened with so many and various illnesses, as the Catholic evil, the Gueux fever, and the Huguenot dysentery, mixed with other vexations...All this we have deserved through our sins; for we are up to our heads in pride and ambition; every one wishes to be called, but not to be, good; every one wishes to teach others, but not to humble himself; to know much and to do little, to dominate others, but not to bow under God's hand. May he be merciful to us, and grant us to see our faults." [6]

This is a quotation from a letter written by Abraham Ortelius to his cousin Emanuel van Meteren in 1567. It expresses what seems to have been the core of Ortelius' religious attitude, and of that of his circle. [7] Disgusted with the horrors of religious war and religious persecution, this group cultivated an inner religion of direct approach to God and attached little importance to outward forms. In their view, a man might belong outwardly to any of the confessions, Catholic or Protestant, whilst stressing his inner attitude more than his outward allegiance, and without attempting to interfere with the allegiances of others. These "Libertinists" were not atheists, as their enemies called them, but rather descendants of the *Devotio moderna* or of the Erasmian tolerance, both religious phenomena native to the Netherlands and now adapted to these later and more terrible times.

It seems not impossible that this attitude, which was particularly characteristic of Ortelius and his circle, might have found a congenial symbol in costume, clothing which alters the external appearance of a man and does not affect his inner personality. We have seen that it was exactly to the circle of Ortelius, Emanuel van Meteren, Hoefnagel, and others of the Antwerp geographical group that Lucas de Heere belonged. We therefore wonder whether possibly in the tapestries the costumes of many countries have in themselves some such "Libertinist" meaning. Looking once again at the "Quintain" we like to fancy, though this can only be a wild surmise, that the debonair man with the mask (Pl. 36) may be the genial Lucas de Heere himself, advancing with a smile to hint at some inner philosophy of costume which he holds in common with the revellers of the French court.

It has recently been suggested that one of Peter Bruegel's pictures, the "Combat between Carnival and Lent" should be related to the Ortelius attitude of inner detachment from the confessions. [8] It is in the form of a tournament between revellers led by King Carnival, a huge pot-bellied figure thought to represent Lutheranism, and Lent, an emaciated female, representing Catholicism, with her followers. This picture, and its interpretation, reminds us of Carel van Mander's curious interpolation on costume in his life of Lucas de Heere where he expatiates on the vagaries of fashion in dress which now commands us to have huge stomachs and now to be unnaturally compressed. [9] Was he hinting at something in that digression, hinting through costume at the deeper attitudes and affiliations of Lucas de Heere?

If there is anything in these guesses, two "politique" or Erasmian and tolerant traditions come together in the Valois Tapestries. The formal imposition of the visual "costume and topography" outlook on the French festival designs, would thus have also a spiritual meaning. Libertinists of the Netherlands are seeing their own outlook in the festivals of that old Erasmian, Catherine de' Medici.

The Man with the Mask in the "Quintain" (p. 106)

We would emphasise that the above remarks are in the nature of hints suggestive of an atmosphere rather than positive statements. As a corrective to them, we remind ourselves that richness of costume is particularly suited for expression in tapestry and that the emphasis on costume in all its variety in the Valois Tapestries contributes largely to their decorative quality, an object which the artist would certainly have had in view.

William of Orange's elevation of Anjou to the sovereignty of the Netherlands is sometimes presented as the unfortunate aberration of an otherwise great man, though thoughtful historians recognise that he had excellent reasons for it. He would not take the sovereignty for himself, both for the private and magnanimous reason that he would not have it said that he had led the Revolt of the Netherlands against their natural prince in order to take the prize for himself, but chiefly for the public and absolutely valid reason that he knew that the hard-won independence of the southern provinces could not be consolidated and defended without outside help and the protection of strong alliances. Anjou seemed absolutely the right choice; he brought with him the foreign protection; he was a Catholic, as was essential for the southern provinces, yet supposedly tolerant. And there were various points of view from which he could be built up as a symbol of national unity. We have begun to see the full splendour of this plan which, if it had succeeded, would have established a liberal bloc in Europe—France and the Netherlands closely joined; England an ally and perhaps also become "politique" in principle through the marriage of the Catholic prince with the Protestant queen; the spirit of Burgundian civilisation revived under new leadership; the spirit of international chivalry revived to present a united front to the dragon of the Spanish tyranny and the threat of Spanish aggression.

Various causes contributed to the failure of the plan. Elizabeth's coquetting with Anjou deceived William of Orange. Yet now that we begin to perceive the full grandeur of the plan, we realise how much there was in it which would have appealed to that most intelligent queen. Its whole ethos was in harmony with some of her own most cherished notions.[10] There is no doubt that she was deeply attracted to the Anjou match and relinquished it with difficulty. She was in love with something in it. Can she really have been in love with that impossible youth? Perhaps she was in love with the ideas of William of Orange, too civilised and too advanced for the age.

The protective power of France was also an illusion, for the French Monarchy itself was on the brink of disintegration and collapse under the Spanish pressure.

But infinitely the worst drawback of all was the character of Anjou. We begin to understand the rôle assigned to him, how he was to become popular with the people as a genial "natural" prince, careful of their rights and privileges, living among them, fostering the revival of their splendid civilisation, like one of the old Dukes of Burgundy come back to heal their wounds. The playing of such a rôle required infinite tact and understanding, it required an attractive and humane personality, the careful nourishing of an equilibrium between the Catholic and Protestant sections of the population on a basis of genuinely tolerant feeling, it demanded self-forgetfulness and love combined with strongly ingrained caution and deep prudence. It is just possible that such a character, in spite of the enormous difficulties, might have succeeded in holding together the southern provinces and holding them against Spain. He would have had to work in closest concert with William of Orange and with full trust in him. Even then the plan might have failed, for huge difficulties and dangers confronted it.

Instead of the character just outlined there was—François d'Anjou. Every effort has been made in the "Barriers" and the "Elephant" to make the best of him but the truth prevails in spite of the artist. Anyone can see at a glance that this man is an impossible person. Why, then, did very clever people like Elizabeth of England and William of Orange fail to see it at a glance? There must have been some element of attractiveness in Anjou, some aura of intelligence and culture which the ridicule and shame of his actions have totally obscured. He was a neurasthenic intellectual, like all his family, and to this difficult temperament was joined a cold egotism and an overweening and childish vanity and ambition. Both his brothers were kings, and he too, the youngest, must be a king too, or as near to one as possible. Hence he snatched at the grand-sounding title which was offered to him without serious thought as to what it involved, and when, as that year in Antwerp progressed, he began to realise that his position was dangerous as well as conspicuous, he panicked and committed a crime and a blunder of the first magnitude, from which he would have been preserved, either if he had had any heart or feeling for those who had trusted him, or if he had had any sense, and sufficient judgment to count the cost of what he had undertaken.

The ridiculous, cruel, and miserable story of the "furie française" of January, 1583, is also an almost unbearably tragic story if one thinks of what it must have meant to Lucas de Heere and his friends.

What a lost and forgotten hour in history this is which the Valois Tapestries hold for us! They represent an abortive aspiration, a candle lighted only to be immediately blown out, leaving no flicker behind it in the ensuing darkness, unless in the Burgundian richness with which French festivals are interpreted in the tapestries.

In the contempt which follows Anjou, and rightly so far as his personal character is concerned, it has been forgotten that he stood in Europe for a while for something important, the "politique" principle. His one year's reign in Antwerp was a reign in which, theoretically, a state was established within which both Catholics and Protestants were to have freedom of worship. Like the Burgundian revival, this too was a candle soon to be extinguished, yet in its light the writing of the Valois Tapestries should be read.

Apart from their splendour as unique and original works of art, these tapestries are a historical document of the first importance, recording in the language of festival a lost moment in history.

PART III

THE SEQUEL

CHAPTER I

THE COLLAPSE OF THE WORLD OF THE TAPESTRIES

So long as we are inside the Valois Tapestries, we are living in a hope, in a vision of what might have been. Anjou as a popular Valois-Burgundian rules as benign protector over the southern provinces of the Netherlands, tolerating both religions. His forthcoming marriage to Elizabeth of England ensures the English alliance. His brother, the King of France, and his mother, look favourably upon him, and the French alliance is safe. In short, a powerful coalition against Spain has been formed, under the protection of which the southern provinces maintain their break away from Philip of Spain, and the way is kept open for their eventual reunion with the northern provinces and the creation of a united Netherlands. These were the hopes which induced Orange to put Anjou into his position, the hopes which the Anjou of the tapestries is to fulfil.

The plan might not have succeeded in any case, but William of Orange thought that it was the only plan which had a chance of succeeding. The person who wrecked it irretrievably was its hero, its symbol, the being to whom Orange tried to transfer his own rôle of knight-champion of the Netherlands—Anjou himself. When Anjou destroyed himself as a symbol, the whole thing became impossible, and the world of the tapestries dissolved into nothingness.

Discontented with what seemed to him the subservient position in which he was placed, and nervous in his exposed position, Anjou planned a coup d'état to be carried out by his French forces upon Antwerp and other cities which was to make him the real master of the Netherlands (so he thought). On January, 17, 1583, French troops fell upon Antwerp shouting "Ville gagnée! Vive la messe!". The latter cry was apparently intended to rally the Catholic inhabitants to the French coup, but failed of this effect. Antwerp rose to a man to turn out the treacherous French. Hundreds of Anjou's Frenchmen were killed, and the noble Duke himself fled from Antwerp, and eventually from the Netherlands, never to return.[1] Instead of playing his rôle of the popular Burgundian-Valois hero and liberator, Anjou had turned upon his subjects, and had let loose on Antwerp a "furie française" of attempted loot and murder which was compared to the "furie espagnole" of 1576, the hated deed of the Spanish tyrants whom he was supposed to replace. As William of Orange wrote to him, the people were now so incensed against him that they were openly saying that they would rather be in the hands of the Spaniards than exposed to perils like these from their protector. With ghastly ingratitude, and incredible folly, Anjou had smashed his own symbol. Where now was the "politique" and tolerant Duke of Brabant? Vanished in the selfish and treacherous Anjou who had unleashed upon Antwerp Frenchmen crying "Vive la messe!"

Though this was not intended as a rallying cry for the massacre of Protestants, it aroused memories of St.Bartholomew's Night. And the "furie française" of 1583 destroyed a liberal hope, wrecked it beyond recall, just as surely as did the massacre of 1572. François of Anjou turned out to be a Charles ix after all.

The deep chagrin of the Burgomaster and Aldermen of Antwerp was expressed in a printed declaration about this horrible event, and its reversal of previous hopes. The Prince of Orange, says this declaration, had delivered the Netherlands from Spain. They chose Anjou to be their Prince because they thought that the King of France would thereby become their ally. And although the "murder committed in France" (that is the Massacre of St.Bartholomew) and the civil wars for religion in that country were causes of great mistrust, yet they were told that "his Highness was a gracious prince. .and not guilty of those matters passed in France. .who often times. .had made peace between the King and the Protestants". They therefore chose him as sovereign and did homage to him when he came out of England "where the Queen had used him very honourably". They had hoped that under him the country might return to its former prosperity, and they were moved "to honour with all manner of triumphs their new lord, who they thought would have been the father of the country, and to give him rich gifts, more than the necessity of the wars and the power of the city, so lately burnt, spoiled, and sacked, and deprived of all property and traffic, suffered. But notwithstanding this, they are now compelled to surmise that his Highness instead of governing the countries and this city with good grace, has purposed nothing else but by crafty practice at the first opportunity with force to overcome them." [2]

This declaration of the citizens of Antwerp after the "furie française" outlines for us both the ideal world of the tapestries and the sordid reality in which it crashed.

Though there were many who had always distrusted Anjou, there were also many who were utterly amazed and confounded by his action. The English ambassador in Paris wrote to Walsingham that, "the manner of Monsieur's proceeding of late at Antwerp has greatly amazed many in France, considering much was before hoped for upon the confidence which was conceived of his princely mind, having been never detected in any such unworthy action as to make an enterprise on those afflicted souls who had fled to him for refuge to be defended from the Spanish tyranny." [3] And Jean Bodin, also writing to Walsingham, casts the blame upon Anjou's evil counsellors, obviously because he finds the whole business almost unbearably painful, and prefers not to believe "that my master, a Prince of so good a House, can have ordered, still less avowed, such an exploit, to wipe out the splendour and lustre of his fine actions. But I fear I may disgust you by refreshing your memory of it, which makes me redden with shame." [4]

And what of William of Orange himself? He wrote to Queen Elizabeth in February, 1583, "I can say with truth that I never loved or honoured prince more than his Highness, insomuch that with great difficulty have I been willing to believe that which I saw." [5]

No city in the Netherlands would receive Anjou, after what had happened at Antwerp, and eventually he made his way back to France, a miserable and abject failure in the eyes of all the world. And in the following year, 1584, this exploded hope of the liberals died, according to d'Aubigné in a state of deepest despondency, regret, and penitence for the utter collapse of his career.[6] That peculiar woman, Elizabeth of England, seems to have been genuinely moved by his death.[7]

Who could believe, looking at the resplendent Anjou of the "Barriers" and the "Elephant", that in two years time he would be nothing, both dishonoured and dead?

Even after the "furie française", William of Orange still urged on the Estates that they must not break with Anjou, for, unless the French alliance were maintained, they must fall back into the hands of the Spaniards. But Orange was losing his popularity in the southern provinces through the odium aroused by Anjou who was considered—and rightly—to be his responsibility. His continued support of Anjou after what had happened increased the wave of feeling against him, and he left Antwerp and retired into what we may now call, not the northern provinces, but Holland. One by one the towns of the southern provinces (which were not to attain independence as "Belgium" until centuries later) were yielding to the Duke of Parma. The Spanish rule was seeping back over all Flanders and Brabant and the refugees were on the move again. Amongst them was Lucas de Heere, if it is true that it was in Paris that he died in August 1584.[8]

William of Orange did not have to spend long in grieving over the trend of events, for, not long after the death of Anjou, he was assassinated at Delft by Balthasar Gerard. Thus it was not only Anjou who was dead two years after the tapestries were designed, but also William of Orange and Lucas de Heere.

Marnix de Sainte Aldegonde, a despairing and broken man, yielded Antwerp to the Spaniards in August, 1585. This meant the end of resistance in the southern provinces where the rule of Spain was re-established. Thousands left Antwerp and the other cities of Brabant and Flanders and took refuge in the northern provinces, which, owing to this influx of able people and to the great increase in trade and economic prosperity (Amsterdam and other Dutch ports took over the trade of Antwerp which became a dead town) made enormous advances in almost every department of human endeavour in the seventeenth century,[9] whilst the south sank back into the inertia of a defeated country. In 1589, the new governors of Brabant and Flanders made their entry into Antwerp.[10] They were the Archduke Albert and his wife Isabella, who was the Spanish granddaughter of Catherine de' Medici, the daughter of her whom she had gone to Bayonne to meet. Devout and sincere Catholics, the Counter Reformation was established in the southern provinces in their time and churches were rebuilt and refurnished. Richness and splendour did not entirely depart from Antwerp for a fruit of the spiritual and material restoration of the Church was the art of Rubens.

The Valois Tapestries by Lucas de Heere are an expression in art of the abortive effort of the southern provinces towards independence of Spain under a French protectorate. The art of Rubens belongs to the Antwerp of the succeeding age.

The French King himself, the Queen Mother, and all the glories of the Valois court were not to last much longer than Anjou and William of Orange. If Anjou was a delusion, Henri III was a broken reed, himself on the brink of ruin. The world of the Valois Tapestries, in so far as it reflects the festivals of the French court, is also a world on the point of collapse. The time was not far off when the Spanish-controlled extremist Catholic faction in France would drive Henri from his throne, leaving Europe bereft of the French Monarchy, the natural antidote to the Spanish Monarchy and its attempt at universal hegemony. Let us see what was soon to happen to the other characters in the tapestries.

The birth of a Dauphin to Henri and Louise might have averted the disasters ahead, but he failed to materialise. At the end of the *Ballet comique*, Louise presented the King with the device of a dolphin, an allusion to the hoped-for Dauphin. Much of the time of Henri and Louise in the years after 1581 was taken up in long pilgrimages to various shrines to implore the heavenly powers for a child. This was the time when penitent processions filled the streets of Paris— White Penitents, Black Penitents, Penitents of all colours were now the masquerade costumes of the court, and the same musicians and singers who had formerly provided music for the ballets now filled the air with religious music, more melodious than had yet been heard, in the street processions.[11] Henri absorbed himself in these religious activities, and his mother complained of them, though she shared the anxiety about the need for influencing heaven for the birth of an heir.

Another anxiety was the difficulty of keeping Marguerite and Navarre together, for the Queen Mother believed that if Navarre abandoned his wife it would be a sign of renewed war with the Protestants. Marguerite was recalcitrant, left Navarre and came to Paris, quarrelled with the King, and was dragged in disgrace back again to Navarre.[12] The happy "politique" family union of the tapestries was not working well.

The death of Anjou was a milestone on the road to the ultimate disaster. In a situation which had already deteriorated since the Joyeuse wedding festivals of 1581, Anjou's sudden and unexpected death in June 1584 was the worst thing that could have happened, for, in the absence of a Dauphin, it meant that the immediate heir to the throne was the heretic, Henry of Navarre. This gave the Catholic extremists an excuse for acting. Unless something could be done, and done at once, about the "fait de la religion" there would be war. At this juncture, or rather just before Anjou's death when they knew that his end was near, Henri III and his mother tried to bring about what was eventually to be the solution of the problem, after the most disastrous war of the century had finished its bitter course. They tried to induce Navarre to become a Catholic, but without success.[13]

Faced with the fact, after the death of Anjou, that a heretic was now heir to the throne, the Duke of Lorraine allowed the Guises and their friends to assemble at Nancy, his capital, in September, 1584, to form a League with the object of preventing the accession of a heretic to the throne of France. This first version of the League was not yet actively seditious, but in the following December, at Joinville the home of the Guises, the treaty of the Holy League was drawn up. No heretic was to succeed to the throne, though a gesture towards the legitimacy of the Bourbon claim was made by nominating the old Cardinal de Bourbon as heir. The League was now overtly offensive, and announced its further aim, beyond safeguarding that a Catholic must succeed in France, of extirpating all heresies both in France and in the Nether- lands. The meeting was attended by a representative of the King of Spain who promised, in his master's name, an enormous annual subsidy for the prosecution of the objects of the League.[14]

So Philip came out into the open at last, the real enemy, the son-in-law of Spain. France was due to fall within his scheme for obtaining the hegemony in Europe, and it was his doubloons which were to make the League what it eventually became, the instrument for driving Henri III from his throne and establishing a Spanish-controlled faction in France at a time to synchronise with his final moves against England.

Philip II's support of the League was at last the open pursuit of that extermination policy in concert with France to which Henri II had lent a willing ear, but which Catherine de' Medici and her children had, on the whole, resisted.

The Netherlands had not given up hope of finding support in the King of France, though he himself was struggling hopelessly in the net which his, and their, enemies were drawing round him. In July, 1584, after the death of Anjou, deputies went to France to offer to Henri III the position which his late brother had held. They were not publicly received, though they had a secret interview with the Queen Mother. They noted that Protestants and Catholics were living together in harmony in France, and leading Huguenots with whom they conferred assured them of the King's good will.[15]

During the rest of that year, as their situation grew more and more menacing, the provinces of the Netherlands debated as to what was to be done and came to the conclusion that the King of France was the only hope. Events had proved William of Orange right in urging the necessity of the French alliance. It was therefore decided that the sovereignty of all the Netherlands—not only of the southern provinces which Anjou had held but of the northern provinces as well—should be offered more or less unconditionally to Henri III. It seems to have been tacitly assumed that he would tolerate both religious parties but, if only he would accept the sovereignty, the provinces were willing to defer the discussion of the terms until afterwards.[16] This was the last time on which the provinces of the Netherlands—soon to be irrevocably divided by the Spanish occupation of the south—acted in concert.

The envoys arrived at Boulogne in January, 1585, and in February they were received at the Louvre. They passed through the four antechambers brilliant with the French court in gala costume and into the royal cabinet where Henri III received them, surrounded by only a few persons the chief of whom was the Duc de Joyeuse. Other meetings and debates followed, but the French king eventually refused this amazing offer of unconditional sovereignty over all the Netherlands. At the parting interview with the ambassadors, Catherine de' Medici wept. They left in March.[17] Four months later, Antwerp surrendered to the Duke of Parma.

Lamentable though this refusal seems, and was, it has to be remembered that Philip II was now turning his full attention to disturbing France. The Netherlands campaign was being comparatively neglected in order that supplies should be sent to the Guises.[18] Henri was now bearing the full brunt of Spanish pressure which was being deflected from the Netherlands to the grandiose projects against France and against England. It was thus really practically impossible for him to accept the proffered sovereignty which would have involved sending a military force to the Netherlands. Yet some in Henri's entourage counselled its acceptance and the acceptance of open war with Spain which it involved, an attempt, even at this late hour, to cut courageously through the meshes of the net which was closing in. De Thou puts the arguments for acceptance into the mouth of a bishop. As reported by that historian, the bishop reminded Henri of the situation of thirteen years ago when Coligny had urged Charles IX to intervene in the Netherlands against Spain. "Would God" cries the bishop, "that this counsel had come from a less suspected source and that it had been followed! If it had been, we would not have fallen into the misfortunes which we have suffered and are now suffering. . ."[19]

Thus the offer of sovereignty in 1585 reminded of past history, raising the same issues as those put forward by the Valois Tapestries. In them, Louis of Nassau reminds of how a pro-Netherlands policy was returned to at Blamont and urges that it should now be taken up again by supporting Anjou in the Netherlands. If the tapestries were not finished in time for their original plea to be made, they could still have spoken and delivered a message if brought by the envoys from the Netherlands who came to Paris in 1585 (or at the less important visit of the deputies in the preceding year). They would now appeal to Henri III to take the sovereignty, with a pathetic reminder of how his dead brother had been honoured in the Netherlands.

The desperate situation in the Netherlands was naturally viewed with grave concern in England. In July, 1584, Sir Philip Sidney came to Paris to offer condolences on the death of Anjou and also to enquire into the attitude of the French court towards the present situation.[20] His report perhaps led to the sending of the Garter embassy of the following year as a sign of Anglo-French friendship in the face of the Spanish menace.

Some years before, Henri had accepted the Order of the Garter from Elizabeth of England, and in February, 1585, a delegation headed by the Earl of Derby came to Paris to confer the Order upon him. After the ceremony, the Protestant Knights of the Order of the Garter and the Catholic Knights of the Order of the Holy Spirit attended vespers together in the church of the Grands Augustins. Ashmole recounts how the route along which they passed through the streets was heavily guarded, for fear of the League mob which was violently antagonistic to the royal friendship with the English heretics and their Queen.[21]

The English embassy was entertained with a series of banquets and festivities, the very last entertainments of the kind staged at the Valois court. New light has been thrown on the reception of the Garter embassy in Paris from the reports of Derby and others which have recently been discovered and published.[22] From these we learn that prominent among the French knights of the Holy Spirit who received and entertained the English knights of the Garter were the Duc de Joyeuse, and the Duc de Montpensier, otherwise the Prince Dauphin who had formerly attended Anjou in Antwerp. When Derby and his train were officially received at the court, he was met in the first chamber by the Duc de Joyeuse, in the second chamber by the Duc de Montpensier, finally passing to the royal chamber where the King himself awaited the Englishmen. Amongst the banquets given in honour of Derby were two, on the same day, at which the hosts were Joyeuse and Montpensier.

Owing to the disturbed state of the city it was not possible to give the usual outdoor events of a series of magnificences but several shows were held within doors. The most costly and sumptuous of these was the masque and ballet given by the King, which Derby and Stafford describe in a letter to Queen Elizabeth written the day after it. There were three shows. In the first, companies of musicians and dancers advanced and retired forming a spectacle most pleasant and delightful "as well for the rarenesse of the musick, both voyces and instrumentes, as strangnes of the attyre and apparele." This was evidently some exotic masquerade the meaning of which the Englishmen have not understood. Next the King himself led in a company of male dancers and himself performed with them an elaborate ballet the figures of which spelled out the letters of his own and the queen's name. Finally, there was a general court ball with mixed couples of men and women.

To form a picture of the latter event, we have only to look at the "Polish" tapestry where the couples, amongst them Henri and Louise, are dancing in the ball after the ballet. We must transform the watching, and deeply impressed, Polish foreigners into Englishmen, but we need not change Joyeuse for he received the English knights.

Though they took place after the tapestries were designed, and after the deaths of Anjou, Orange, and Lucas de Heere, the entertainments for the English Garter embassy of 1585 throw a retrospective light on the tapestries. They are, as it were, still within the world of the tapestries; they are the last dying embers of the festival art of the Valois court; they represent the same political and spiritual alignment. Anjou had gone but the Prince Dauphin was there, and the emissaries from the Netherlands who had come to ask Henri III to assume the sovereignty were in Paris. The Garter embassy was, in part, designed as a taking up of position with France by England in regard to the situation in the Netherlands. Though Henri would not take the sovereignty, he was willing to show, as far as he dared, his sympathy with the anti-Spanish alliance by his brilliant reception of the English ambassadors.

We have thought much on the Valois Tapestries in relation to festivals of the past, and to festivals of their present, but the festivals for the English Garter embassy are in the future with regard to them, not yet enacted when they were designed. Yet these festivals of 1585 certainly have something to tell us about the tapestries. They are an event in which international chivalry overrides differences in religion in the interests of an anti-Spanish alliance, as at Anjou's entry. They seem to confirm that the identification of the man in the velvet hat in the "Polish" tapestry with Joyeuse is correct. The prominence of Joyeuse in the reception both of the envoys from the Netherlands and of the English Knights of the Garter shows that he belongs within the political and spiritual alignment of the tapestries and has a rightful place in them. The Garter festivals also tend to strengthen the probability that an Englishman must be somewhere represented in the tapestries, to include England in the alignment.

Above all, these latest festivals at the Valois court for the Garter embassy show us that the tapestries give a correct reading of the mind of Henri III as secretly in favour of the cause for which they plead. In his brilliant and desperate dancing at these last ballets, this hunted King stated his position in the language of festival. The mud thrown at him by his enemies has clung too long to the memory of Henri III. He has received no credit for his sincere effort to guide the Counter Reformation in France along non-violent lines, emphasising in his processions and religious activities the virtue of charity. His policy of raising men like Joyeuse to counteract the influence of the Guises has never been seriously examined. The mystery which surrounds this King—the enigmatic figure whom we see in the "Quintain" tapestry surrounded by the costumes of many nations—may be a mystery worthier of respect than has been supposed. The Last of the Valois was a prince with a Hamlet-like profundity of insight into the problems which bore so unbearably upon him, over sensitive and over artistic for the rough tasks with which he was faced, but with more courage than he has been given credit for. It took courage, of a Hamlet-like variety, to dance the ballet for the English ambassadors under the menacing eyes of the Spanish ambassador.[23]

The festivals for the Garter embassy differ from all the preceding great festivals in one important respect; no Guises were present at them. The handsome and active scions of the House of Lorraine had always been conspicuous at the festivals, splendid looking personages, most apt at all knightly sports, sullenly averse to all conciliation, secretly envious and disloyal. Now they had given up all pretence and were away mobilising the forces of the League. They had carried the Duke of Lorraine with them; the handsome presence in the "Whale" was among the absentees from the last of the festivals.

But poor old Catherine was there, watching; and Louise de Lorraine doubtless danced at the balls.

In the very next month—March, 1585—the Duke of Guise began to move, massing troops and occupying towns and provinces, and in the same month—alas! for the united family—Marguerite broke out again. She left her husband and went to the Catholic town of Agen where she declared for the League—a rebel against both the King her husband and the King her brother—raised troops and sent to Spain for doubloons, which she did not get.[24] This amazing action of Marguerite's is probably very revealing for the whole of the previous family history. It was said that her first love was the Duke of Guise; she had married Navarre at the behest of her mother and Charles IX; she had received a severe psychological shock through the massacre at the time of her wedding; she had been forced to play the rôle of decoy to Navarre, all the more humiliating since the decoy failed to function; it is possible that he had insulted her at their last reunion by refusing to resume conjugal relations. So, in what sounds like a fit of nervous rage (of a kind to which the family was subject), she turned on her mother, her brother, and her husband and declared for the League and the Duke of Guise.

The Queen Mother's letters at this time are full of moanings almost beyond utterance. Her anxieties about "my daughter the Queen of Navarre" and the "new troubles" seem likely to kill her. No day passes without some new alarm. Her daughter has written to "my son the Duke of Lorraine, I have seen the letters, to ask him to receive her into his country." This she feels as a blow; Marguerite, then, wanted definitely to place herself on the opposite side of the family split. She will write to her son the King of Navarre to try to placate him about his wife's behaviour.[25] Navarre was not worrying in the least about his wife, but raising troops. What future strains and stresses were latent in that family group of the Duke of Lorraine and the King and Queen of Navarre which we see in the "Whale"!

Henri and Catherine made a treaty with the Leaguers, the Treaty of Nemours (July, 1585). Catherine, though very ill, did all the negotiating [26] and she was obliged, in order to placate them, to agree to rescinding the Edict which had afforded some degree of protection and toleration to the Huguenots. Navarre immediately felt himself threatened. The uneasy peace lasted only a short while and then came the war, sometimes called the "War of the Three Henries", Henri III, Henri de Guise, Henri de Navarre. In this three-cornered contest, with both Huguenots and Leaguers against him, the French King went down to ruin.

In 1587, Joyeuse was defeated and killed at the battle of Coutras in which he led the royalist forces against those of Navarre. The resplendent bridegroom of the "Polish" tapestry has thus now disappeared. Early in 1588, the heads of the League met again at the Duke of Lorraine's capital, Nancy, and determined on more extreme measures. In May of that year, Henri III was driven out of Paris by a revolt fomented by the League, an event which roughly synchronised with the sailing of the Spanish Armada against England. (The coasts of the Spanish-controlled Netherlands were full of ships preparing for the invasion of England after the expected naval victory.) The League demanded a meeting of the Estates General, and this was held at Blois. Feeling himself falling utterly into the power of his enemies, Henri III, with the typical sudden nervous action of the family, caused the Duke of Guise and his brother, the Cardinal, to be assassinated (December, 1588).

In the last terrible months, the Queen Mother had been wretchedly conciliating the Spanish-Guise party, with which her son-in-law of Lorraine was associated, though not in quite such a seditious spirit as the Guises. She thought that this was the stronger side, and she also remembered that she had a Spanish granddaughter. Yet had the defeat of the Armada come earlier, Henri and his mother might have openly cast in their last lot with Navarre and England; as it was, the Virgin Queen's victory came too late to save them. After her son's assassination of the Guises, the Queen Mother tottered out on her last negotiation. She called on the Cardinal de Bourbon to attempt to explain and palliate what had happened. The old Cardinal, the figure-head of the League, reproached her with having laid a murderous trap for himself and the Guises.[27] This seems to have been the last straw. The old woman, who was already very ill, took to her bed and died on January 5, 1589. The presiding genius of all the festivals in the Valois Tapestries has gone.

However much he may at times have resented his mother's interference the Last of the Valois must now have felt utterly alone. In August, 1589, he was assassinated by an emissary of the League, and died after having named Navarre as his heir. There would be many years of fighting before Navarre conquered the League and its Spanish auxiliaries and made good his claim to the throne as Henri IV. And in the interim, there was no crowned King of France in Europe. The Henri III of the Valois Tapestries was to be engulfed in the same rising tide of Spanish agression as the Netherlands, and with his disappearance the French Monarchy itself disappeared for a while from history.

CHAPTER II

THE TAPESTRIES GO TO FLORENCE

The Duke of Lorraine's eldest daughter, Christina, was a great favourite with her grandmother, by whom she had been adopted after her mother's death in 1575.[1] Since that time, Christina had lived at the French court, being "nourished in affairs and public counsels" by the Queen Mother [2], whom she somewhat resembled both in appearance and character. She would well remember the Lorraine-Joyeuse wedding festivals of 1581, so closely associated with her family. Though her name does not appear among those who took part in the *Ballet comique*, her young brother, the Marquis du Pont, was present at it and received a device, as did also her father, the Duke of Lorraine. She was, of course, also related to Joyeuse's bride and her sister Queen Louise.

Perhaps Catherine de' Medici gave the Valois Tapestries to Christina of Lorraine because they contained portraits of her father and of Louise de Lorraine and alluded to the Lorraine-Joyeuse wedding festivals. We know, at any rate, that they were given to Christina by Catherine whilst the latter was still alive, together with a number of other valuables. They went with Christina to Florence when she married the Grand Duke Ferdinand I of Tuscany, and there they have remained until this day. In this transference, they lost their original meaning, as the monument of Anjou's venture in the Netherlands, and acquired a new meaning, as a family heir-loom to remind the young bride of her French relations and of the festivals at her grandmother's court in the country to which she was going.

From every point of view, the destiny of the Valois Tapestries is very singular. They missed their immediate historical mark, for the situation in view of which they were designed collapsed, perhaps before the weaving of them was completed, with the exit of Anjou from Antwerp, and his subsequent death rendered them still further out of date. We have seen that they might still have delivered their message as a plea from the Netherlands to the French court, though in a form altered by the situation, if they were taken to Paris by the envoys who went to implore Henri III to assume the sovereignty. If they were then seen for the first time by Henri and his mother, they would have acted on them only in the sense of adding poignancy to the refusal of the sovereignty. After the southern provinces had finally gone under to Spain, they would be merely purposeless reminders of lost opportunities.

Catherine saw a way to use them, by giving them to Christina, and this must have early obscured their historical meaning. It is true that the Grand Duke Ferdinand, Christina's husband, was pro-French and anti-Spanish in sympathies and might have been able to recognise something of the meaning of the tapestries when these reached Florence among the belongings of his bride. In his earlier days, as Cardinal de Medici, he had received the Duc de Joyeuse when in Rome on his secret mission from the French court to the Pope, and had accompanied him as he left the Vatican.[3] But the tapestries do not go to Florence as a diplomatic appeal to the

Grand Duke. They go, together with other objects, as things of value belonging to his bride, and as such they join the grand-ducal collections. In the grand-ducal halls in Florence, who would recognise Louis of Nassau or understand the Orange context in which the tapestries were made? Yet there is a certain artistic justice to be perceived in the journey of the tapestries to Florence, for they were the record of the artistic life-work of a daughter of the Medici in France, now going to find their permanent home in the city of the Medici.

The basic document concerning the gift of the Valois Tapestries by Catherine de' Medici to Christina of Lorraine is to be found in the records of a Florentine notary, Zanobi Paccali. Amongst these records is a list of objects belonging to Christina which had arrived in Florence and of which an inventory and valuation were made in the Pitti Palace on May 29th, 1589.[4] In a preamble to the list,[5] the objects contained in it are stated to have been given to the Grand Duchess by the Queen Mother of France whilst the latter was still alive, "date attualmente in uita dalla detta Christianissima Regina alla detta Serenissima Gran Duchessa". This statement was made by a certain Sieur de St.Martin, seigneur de Puylobier, described as formerly major-domo to the Queen Mother of France, who had these valuables in his custody. The inventory describing the various objects was made by Ascanio Rasi, and whilst it was being made, each item was valued. The jewels were valued by a jeweller, and the other objects by Benedetto Buonmattei and his son, Vincenzo, and by Bernardo Vechietti. In this list, there are three entries relating to Flemish tapestries, "arazzerie fatte in Fiandra". The first describes a set of seven pieces, the subject of which is the virtues, and which was valued at 3,480 scudi; the second is a set of five pieces, "a figure piccole a fantasia", valued at 3.696 scudi. The third entry is as follows:—

> "Un paramento d'Arazzeria a figure di pezzi n⁰ otto alti braccia sei e mezzo, et a lungo sono braccia sessanta, a figure (*sic*) con oro stame, e seta e fregio a grottesche, et altro bianchi, et d'altri colori stimato scudi tremila cinque cento dieci."[6] (A set of tapestries with figures, consisting of eight pieces, six and a half "braccie" high and sixty "braccie" long, of gold, wool, and silk, with a border of grotesques, white and other colours, estimated at three thousand five hundred and ten scudi.)

Six and a half "braccie" is the equivalent of about 3.80 metres; sixty "braccie" of about 35 metres. The average height of the Valois Tapestries is about 3.80 metres; their total length, about 36 metres. The measurements of the eight pieces in this list thus correspond very closely to those of the Valois Tapestries as Cecilia Lisi was the first to observe.[7] In an Italian catalogue of 1884, the Valois Tapestries are described as "tessuto in oro, argento, seta e stame",[8] almost exactly the same terms as those used of the materials of the eight tapestries in the inventory of 1589. The borders of the Valois Tapestries are decorated with the kind of designs technically known as "grotesques". And moreover the "white" effect which Ascanio Rasi noted of the eight tapestries just arrived from France in 1589 is a striking characteristic of the Valois Tapestries, the white foundation of both the borders and the central panels giving a general effect of "white and other colours."

Here is an entry in a list of objects given to Christina of Lorraine by Catherine de' Medici which corresponds closely to the Valois Tapestries; these tapestries have been in Florence from time immemorial. The conclusion seems inevitable that they went there with Christina.

In the same document there is another list of objects, inventoried and valued at the same time and by the same people, but which are stated (by the same major-domo) to have been "left by will" to Christina by Catherine.[9] We know, in fact, that on the day of her death Catherine made a will in which she left all her property in Italy to Christina, also her house in Paris, and half of all the "meubles", jewels, and other objects in her possession; the other half was to go to the Grand Prior of France, the illegitimate son of Charles IX.[10] In Florence, under the guidance of the major-domo, they were careful to distinguish in two different lists the property of Christina which had been given to her by Catherine in her life-time and that which she had obtained under Catherine's will. The Valois Tapestries come under the first category; they were given to Christina while her grandmother was still alive. In the list of objects which came to her through her grandmother's will, there is no mention of any tapestries of any description.

Light is thrown on the distinction made by these two lists by the inventory of the contents of Catherine de' Medici's house in Paris, which was made after her death.[11] This house, which Catherine had enlarged from an old convent, was full of riches of all kinds, and of the artistic treasures which she had accumulated during her long life. The Duke of Mayenne, brother of the Guises and governor of Paris in the revolutionary fury of the League, cast greedy eyes on this house and its contents, and so did his mother and sister. These two women installed themselves in it and began appropriating its furnishings; Mayenne also took an apartment in it and demanded that "aulcuns meubles de tapisserie et aultres" [12] should be handed over to him. The officials of the Chambre des Comptes were embarassed by these demands, which they dared not disobey, though they were trying to hold the house and its contents as the property of the late Queen's creditors and heirs. They could not prevent the plunder, but they endeavoured to maintain some vestiges of legal procedure by making an inventory of the contents of the house.

The officials began to make this inventory on July 15th, 1589, and their first care was to ascertain what had been taken out of the house since the Queen Mother's death, which had occurred six months previously. They were informed by the wife of the concierge that:

"il en a esté transporté l'ameublement de Madame la Princesse de Lorraine qui estoit en ladicte maison, que ladicte dame royne luy avoit donné de son vivant et faict mestre en une chambre à part pour luy estre délivré." [13]

Other witnesses confirmed that the "ameublement de Madame la Princesse de Lorraine" had been taken out of the house, in accordance with an order of the Chambre des Comptes of March 2nd, 1589.[14]

This, then, is the explanation of the list at Florence of the objects given to Christina whilst Catherine was still alive. Catherine had selected and put aside in a room in her house in Paris the things which she was giving to Christina, amongst which were the Valois Tapestries. This "ameublement" had been got out of the house after Catherine's death at Blois, before the inventory was made, and before the harpies began their plunder. Perhaps some fraction of the half of the contents of the house left to Christina under the will was also got out [15], since the other list at Florence is of goods which had reached her in this way.

Thus it is that the Valois Tapestries survive. Had they not been salvaged by the powerful Lorraine influence from Paris under the League, they would have disappeared as did most of the treasures in Catherine's house. The "Arthémise" tapestries, for example, were almost certainly in it,[16] but only the drawings for them by Caron and others have come down to us. There is also a mention in the inventory of:

"Huit pièces de tapisserie de haulte lisse à crotesques, le fondz blanc." [17]

One wonders whether this was another set made in the same atelier as the Valois Tapestries. It was among the "meubles" appropriated by Mayenne and his female relatives.[18]

Christina of Lorraine's marriage to the Grand Duke of Tuscany, one result of which was the saving of the Valois Tapestries for posterity, is most strangely mixed up with the last act of the tragedy of the House of Valois at Blois.

To Blois there had come, on October 23rd, 1588, Orazio Rucellai, member of a famous Florentine family, to conclude the negotiations concerning the marriage.[19] The Queen Mother received him every day and many careful discussions were held. The King wished that the betrothal should take place in France and suggested that the following persons should stand as proxies for the Grand Duke at the ceremony—the Duc de Mercoeur, the Duc de Guise, and Guise's eldest son, the Prince de Joinville. Since these were all relatives of the bride, the choice seems suitable. Bassompierre was also to be a proxy, representing her father.

In December the Queen Mother became ill. The King wished to hurry the betrothal, but the Grand Duke would not allow it to be held until four days before his fiancée's departure for Florence.[20] These apparently delaying tactics worried Their Majesties; and it was rumoured that the King of Spain was sending someone to break the match. The marriage contract was however signed in December. It was agreed that a dowry of 600,000 scudi was to be settled on Christina; 50,000 of this amount was to be in jewels of which an inventory and valuation was to be made by expert persons after her arrival in Florence. In the contract as actually signed at Blois the phrase is added that part of the dowry is to consist "soit en bagues ou autres choses".[21] This phrase "other things" might include the "meubles" which had been given to Christina whilst Catherine was alive, amongst which were the Valois Tapestries, which may, therefore, have been part of her dowry. This is, however, not quite clear from the documents. The marriage contract was probably the last important official document which Catherine de' Medici signed; the list of signatures is headed by those of "Henry" and "Caterine"; it was also signed by the papal legate, Carlo Morosini; by Orazio Rucellai for the Grand Duke; and by Bassompierre, for the Duke of Lorraine. The day of the month is not given in the date on the contract, but it must have been before December 23rd.

On December 23rd, splendid jewels arrived from Florence as a gift from the Grand Duke for Christina, and were much admired[22]. Things now seemed to be going well, and everyone expressed pleasure over the match. But this was the very day (it must have been after the arrival of the jewels) on which Henri III had the Duc de Guise assassinated. This desperate deed has made much noise in history, but from the point of view of Christina of Lorraine it was heavy with personal anxiety—for her uncle had destroyed the chief of the proxies whom he had himself chosen to stand for the Grand Duke at her betrothal. (Was Henri already planning the deed when he made that choice?) Mercoeur and Bassompierre (who had recently signed the marriage contract) fled from Blois.[23] There are no proxies now to serve at Christina's betrothal. Anxious to avoid new delays, she begins to take a hand in the matter herself, and urges that the Grand Duke should name his own proxies; or that Rucellai should perform this office. Rucellai demurred, on the ground that he was not noble, which somewhat irritated Christina.[24]

Meanwhile the double assassination (the Cardinal de Guise was killed on December 24th) of which her son had not warned her, had proved too much even for the staying powers and the resilience of the Queen Mother. On January 5th, 1589, she made the will already described, and at one-thirty on the same day she died. Of all that large Family for which she had laboured all her life, most were dead, and the only two who were with her at the end were the desperate Henri III and Christina of Lorraine. Both showed signs of uncontrollable grief.[25]

Genuinely distressed though she undoubtedly was, Christina was also anxious to get away, and one cannot blame her. Yet the uncle who had murdered her relatives and her proxy also felt for her. Cavriana, another of the Grand Duke's agents, writes that both the Grand Duchess (Christina) and the King are continually wishing that she could be out of it all and in Florence. "Happy are you my niece" said Henri, "for you will be in a peaceful land and will not see the ruin of my poor kingdom." [26] Preparations were being made for her journey, though, says Cavriana, "such terrible things are happening from moment to moment that everything is in confusion." [27]

Amongst these terrible things was the outbreak of mob fury in Paris when news reached it of the assassination of the Guises. It was threatened that if the Queen Mother's body was brought to Paris for burial it would be torn to pieces. This was the time when every monument and work of art associated with Henri III which the crowds could lay hands on was defaced and destroyed. And the Valois Tapestries were still in Paris, in the Queen Mother's house.

The uproar in Paris delayed Christina's departure. The horses and equipment which the Grand Duke had hired for her journey were in the capital and had to be somehow extricated, and then there was the problem of how to get hold of her property in the Queen Mother's house. Early in February, Rucellai reports anxiously to the Grand Duke that the Parisians hold his money and horses for the journey "ainsi que tous les meubles légués à la princesse de Lorraine par la Reine mère." [28] Next we hear that everything belonging to the Grand Duke is lodged in the Hôtel de Ville in Paris, and that "the princess (Christina) has addressed her complaints to Monsieur de Mayenne". [29] And on February 17th we learn that "Monsieur de Lenoncourt has obtained an order from the Duc de Mayenne for the restitution by the Parisians of the horses and objects belonging to the Grand Duke." [30] Lenoncourt was the Duke of Lorraine's man; [31]

the Lorraine influence is at work in protecting Christina's interests in Paris under the League. And the duke, her father, would protect his daughter's journey through France in the throes of civil war. "Au besoin, le duc de Lorraine saura défendre sa fille". [32]

Now, at last, they could be off, to the great relief of the "serenissima sposa". Henri bade her farewell—not the Henri whom we see in the "Fontainebleau" tapestry, but the white-haired prematurely aged man of the late portraits. Louise de Lorraine, too, was there at Blois. Some of Christina's Italian suite were struck by the tragic situation of the King of France whom they were leaving in such a plight. Cavriana prays God for the King; only God can rid him of the universal perfidy and poverty amongst which he finds himself. [33] There was one more ceremony to be gone through, the "fiançailles" which took place on February 27th at Cheverny, [34] celebrated by the Cardinal de Gondi; a proxy had been found; he was the young Charles de Valois, the "bâtard" who, according to Catherine's will, was to have shared her personal property with Christina. On the next day, the final departure for Florence took place.

It is like the last act of a Shakespearean tragedy, with the stage strewn with the dead and dying, but as often in those last acts there is something to remind us that, outside the nightmare, normality still exists. The world of the Valois has collapsed; but Christina departs for safety and for Florence.

The record of that dying world, the Valois Tapestries, also escaped destruction in the nightmare. Since Christina's "ameublement" was not released by a special order from the house in Paris until March 2nd, [35] which was after the date of her departure, the tapestries did not actually leave Blois with her in her personal train, but they were safely in Florence in May. Melchior de Saint Martin, seigneur de Puylobier, who had often in the old days carried confidential despatches for Catherine, [36] faithfully carried out the wishes of his late mistress when he carefully handed over, distinct from the other property, the "meubles" which she had set aside for her granddaughter whilst she was still alive.

Christina's journey from the tragic remains of the French court at Blois to her new home took about six weeks; she entered Florence in state on the last day of April, 1589. Architects and artists must have been working with feverish haste to finish the triumphal arches which were erected in the streets of Florence for her entry. From the full descriptions of these, published by Raffaele Gualterotti, [37] we realise that the Grand Duke Ferdinand I, who was strongly pro-French and anti-Spanish, made the occasion an expression of reverence for that famous daughter of the house of Medici, the Queen Mother of France, and of respect for the French Monarchy, now at the very nadir of its fortunes.

There was a very large triumphal arch near the Arno. [38] On the side of it not facing the Arno, which was the side first seen by Christina and her entering train, was a picture of a huge group dominated by Catherine de' Medici. There Christina saw the Queen Mother, once more in the centre of things as of old, and now seen through the eyes of her compatriots as the singular glory of her native land who has joined through marriages "the greatest princes of the world with the royal family of the Medici." Catherine was shown crowned, seated on a throne under a canopy, and wearing a blue gown covered with the fleur-de-lys. Behind her were the popes and cardinals to whom she was related; on her left were her Medici relations; and on her right and spreading also to the left and around was the whole royal family of France. There was François I, her father-in-law; Henri II, her husband. Then her own three sons as Kings of France, with their Queens. Then her daughters with their husbands—Claude with the Duke of Lorraine "who looked very pleased at being the son-in-law of such a Queen and the father of our Grand Duchess." How the Queen Mother would have rejoiced to see this admiring recognition of her life-long labours in dynastic match-making! The artist was Cosimo Gamberucci, and the sketch of the picture reproduced in the description of the entry by Gualterotti is, one must admit, disappointing.

When she had passed through the arch, towards the Arno, and looked back at its other side, Christina saw a huge painting representing her own betrothal to the Grand Duke.[39] What would still be so fresh in her mind as the last hurried ceremony before that agonising departure, has now here become history, a great state picture, and one evidently set up with the deliberate purpose of vindicating before the Florentine crowds the despised and rejected King of France. For the betrothal picture improved on actual events and was edited in order to enhance the dignity of the French King.

It showed Henri III standing under a dais, pointing towards Christina who bowed reverentially towards him as she received the ring from the young proxy, Charles de Valois. The Queen Mother was in the picture, though of course she was in fact dead before the actual betrothal took place. Her face is described as showing "rare majesty and grandeur joined with affable liberality and magnificence", while the figure of the King is said to be full of royal dignity as he points affectionately towards his niece. Again the sketch in the printed description of the entry of this picture by Giovanni Cosci, is disappointing. The interest of it lies in the fact that the awkward movement of the bride as she bows to the King as she stands beside the proxy is obviously intended to make of the picture of the betrothal a mark of respect to the King of France—to Henri III whom Spain and the Catholic League were bent on destroying, and who in three months' time would be assassinated.

On the day after the entry, the festivals for the wedding began and continued throughout the month of May. As in France, so also in Florence, a new type of court entertainment had been developing within the context of a series of magnificences. The festivals for the Medici-Lorraine wedding included the traditional Florentine *calcio;* a hunt of lions and bears on one of the piazze; a "sbarra" or barriers; a "corso al Saracino" or quintain; a naumachia, or water-festival; but above all and crowning all as the jewel of the series, the famous *Intermezzi.*[40]

The *Intermezzi* of 1589 are rightly considered as a landmark in the history of court festival, for with them the new European genre of opera comes to birth. The six mythological shows were set to music, the actors brilliantly costumed, the stage settings probably beyond anything hitherto seen, and making use of the new techniques and machines for obtaining astonishing transformation scenes. The subject of the first intermezzo was the harmony of the spheres, and all the others were related to the theme of harmony. The opening scene showed a Doric temple and above, on a cloud, a lady representing harmony descending from the celestial spheres to mortals; when this cloud disappeared, the whole starry heaven was revealed; then there appeared on clouds the Sirens, who, according to Plato, are the movers of the spheres. The whole was a representation, appealing simultaneously to ear and eye, of cosmic harmony, and turned as a compliment to Ferdinand and Christina, at whose union the righteous harmony returns to earth.

In Catherine de' Medici's series of French court festivals, the Sirens were, since Fontainebleau, a traditional feature. The French Sirens were not of the bird type, used in the *Intermezzi*, but the fish or mermaid type.[41] Yet, like the bird Sirens of the *Intermezzi*, the French Sirens were good creatures, assimilated to the harmony of the spheres. At the *Ballet comique*, their music was answered by the music of the "voûte dorée" which represented the harmony of heaven. These were Sirens singing the praises of the French Monarchy through which harmony is to be established, reflecting the cosmic harmony.

The *Ballet comique* is in many ways the French counterpart of the *Intermezzi*; both are products of influences of musical humanism running independently of one another in France and Italy. There is no question of the one "influencing" the other. Yet there may be, it is now suggested, a possibility of a deliberate compliment. We have seen that the Grand Duke went out of his way at Christina's entry to express solidarity with the French Monarchy. Might he not have thought it a graceful compliment to take up the harmony theme of the French festivals at the Joyeuse-Lorraine wedding—where the harmonies and harmonious Sirens were in honour of the French King—at his own Medici-Lorraine wedding? Such an idea could have been arrived at merely by consulting a printed copy of the *Ballet comique*.

We do not wish to stress this point, but rather to meditate with wonder on the strange experiences of Christina of Lorraine, probably the only person who saw both the *Ballet comique* in Paris, when she was sixteen, and the *Intermezzi* for her own wedding in Florence, and also the person who brought to Florence the Valois Tapestries. Gazing once again at the "Whale" tapestry, it now seems a nodal point in the whole history of court festival—looking backward from the Joyeuse Magnificences to Bayonne, looking prophetically forwards, through the presence of Duke Charles of Lorraine, to the *Intermezzi* at his daughter's wedding. We seem to see this wonderful tapestry as a fundamental revelation of the ethos of Renaissance court festival which seeks, through semi-magical identification with the figures of classical mythology, to draw the forces of nature—the cosmic harmonies themselves—into the service of the prince. Strange indeed it is to think that this glorification of the festivals of Catherine de' Medici, made in Antwerp in the circle of William of Orange, should have arrived in Florence at the time of the *Intermezzi* of 1589.

Christina must have been astonished by the Italian spectacle, for the transformation scenes would be new to her. Perhaps they seemed like a confirmation of her grandmother's belief in magic. Prospero's words to Ferdinand and Miranda after his magical shows come to mind. Ferdinand and Christina, too, saw a wondrous pageant of cloud-capped towers and gorgeous palaces, of solemn temples and the great globe itself. Thinking of her terrible experiences in France, Christina might have drawn Prospero's dreamy comparison with the insubstantial pageants of life.

We take our story one stage further, to the year 1600 when the eyes of all Europe were turned towards Florence, brilliant with festivals for the marriage, by proxy, of Henri IV, King of France and Navarre, with Maria de' Medici, the niece of the Grand Duke Ferdinand.

Ferdinand's sympathy with the French Monarchy, and antipathy to Spain,[42] had taken the form, in the years following the assassination of Henri III, of assisting Henry of Navarre in his struggles against the League with money, and even with troops. After the latter's victory and conversion, he used his influence in Rome for the reconciliation of the ex-heretic with the Papacy, and his influence with the House of Lorraine for his reconciliation with that family and with his French Catholic subjects. Ferdinand de' Medici was a power behind the scenes in all those complicated manoeuvres and negotiations which made possible the accession to the throne of France of the ex-Huguenot, Henry of Navarre, as Henri IV. All this was sealed with a marriage. The French King divorced his first wife, Marguerite de Valois, and married Maria de' Medici.

Of all the members of the French royal family in the Valois tapestries, Navarre alone had a future. He it was, too, who would achieve some kind of "politique" solution of the religious situation by accepting conversion to Catholicism for himself and ensuring protection for Protestants, within certain delimited areas, by the Edict of Nantes. Meagre though this solution was, it was brought about with a genuinely "politique" intention by Henri IV, who was in some respects, though not in all, slightly akin in spirit to William of Orange. His famous saying that "Paris is worth a Mass", can be interpreted, not merely as cynically ambitious, but also as a genuinely humanitarian concern to end the fearful suffering caused by the wars of religion in France in the only way possible, namely his conversion.

Henri IV and his Medici wife were to be glorified in the art of a great Antwerp painter, Rubens, and it is curious to reflect that the Valois Tapestries, in which Henri appears with his Valois wife, had also emanated from Antwerp, though at a date and in a context which seem such worlds apart from the atmosphere of the court of the governors of the Netherlands in Rubens' time, who were Catherine de' Medici's Spanish granddaughter, Isabella, and her husband.

The "Whale" tapestry, with Navarre and Marguerite in the foreground, must have been in Florence, somewhere in the grand-ducal palaces, when the festivals celebrating Henri IV's marriage to Maria de' Medici were going on. The palaces were decorated with all their richest furnishings and tapestries for this great occasion,[43] but in the description of the tapestries displayed, there is nothing corresponding to the Valois Tapestries. Indeed it would not have been suitable to show these, with their portraits of his first wife (recalling the ill-starred festivities at his first wedding) at such a time.

The wonderfully fresh condition of the tapestries, the unfaded brilliance of their colouring, has given rise to the conjecture that they must have passed much of their existence rolled up in storage. Possibly it was after the second marriage of him who was now Henri IV, King of France, that they were banished from the public view.

It is idle, but fascinating, to wonder how much Christina knew about their real meaning. Catherine would have known their true history, would have recognised Louis of Nassau. Did she tell Christina who the three men in the "Journey" are? We cannot know; but after Christina was dead there would be no one to give any account of them. And if they were rolled up in some cellar it would not matter. They slept through the centuries, keeping their secrets.

The tapestries of the grand-ducal collections remained in the various Medici palaces until the Risorgimento. Under the premiership of Baron Bettino Ricasoli, successor of Cavour, all objets d'art were declared to be the property of the State, and it was at this time that the treasures of the grand-ducal collections were assembled in the Palazzo Vecchio and there put into storage.[44] In 1864, the government ceded some of this material, including the tapestries, to the royal galleries and museums, and part of it was provisionally put on public exhibition in the Vasari corridor between the Uffizi and the Palazzo Pitti. This temporary exhibition was on view from 1866 to 1882, and there can be little doubt that it included the Valois Tapestries, for in Gotti's catalogue of the Florentine galleries, published in 1872, it is said that in the corridor there are drawings, prints, and tapestries; amongst the latter, towards the end of the corridor, there are "eleven Gobelins tapestries representing public festivals at the time of Henri III and Henri IV".[45] Recognising the subjects as French, Gotti has assumed (without looking at the marks) that these are Gobelins tapestries, but this can be forgiven him since he has recognised Henri III in the foregrounds, a correct identification which was soon afterwards lost sight of. Three other tapestries must have been mixed in with Christina's set of eight to reach the number eleven.

According to Gotti, the corridor was opened to the public in 1866 and was filled with objects which had been unpacked from the state stores.[46] It was thus in 1866 that the Valois Tapestries appeared before the public eye, in all their freshly unpacked splendour, and they presumably remained on view in the corridor until 1882.

It was then decided to establish a special museum for tapestries in the Palazzo della Crocetta (now the Museo Archeologico); and a catalogue of this "Galleria degli Arazzi" was published by C. Rigoni in 1884. Four of the Valois Tapestries were on exhibition here, namely the "Journey", the "Fontainebleau", the "Tournament" and the "Elephant". The other four ("Barriers", "Quintain", "Whale", and "Polish") were not exhibited but kept in store.[47] Rigoni's catalogue gives a correct technical description of the four tapestries exhibited and reproduces their marks.[48] He gives one generic title for the subjects of all four, namely "Festivals of Henri II and Catherine de' Medici". He thinks that he can see Henri II in a foreground. This is a retrograde step from Gotti, who had recognised Henri III.

The first publication of any of the tapestries was made in A. Pinchart's *Histoire de la tapisserie dans les Flandres*, 1878-85, where the "Tournament" and the "Journey" are reproduced in photogravure and described as "Les Fêtes d'Henri II", following Rigoni's catalogue. Thus the tapestry containing Louis of Nassau was one of the first two to be published. How totally all has been forgotten during their long sleep, and they enter the learned world of the late nineteenth century as "Festivals of Henri II"!

In 1924, the tapestry museum was dismantled to make way for the Museo Archeologico, which the Palazzo della Crocetta was enlarged to hold. The eight Valois Tapestries then went to the Uffizi Gallery, where they hang to-day.

NOTES

INTRODUCTION

[1] A. Warburg, "Medicäische Feste am Hofe der Valois auf Flandrischen Teppichen in der Galleria degli Uffizi". Lecture delivered in Florence in 1927, published in abridged form in *Gesammelte Schriften*, Leipzig, 1932, I, pp. 255-8, 392-3.

[2] N. Ivanoff, "Les Fêtes à la Cour des Derniers Valois d'après les tapisseries flamandes du Musée des Offices à Florence", *Revue du seizième siècle*, XIX, 1932-3, pp. 96-101.

[3] J. Guiffrey, *Histoire générale des arts appliquées à l'industrie*, VI, Les Tapisseries, Paris, 1911, pp. 122, 154-6.

[4] J. Ehrmann, "Caron et les tapisseries de Florence", *Revue des Arts*, 1952, pp. 27-30, and *Antoine Caron*, Geneva-Lille, 1955 (publications of the "Fontainebleau" drawing); "Les Tapisseries des Valois du Musée des Offices à Florence", in *Les Fêtes de la Renaissance*, Centre National de la Recherche Scientifique, Paris, 1956, pp. 93-100 (publication of the "Whale" drawing); "Caron et les tapisseries des Valois", *Revue des Arts*, March 1956, pp. 9-16 (publication of "Whale", "Anet", and "Polish Festival" drawings); "Dessins d'Antoine Caron pour les tapisseries des Valois du Musée des Offices à Florence", *Bulletin de la Société de l'Histoire de l'Art Français*, Année 1956, pp. 115-25 (publication of the "Tournament" and "Quintain" drawings); "Drawings by Antoine Caron for the Valois Tapestries", *Art Quarterly*, XXI, no.I, 1958 pp. 47-65 (publication of all the drawings with the tapestries).

[5] "Dessins d'Antoine Caron", *Bull. de la Soc. de l'Hist. de l'Art Fr.*, 1956, pp. 124-5.

[6] J.-H. Mariéjol, *Catherine de Médicis*, Paris, 1922, p. 242.

[7] These suggestions are made in the three articles of 1956 and the translation of 1958 listed in note 4 above.

[8] The most obvious of the portraits were recognised by H. Bouchot, *Catherine de Médicis*, 1899. The best study of the portraits is that by L. Dimier, *Histoire de la peinture de portrait en France*, Paris, 1926, III, pp. 270-2.

[9] Ivanoff, in particular, drew attention to this, and made a suggestion to account for it which came very near to the truth. This aspect of the tapestries has been discussed, since the discovery of the Caron drawings, by P. Francastel, "Figuration et spectacle dans les tapisseries des Valois", in *Les Fêtes de la Renaissance*, Centre National de la Recherche Scientifique, Paris, 1956, pp. 101-5.

[10] G. T. van Ysselsteyn, *Geschiedenis der tapijt-weverijen in de noordelijke Nederlanden*, Leyden, 1936, I, p. 236; II, p. xxx.

PART I, CHAPTER I
THE CARON DESIGNS

[1] *Catalogue of an Exhibition of Landscape in French Art* (by A. F. Blunt), Arts Council of Great Britain, 1949, p. 124, no. 525. When Professor Blunt was preparing this catalogue he sent me a photograph of the drawing and I had the pleasure of being able to point out its connection with the Uffizi tapestry. My interest in the Valois Tapestries dates from that moment.

[2] The provenance of these drawings is not clear. The one in the National Gallery of Scotland reached the gallery as part of a bequest of many drawings by David Laing, an antiquarian and bookseller. It is perhaps likely that Laing acquired it in Scotland. The five drawings sold at Colnaghi's may also have come from Scotland.

[3] On this picture see J. Ehrmann, "Tableaux du carrousel à l'éléphant et des astronomes étudiant une éclipse", *Bull. de la Soc. de l'Hist. de l'Art Fr.*, année 1949, pp. 21-7; and *Antoine Caron*, 1925, pp. 27-9. He discusses its relation to the "Elephant" tapestry" in "Dessins d'Antoine Caron", *Bull. de la Soc. de l'Hist. de l'Art Fr.*, Année 1956, p. 120, and in his *Art Quarterly* (1958) article.

[4] The unusual character of the Valois Tapestries in this respect is stressed by M. and V. Viale, *Arazzi e Tappetti Antichi*, Turin, 1952, pp. 33-4.

[5] *Recueil des choses notables faites à Bayonne à l'entrevue de Charles IX avec la Royne Catholique sa soeur*, Paris, 1566, pp. 49 *verso*-53 *recto*.

[6] *Recueil*, pp. 8 *verso*-16 *verso*.

[7] On Caron, see J. Ehrmann's book where a full bibliography is given, and A. F. Blunt, *Art and Architecture in France*, London, 1953, pp. 102-3.

PART I, CHAPTER II
THE FRENCH PORTRAITS

[1] The engraving is by L. Gaultier (Cabinet des Estampes, *Inventaire du fonds français, graveurs du*

seizième siècle, Vol. I, by A. Linzeler, number 241).
Louise also wears the same necklace in a drawing
at Lille (reproduced in E. Moreau-Nelaton, *Les
Clouet*, Paris, 1924, II, fig. 440) and in the portrait
in the Ambras Collection at Vienna.

[2] L. Dimier pointed out (*Histoire de la peinture de
portrait en France*, Paris, 1926, III, pp. 270-2) that the
same head of Marguerite has been used three times.

[3] Dimier (*Op. cit., loc. cit.*) accepts the identification
of this man with Navarre.

[4] This comparison was first made by Dimier, *Op.
cit., loc. cit.*

[5] N. Ivanoff, "Les Fêtes à la cour des Derniers
Valois d'après les tapisseries flamandes du Musée des
Offices", *Revue du seizième siècle*, XIX, 1932-3, p. 114.

[6] See further below, pp. 82-5.

[7] Evidence to be brought forward later will confirm
that this group does allude to Louise with her sister
at the *Ballet comique*. Since the artist does not show
the face of Marguerite de Lorraine, Duchesse de
Joyeuse, he probably had no portrait of her.

[8] Carel van Mander, *Le Livre des Peintres*, trans. H.
Hymans, Paris, 1885, II, p. 22.

PART I, CHAPTER III
COSTUME AND TOPOGRAPHY

[1] For the bibliography of Abraham de Bruyn's
costume manuals, see *Katalog der Freiherrlichen von
Lipperheide'schen Kostümbibliothek*, Berlin, 1896-1905,
nos. 9-12, 2897-9; R. Colas, *Bibliographie générale du
costume et de la mode*, Paris, 1933, nos. 468-78. Cf. also
A. J. J. Delen, *Histoire de la gravure dans les anciens
Pays-Bas*, Paris, 1935, II, Graveurs d'Estampes, p. 113.

[2] "Les Tapisseries des Valois", *Fêtes de la Renaissance*, p. 95, pl. viii.

[3] Abraham de Bruyn, *Omnium poene gentium ima-
gines*, Cologne, 1577. The same figures occur in an
edition of Antwerp, 1581, from which Ehrmann's
plate is taken.

[4] Abraham de Bruyn, *Omnium pene Europae, Asiae,
Aphricae atque Americae gentium habitus*, Antwerp, 1581.

[5] Abraham de Bruyn, *Diversarum gentium armatura
equestris, ubi fere Europae, Asiae atque Africae equitandi
ratio propria expressa est*, Cologne, 1577. There were
various editions of this book with varying numbers
of plates; see Lipperheide, nos. 2897-9; Colas, nos.
468-71.

[6] The German rider is found both in the first
editions and in the later enlarged edition; the noble
Polish rider is only in the later enlarged edition.

On this later enlarged edition, in which some of the
riders are portraits, see below pp. 46-7 and Pl. 21,
a, b, c, d.

[7] See, *inter alia*, H. Wauwermans, *Histoire de l'école
cartographique belge et anversoise du XVIe siècle*, Brussels,
1895, II, pp. 109 ff.; J. Denucé, *Oud-Nederlandsche

kaartmakers in betrekking met Plantijn, Uitgaven der
Antwerpsche Bibliophilen, nos. 27-8, Antwerp, The
Hague, 1912-13, II, pp. I ff.

[8] On the *Civitates orbis terrarum*, see Wauters, *Op.
cit.*, II, pp. 33 ff.; Denucé, *Op. cit.*, I, pp. 266 ff.;
A. E. Popham, "George Hoefnagel and the *Civitates
Orbis terrarum*" in *Maso Finiguerra*, I, 1936, pp. 183-
201; A. Hind, *Engraving in England in the Sixteenth
and Seventeenth Centuries*, Cambridge, 1952, pp. 65, 67,
72.

[9] *Civitates orbis terrarum*, I, 1572, preface; quoted
by Popham, article cited, p. 185.

[10] See above, p. 4.

[11] See M. and V. Viale, *Arazzi et Tappeti Antichi*,
Turin, 1952, pp. 33-4.

PART I, CHAPTER IV
LUCAS DE HEERE

[1] Van Mander's book was first published in 1604.
In the modern edition of the Flemish text (*Het Schil-
der-Boek*, ed. A. F. Mirande and G. S. Overdiep,
Amsterdam, 1936), the life of Lucas de Heere is on
pp. 350-6. In the French translation by H. Hymans
(*Le Livre des Peintres*, Paris, 1884) it is in II, pp. 1-6.

[2] Van Mander's own work probably owed something to the researches of his master; see Hymans'
introduction to *Le Livre des Peintres*, I, p. 2.

[3] G. T. van Ysselsteyn, *Geschiedenis der tapijt-weverijen in de noordelijke Nederlanden*, Leyden, 1936, I,
p. 236; II, p. xxx.

[4] L. Cust, "Notice of the Life and Works of Lucas
de Heere", *Archaeologia*, LIV, 1895, p. 63, note.

[5] Flemish version: *De eerlicke incomste van onsen
ghenadighen ende gheduchten Heere, my heer Fransoys van
Vranckerycke, des conings eenich broeder, by Gods ghenade
hertoghe van Lothryc, Brabant, van Anjou, Alenchon,
Berry & c. Grave van Vlaendren, & c., in zyne vermaerde
hoofstad van Ghendt, de XX Augusti 1582*, Ghent,
1582. French version: *L'Entrée Magnifique de Monseigneur Francoys filz de France, frere unique du Roy, par
la grace de Dieu Duc de Lothier, de Brabant, d'Anjou,
d'Alençon &c. Comte de Flandres &c. Faicte en sa
Metropolitaine & fameuse Ville de Gand le XX d'Aoust,
Anno 1582*, Ghent, 1582.

In the preamble to both versions, Lucas de Heere
names himself as the designer and artist of the entry.

[6] Berlin State Museum, Print Room, ms. 78 D 6.
See P. Wescher, *Miniaturen, Handschriften und Einzel-
blätter des Kupferstichkabinetts der staatlichen Museen
Berlin*, Leipzig, 1931, pp. 185-6. The manuscript,
formerly in the library of the Duke of Hamilton,
was purchased in France in 1821.

[7] Blank in the manuscript.

[8] The life of Lucas de Heere will be discussed more
fully in the next chapter.

[9] Additional, 28,330.

[10] Lucas de Heere, *Beschrijving der Britsche Eilanden*, ed. T. M. Chotzen and A. M. E. Draak, Antwerp, 1937. The editors arrive at the dates 1573 to 1575 as those between which the work must have been composed on p. xxiv of their introduction.

[11] It is taken from the first editions of 1570; see *ibid.*, p. xxv.

[12] Ghent University Library, ms. 2466. It was acquired at a sale in France in 1865, and seems to have been taken from Belgium to France by the French painter, Louis David. See E. de Busscher, *Recherches sur les peintres et sculpteurs à Gand au XVIe, XVIIe et XVIIIe siècles*, Ghent, 1866, pp. 186-7.

[13] Pieter Koeck, *Ces Moeurs & fachons de faire des Turcz...*, engraved in 1533: Guillaume du Choul, *Discours de la religion des anciens romains, De la castramentation & discipline militaire d'iceux etc.*, first editions, Lyons, 1556-7.

[14] H. van de Waal, *Drie Eeuwen Vaderlandsche Geschied-Uitbeelding*, The Hague, 1952, I, p. 167; II, pl. 50.

[15] Andrew Boorde, *The Fyrst Boke of the Introduction of Knowledge* (dedication to Mary Tudor dated 1542, supposed date of publication 1547). Horace Walpole pointed out the origin of the "naked Englishman" jest in Boorde (*Anecdotes of Painting*, ed. Wornum, I. p. 157); but the extremely close correspondence between Lucas' drawing and the wood-cut has not been noticed.

[16] A curious feature of the volume is that on the inside cover are drawn the arms of England over which those of De Wackene have been pasted. De Busscher thought that this indicated that the collection was begun before 1568 in England (*Recherches* pp. 189, 192-3).

[17] F. Deserpz, *Recueil de la diversité des habits*, Paris, 1562. See H. F. Mc Clintock, *Old Irish and Highland Dress*, Dundalk, 1950, p. 16.

[18] In their edition of the *Beschrijving*, p. lxxvii, and pl. B.

[19] The original drawing is in the British Museum; see Hind, *Engraving in England in the Sixteenth and Seventeenth Centuries*, p. 72.

[20] This volume did not appear until after 1594, which is the date of the fourth volume.

[21] See Hind, *Op. cit.*, pp. 67, 72.

[22] The problem is a very interesting one, and is perhaps related to the problem of how Lucas de Heere's "Ancient Britons" achieved publication, through John White, in De Bry's *America*, which does for the New World what the *Civitates orbis terrarum* does for the Old World. On White's drawings see Laurence Binyon, "The Drawings of John White", *Walpole Society*, XIII, 1925, pp. 19-24; Chotzen and Draak, edition of the *Beschrijving*, pp. lxxviii-lxxix; Van de Waal, *Op. cit.* I, p. 92; II, pl. 36.

[23] See Ellis Waterhouse, *Painting in Britain 1530 to 1790*, London, 1953, pp. 24 ff.

[24] With the exception of the "Gideon and the Angel", which is reproduced in the Catalogue of the Berlin Print Room (see note 6 above) they have not been published.

PART I, CHAPTER V
LUCAS DE HEERE LEADS TO WILLIAM OF ORANGE

[1] Van Mander, Life of Floris, *Livre des Peintres*, I, p. 339.

[2] On the life of Lucas de Heere see E. de Busscher, *Recherches sur les peintres et sculpteurs à Gand au XVIe, XVIIe et XVIIIe siècles*, Ghent, 1866, and De Busscher's article on De Heere in *Biographie Nationale (de Belgique)*; Lionel Cust, "Notice on the Life and Works of Lucas de Heere", *Archaeologia*, LIV, 1895, pp. 59-80, and Cust's article on De Heere in the *Dictionary of National Biography*. To these must now be added the invaluable introduction and notes by Chotzen and Draak to their edition of the *Beschrijving*.

On the attribution to Hans Eworth of works signed "HE" formerly attributed to Lucas de Heere, see Lionel Cust, "The Painter HE, Hans Eworth", *Walpole Society*, 1912-13, pp. 1-44.

[3] *Beschrijving*, *ed. cit.*, pp. 68 ff. Some of Lucas' information is derived from printed sources, as the editors show, but there is a strong personal accent in his narrative, and moreover several of the events which he selects for inclusion were those in which Admiral Clinton (whom we know from Van Mander to have been his patron) took a leading part.

[4] De Busscher, *Recherches*, p. 29; Cust, *Archaeologia*, LIV, p. 63.

[5] *Liure de lordre du Thoison dor*, Brussels, Bibl. Royale, ms. 9080

[6] See E. Auerbach, *Tudor Artists*, London, 1954, p. 90.

[7] Compare "Solomon and the Queen of Sheba" engraved by Coornhert after Frans Floris, reproduced in Delen, *Hist. de la gravure dans les anciens Pays-Bas*, II, Les graveurs d'estampes, pl. XXIX; and Holbein, "Solomon and the Queen of Sheba", reproduced in K. T. Parker, *The Drawings of Hans Holbein in the Collection of His Majesty the King at Windsor Castle*, Oxford and London, 1945, Frontispiece.

[8] See above, pp. 18-19.

[9] *Apologie ou Defense de Tres Illustre Prince Guillaume par la grace de Dieu Prince d'Orange etc.*, (Leyden), 1581, pp. 49-51.
Henri II supposed that Orange was informed of the secret plans of Philip and Alva; cf. C. V. Wedgwood, *William the Silent*, London, 1945, pp. 28-30.

[10] Cf. J.-H. Mariéjol, *Catherine de Médicis*, Paris, 1920, pp. 101 ff.; L. Romier, *Catholiques et huguenots à la cour de Charles IX*, Paris, 1924, pp. 177 ff.; F. A.

Yates, *The French Academies of the Sixteenth Century*, London, 1947, pp. 200 ff.

[11] Cust, *Archaeologia*, LIV, p. 65.

[12] *Ibid.*, p. 66.

[13] De Busscher, *Recherches*, pp. 39-40.

[14] *Livre des Peintres*, I, p. 343.

[15] *Publications of the Huguenot Society of London*, X (i), p. 370.

[16] In a Return of Aliens made in November, 1571, Lucas de Heere is described as having "come hither five years ago for religion" (*Hug. Soc.* X(ii), p. 40), which would give late in 1566 as the date of his arrival. The date 1568 which is usally given as that of his arrival seems to have been based only on *Hug. Soc.* X (i), p. 441 and *Hug. Soc.* X (iii), p. 394. It conflicts with the Dutch Church Register which says that he was here in 1567; and also 1568 would have been too late to escape from Alva.

[17] See Chotzen and Draak, introduction, pp. xii-xv.

[18] Douce 68.

[19] Ms. G. 3521.

[20] The Siren from the Van Meteren album (Bodleian, Douce 68) is reproduced by Cust in his *Archaeologia* article on Lucas de Heere; the one from the Vivianus album (The Hague, MS. 74 F 19), is reproduced by Chotzen and Draak in their edition of the *Beschrijving*.

[21] *The Diary of Henry Machyn*, ed. J. G. Nichols, Camden Society, 1848, p. 207. I am indebted to R. Strong for this reference.

[22] *Documents Relating to the Office of the Revels in the time of Queen Elizabeth*, ed. A. Feuillerat, Louvain, 1908, pp. 106-7; the painter named here is Richard Bosum (on whom see E. Auerbach, *Tudor Artists*, London, 1954, p. 155); Clinton's painters would not have been mentioned in the court accounts, since he would be paying them. Machyn says that the Admiral had "kept a great many painters a great while in the country" preparing this banqueting-house.

[23] West Horsley Manor was the property of Clinton's third wife, Elizabeth Fitzgerald and he habitually resided there; see *Victoria County History, Surrey*, III, p. 354.

[24] Queen Elizabeth also visited West Horsley in the summer of 1571 (Nichols, *Progresses*, I, p 291). We need not, however, assume that the costume gallery was at West Horsley. Since Van Mander speaks of the "Admiral of London" showing the gallery to Elizabeth, it was perhaps in Clinton's London house, which seems to have been at Westminster (Nichols, *Progresses*, I, p 275, note).

[25] Cf. F. A. Yates, "Elizabethan Chivalry: The Romance of the Accession Day Tilts", *Journal of the Warburg and Courtauld Institutes*, XX, 1957, pp. 4-25.

[26] *Ibid.*, pp. 6-7. Von Wedel's description of this tilt is quoted in E.K. Chambers, *Elizabethan Stage*, Oxford, 1923, p. 143, note 3.

[27] *Beschrijving, ed. cit.*, p. 86.

[28] *Ibid.*, pp. 81-4.

[29] Bibl. Nat., ms. Fr. 32881

[30] Papiers d'Etat et de l'Audience, Liasse no. 161. The latter was printed in full by C. A. Rahlenbeck, "Quelques notes sur les réformés flamands et wallons du 16e siècle réfugiés en Angleterre", *Proceedings of the Huguenot Society of London*, IV (1893-1), p. 39 note. Cf. Cust's article in the *Proceedings of the Huguenot Society*, VII (1901-4), p. 49; Chotzen and Draak, introduction to *Beschrijving*, p. xv.

[31] *Album amicorum Joanni Rotarii*, Ghent University Library ms. G. 3521, f. 69. Published by Paul de Keijser, "Marnix als Psalmvertaler" in *Marnix van Sinte Aldegonde. Officieel Gedenkboek*, Brussels, 1939, pp. 370-1. Cf. Cust, *Archaeologia*, LIV, p. 67; De Busscher, *Recherches*, p. 35; Chotzen and Draak, p. xv.

[32] H. Pirenne, *Histoire de la Belgique*, Brussels, 1911, IV, p. 36.

[33] *Ibid.*, p. 82.

[34] Many refugees returned to Ghent at the time of the Pacification; cf. *ibid.*, p. 127.

[35] "Lucas Dheere, greffier van de rekeningcamere, pensionnaris van den prince van Oraignen en Saint-Aldegonde, getaxeert op 1050 ff. tourn.", Archives communales de Gand, Comptes et livres échevinaux, 1585. This document was first published by P. Blommaert, *Levensschets van Lucas D'Heere, Kunstschilder te Gent*, Ghent, 1855, p. 23; also in P. Blommaert, *De Nederduitsche Schryvers van Gent*, Ghent, 1861, p. 143. Cf. De Busscher, *Recherches*, pp. 40-2; Cust, *Archaeologia*, LIV, p. 69.

The sum for which Lucas de Heere was taxed was part of the total of 600,000 florins (=200,000 gold crowns) which the town of Ghent was ordered to find after its capitulation to the Duke of Parma (see Pirenne, *Histoire de la Belgique*, IV, p. 187). The enormous amount of 1050 florins (=350 gold crowns) demanded of Lucas de Heere is one of the heaviest taxes in the list. However, he never paid it, for he had died in August, 1584 (see Van Mander). They did not know in Ghent that he was dead (see De Busscher, *Recherches, loc. cit.*).

[36] See S. W. A. Drossaers, *Het Archief van den Nassauschen Domeinraad*, The Hague, 1948, introduction.

[37] *Livre des Peintres*, II, p. 3.

[38] *Beschryvinghe van het ghene dat vertoocht wierdt ter incomste van d'Excellentie, des Princen van Oraengien, binnen der Stede van Ghendt*, Ghent, 1578. There may have been more than one edition of this pamphlet (see Blommaert, *Schryvers*, p. 151; De Busscher, article on Lucas in *Biog. nat.* V, p. 164). Motley says that he had seen an illustrated copy in the Royal Library at the Hague (J. H Motley, *The Rise of the Dutch Republic*, Everyman Edition, III, p. 194, note). It has not been possible to trace this. The copy in

the British Museum which I have used is unillustrated.

[39] Sig. A ii *recto*.

[40] Sig. A iii *recto*.

[41] Everyman ed., III, pp. 194-5.

[42] On the alternate use of the same symbol for the triumph of Catholic or Protestant truth, see F. Saxl, "Veritas Filia Temporis" in *Philosophy and History, Essays presented to Ernst Cassirer*, Oxford, 1936, pp. 203 ff. There is, however, an essay on religious toleration which uses the symbol: see *Temporis Filia Veritas, A mery devise*, 1589, ed. F. P. Wilson for the Luttrell Society, Oxford, 1957.

[43] Blommaert, *Schryvers*, pp. 153-4; De Busscher, *Biog. nat.*, V, p. 167; Cust, *Archaeologia*, LIV, p. 69. I have not been able to see a copy of this book.

[44] On Lucas and English theologians, see Chotzen and Draak, introduction to the *Beschrijving*, pp. xix-xx.

[45] The source material on Anjou's relations with the Netherlands is collected in P. L. Muller and A. Diegerick, *Documents concernant les relations entre le Duc d'Anjou et les Pays-Bas*, The Hague, 1889; cf. Kervyn de Lettenhove, *Les Huguenots et les Gueux*, Bruges, 1885, vols. V and VI (still the fullest study of French relations with the Netherlands in the period but not always reliable); Pirenne, *Hist. de la Belgique*, IV, pp. 169 ff.; P. Geyl, *The Revolt of the Netherlands*, London, 1932, pp. 181 ff.

[46] There is no serious study of Anjou from this point of view.

[47] On Bodin and Anjou, see Pierre Mesnard's introduction to Bodin's *Oeuvres philosophiques*, Presses Universitaires de France, 1951.

[48] On Anjou's circle of musicians, see the preface by D. P. Walker and F. Lesure to Claude Le Jeune's *Airs* (1608), Rome, 1951. On the possible connection with Anjou's circle of La Primaudaye's *Académie Française*, see Yates, *French Academies of the Sixteenth Century*, p. 124.

[49] Muller and Diegerick, *Documents*, III, p. 497; cf. Kervyn de Lettenhove, *Op. cit.*, V, p. 573.

[50] Muller and Diegerick, *Documents*, V, pp. 258-9; Kervyn de Lettenhove, *Op. cit.*, VI, p. 226.

[51] J. F. Willems, *Mengelingen*, Antwerp, 1827-30, pp. 107-8; Kervyn de Lettenhove, *Op. cit.*, *loc. cit.*

[52] P. de Kempenaere, *Vlaemsche Kronijck of dagregister*, 1566-1585, ed. P. Blommaert, Ghent, 1839, p. 290; cf. De Busscher, *Recherches*, pp. 36-7.

[53] On the virgin imagery used of Queen Elizabeth see Yates, "Queen Elizabeth as Astraea", *Journal of the Warburg and Courtauld Institutes*, X, 1947, pp. 27-82. Her imagery is fused with that of the virgins of the Netherlands in the well-known print of "Queen Elizabeth and the Pope as Diana and Calisto", reproduced *ibid.*, pl. 20b, and discussed p. 76.

[54] *La Joyeuse & magnifique Entrée de Monseigneur Francoys Fils de France et frere unicque du Roy, par la grace de Dieu, DUC DE BRABANT, d'Anjou Alencon Berri & en sa tresrenommee ville D'ANVERS* Antwerp, Plantin, 1582. An English translation of the text of this entry is given in Nichols, *Progresses of Queen Elizabeth*, II, pp. 354-85.

[55] These artists are not mentioned by name in the entry, but appear in the city archives in connection with preparations and payments for it: see *Antwerpsch Archivienblad*, ed. F. J. van den Branden, vol. XXIV, p. 322; F. J. van den Branden, *Geschiedenis der Antwerpsche Schilderschool*, Antwerp, 1883, p. 240.

[56] J. Ehrmann, "Les Tapisseries des Valois" in *Fêtes de la Renaissance*, 1956, pp. 97-8; "Dessins d'Antoine Caron", *Bull. de la Soc. de l'Hist. de l'Art français*, Année 1956, p. 121.

[57] See A. J. J. Delen, *Histoire de la gravure dans les anciens Pays-Bas*, Paris, 1934, II, Les Graveurs Illustrateurs, pp. 160-1.

[58] See above p. 24.

[59] See above, p. 19.

[60] See further, below pp. 89-101.

[61] *Le Livre des Peintres*, I, p. 258. No work by Enghelrams seems to be known; see the article on him in *Biographie Nationale (de Belgique)*. Van Mander says that he died in 1583, though this date is contested in Hymans' note on the passage.

[62] See Thieme-Becker, *Lexikon der Bild.Künstl.*, sub nom.

PART I, CHAPTER VI
ANTWERP UNDER ANJOU

[1] The pieces vary slightly in size: their precise dimensions, in metres, are as follows:

	Height	Width
Fontainebleau (I)	4.03	3.39
Tournament (II)	3.87	6.08
Whale (III)	3.55	3.94
Polish (IV)	3.81	4.02
Journey (V)	3.83	5.34
Quintain (VI)	3.87	4.00
Barriers (VII)	3.86	3.28
Elephant (VIII)	3.87	6.70

These dimensions are copied from the fiches in the Uffizi relating to the tapestries, which the authorities kindly allowed me to consult.

[2] This is taken for granted in the standard work by H. Göbel, *Wandteppiche, Die Niederlande*, Leipzig, 1923, I, pp. 173, 174, 423, 523.

[3] For the references to the articles in which these views are put forward, see Introduction, note 4.

[4] A. Wauters, *Les tapisseries bruxelloises*, Brussels, 1878, pp. 144-9, 282.

[5] M. and V. Viale, *Arazzi e tappeti antichi*, Turin, 1952, pp. 33-4, 54-5.

[6] Pierre Colins, *Histoire des choses les plus memorables advenues en l'Europe depuis l'an onze cens XXX iusques a nostre siecle. Digerées & narrées selon le temps & ordre qu'ont dominé les Seigneurs d'Enghien etc.*, Tournai, 1643,

p. 549. Quoted by A. Pinchart, *Histoire de la tapisserie dans les Flandres* (*Histoire générale de la tapisserie*, Paris, 1878-85), p. 91.

[7] J. Guiffrey, *Histoire générale des arts appliqués à l'industrie*, VI, Les Tapisseries, Paris, 1911, pp. 122, 154-6.

[8] Wauters, *Op. cit.*, pp. 172-6; Pinchart, *Op. cit.*, p. 91.

[9] Pinchart, *Op. cit.*, p. 92.

[10] Colins, *Op. cit.*, pp. 726-8.

[11] J. Guiffrey, *Histoire de la tapisserie en France* (*Histoire générale de la tapisserie*, Paris, 1878-85), pp. 88-9.

[12] See J. Denucé, *Sources pour l'histoire de l'art flamand*, IV *Les tapisseries anversoises*, Antwerp, 1936.

[13] Marthe Crick-Kuntziger, "Marques et signatures de tapissiers bruxellois", *Annales de la Société Royale d'Archéologie de Bruxelles*, XL, 1936, pp. 166-83.

[14] *Ibid.*, pp. 169-70.

[15] See in particular, those published by G. T. van Ysselsteyn, "Tapisserieën uit de weverij van François Spiering", *Oud-Holland*, LIV, 1937, pp. 165-72.

[16] Article cited.

[17] G. T. van Ysselsteyn, *Geschiedenis der tapijt-weverijen in de noordelijke Nederlanden*, Leyden, 1936, I, p. 56, II, pp. 32-3. I am indebted to Dr. van Ysselsteyn for her kindness in translating these documents into English for my benefit.

[18] *Antwerpsch Archivienblad*, ed. J. van den Branden, XXIV, p. 323.

[19] F. Donnet, "Documents pour servir à l'histoire des ateliers de tapisserie de Bruxelles, Audenarde, Anvers etc.", *Annales de la Société Royale d'Archéologie de Bruxelles*, X, 1896, p. 336.

[20] His mark is reproduced in M. and V. Viale, *Arazzi e tappeti antichi*, p. 48.

[21] *Op. cit.*, p.xxxviii.

[22] Stafford in a letter to Walsingham mentions that the Queen Mother, according to the custom of France "where the mothers inherit their sons' purchases" will take the matter of Cambrai in hand (*Cal. S. P. Foreign*, July 1583-July 1584, pp. 535, 537). Cf. also M. Gachard, *Correspondance de Guillaume le Taciturne*, Brussels, 1866, VI, pp. 248-9.

[23] There is a copy of Anjou's will in the P. R. O. (*Cal. S. P. Foreign*, vol. cited, p. 519). It contains no mention of any personal property whatever, except debts which he implores his brother to pay.

[24] "Les Tapisseries des Valois", *Fêtes de la Renaissance*, p. 97; "Dessins d'Antoine Caron", *Bull. de la Soc. de l'Hist. de l'Art Fr.*, Année 1956, pp. 121-2.

[25] These documents are published in M. de Maeyer, "Otto Venius en de Tapijtenreeks 'De Veldslagen van Aartshertog Albrecht'", *Artes Textiles*, Ghent, II, 1955, pp. 105-111.

[26] *Antwerpsch Archivienblad*, ed. J. van den Branden, XXIV, pp. 247-472.

[27] That is to say, no payments for tapestries ordered to be made. The payments to Herseel and others are for tapestries purchased.

[28] Cf. Kervyn de Lettenhove, *Les Huguenots et les Gueux*, IV, pp. 14-15; V, pp. 47, 68-9, 112-3, 595. VI, pp. 140, 345.

[29] See below pp. 115-6 for further discussion of this.

[30] Apart from the fragmentary attempt by Kervyn de Lettenhove (*Les Huguenots et les Gueux*, VI, pp. 305-19) to reconstruct Anjou's court at Antwerp, there is little else on the subject.

[31] See *Biographie universelle* under Montpensier. He was a "politique" Catholic, thus characterised in despatches from the English embassy in Paris in 1584: "Duke Montpensier. Greatly loving the state and commonwealth, affecting the peace of the realm, enemy to Spain and to Guise, secretly a friend to the princes of the Religion, for the love he beareth to themselves, not for the Religion, being in his religion extremely addicted, better for execution than for counsel" (*Cal. S. P. Foreign*, July 1583-July 1584, p. 619).

[32] *Antwerpsch Archivienblad* XXIV, pp. 322, 324-5. They were furnished with tapestries bought from Herseel.

[33] See below, p. 59.

[34] See below, p. 72.

[35] See below, p. 91.

[36] The story of the attempted assassination is given in a contemporary pamphlet, *Bref recueil de l'assassinat commis en la personne du tres illustre prince d'Orange etc.*, Antwerp, 1582.

[37] This detail comes from Brantôme's life of William of Orange, *Oeuvres*, ed. Merimée, II, p. 176.

[38] A. Ortelius, *Theatre de l'Univers*, Antwerp, 1581, "Au Prudent Senat et Peuple d'Anvers, Christophe Plantin". The enlarged edition of Abraham de Bruyn's costume-manual, with its title-page showing the Four Quarters of the Earth, was also published at Antwerp in 1581. See above, p. 13.

[39] *Antwerpsch Archivienblad*, XXIV, p. 299.

[40] See above pp. 13-14.

[41] This enlarged edition (Colas, no. 470) contains 77 plates, whereas the earlier editions contained only 52 plates. The "portrait" riders are among those added to the enlarged edition. I am indebted to Dr. Nienholdt, of the Lipperheide'sche Kunstbibliothek, Berlin, for the information that the portrait riders are not in the earlier editions, which I have not been able to see.

A somewhat comparable use of the portrait in a costume book can be seen in the sketch-book of an Italian tailor who used the Emperor Charles V to illustrate his styles for noblemen; cf. F. Saxl, *Costumes and Festivals of Milanese Society under Spanish Rule*, British Academy Lecture, 1937.

[42] In some copies, this rider is actually labelled

as a portrait of the Prince of Orange; see E. A. van
Beresteyn, *Iconographie van Prins Willem I*, Haarlem,
1933, pl. xxiv.

PART II, CHAPTER I
FESTIVALS OF CHARLES IX

[1] Brantôme, "Discours sur la Royne Mere",
Oeuvres complètes, ed. P. Mérimée, Paris, 1890, X, pp.
72-6.

[2] The main sources for the Fontainebleau festivals
are: Abel Jouan, *Recueil et discours du voyage du roy
Charles IX*, Paris, 1566, reprinted by L. Menard,
Pièces fugitives pour servir à l'histoire de France, Paris,
1759, I (I), pp. 1-74; Anon., *Le Recueil des triumphes
et magnificences qui ont estez faictes au logis de Monseigneur
le Duc d'Orleans..estant à Fontainebleau..*, Troyes,
1564, partially reprinted in J. Madeleine "Quelques
vers de Ronsard", *Mélanges offertes à M. Gustave
Lanson*, Paris, 1922, pp. 121-7; Michel de Mauvissière, *Mémoires*, ed. Le Laboureur, Paris 1659, I,
pp. 168-9 (ed. Michaud et Poujoulat, IX, p. 498);
Brantôme on Charles IX, *Oeuvres, ed. cit.* VI, pp. 289-
90; Ronsard, *Oeuvres complètes*, ed. P. Laumonier,
1914-19, III, pp. 475-9. Cf. H. Prunières, *Le Ballet
de Cour en France*, Paris, 1914, pp. 45, 50; P. Laumonier,
Ronsard poète lyrique, Paris, 1909, pp. 219-21; P.
Champion, *Ronsard et son temps*, Paris, 1925, pp.
207-11; H. Chamard, *Histoire de la Pléiade*, Paris,
1939-40, III, pp. 7-12; Yates, *French Academies of the
Sixteenth Century*, pp. 251-3.

[3] Mauvissière, *loc. cit.*

[4] Madeleine, article cited, p. 126.

[5] Ronsard's work for the Fontainebleau and other
festivals is discussed by H. Prunières, "Ronsard et
les fêtes de cour", *Revue musicale*, 1924.

[6] This is stated by Mauvissière.

[7] Reproduced in W. H. Ward, *French Châteaux and
Gardens in the Sixteenth Century*, London, 1909, Pl. IX.

[8] *Oeuvres, ed. cit.*, III, p. 485.

[9] So far as I know, there is no detailed study of
the history of the use of this term. According to the
Cambridge Modern History (III, pp. 7-8) it was at this
very time, around 1564-5, that it came into existence
as the definition of "the group which, while remaining
within the Catholic religion and, when called upon,
bearing arms on the side of the King, were opposed
to all coercion in matters of religion."

[10] *Mémoires*, ed. Le Laboureur, I, p. 170.

[11] There is an excellent presentation of the political situation behind the Fontainebleau festivals, based
on the reports of the Spanish ambassador, in P.
Champion, *Catherine de Médicis présente à Charles IX
son royaume*, Paris, 1937 pp. 58-68.

[12] For the sources for the Bar-le-Duc festivals,
see Chamard, *Histoire de la Pléiade*, III, p. 13.

[13] For a bibliography of the various entertainments and entries staged throughout France in the
course of this progress, see Champion, *Op. cit.*
pp. 7-11.

[14] *Oeuvres, ed. cit.*, X, p. 73.

[15] The printed sources for the Bayonne festivals
are: *Recueil des choses notables faites à Bayonne à l'entrevue de Charles IX avec la Royne Catholicque sa soeur*,
Paris, 1566 (partly reprinted in Laumonier, *Ronsard
poète lyrique*, pp. 743-54); Abel Jouan, *Ample discours
de l'arrivee de la royne catholique, soeur du roy à Sainct
Jehan de Lus; de son entrée à Bayonne, etc.*, Paris, 1566
(reprinted in L. Menard, *Pièces fugitives pour servir à
l'histoire de France*, Paris, 1759, I (2), pp. 13-23); *Li
grandissimi apparati e reali Trionfi fatti per il Re e
Regina di Francia nella Citta di Baiona*, Padua and
Milan, 1565. Cf. A. Warburg, *Gesammelte Schriften*
I, pp. 257-8, 392-3; Prunières, *Op. cit.*, pp. 44 ff.;
Champion, *Ronsard et son temps*, pp. 215 ff.;
Chamard, *Op. cit.*, III, pp. 13-14; Yates, *Op. cit.*,
pp. 253-4.

Of the three printed accounts, only the *Recueil des
choses notables* was used by the artist of the tapestries.

[16] *Recueil des choses notables*, pp. 28 recto-49 recto
(Laumonier, *Ronsard poète lyrique*, pp. 745-51)

[17] *Recueil*, p. 49 recto

[18] See Abel Jouan, *Voyage*, p. 26.

[19] *Recueil*, p. 45 verso.

[20] *Ibid*, pp. 49 verso-56 verso (Laumonier, *Op. cit.*,
pp. 751-4).

[21] See pp. 4, 15 above.

[22] *Mémoires de Marguerite de Valois*, in Michaud and
Poujoulat, *Nouv. Coll. des Mémoires pour servir à l'Hist.
de France*, X, p. 403.

[23] *Ibid.*, *loc. cit.*

[24] He was one of the Knights in the Tournament
(*Recueil*, p. 45 recto), and led the masqueraders dressed
as "femmes à l'antique" in another show (*Recueil*,
pp. 2 verso, 11 recto and verso). Cf. J. Ehrmann, "Dessins d'Antoine Caron", *Bull. de la Soc. de l'Hist. de
l'Art Fr.*, 1956, pp. 119-20.

[25] *Recueil des choses notables*, pp. 8 ff.

[26] This drawing is reproduced in H. W. Ward,
French Châteaux and Gardens in the Sixteenth Century,
London, 1909, pl. XX b. I am indebted to Professor
A. F. Blunt for this comparison.

[27] Though not much like our idea of Catherine,
the figure is like the type used for Catherine in the
drawings for the "Histoire d'Arthémise" tapestries,
some of which are by Caron.

[28] See below, pp. 83-4.

[29] Alva's letters are printed, with a French translation, in *Papiers d'Etat du Cardinal de Granvelle*, Paris,
1852, IX, pp. 281-330. Cf. Motley, *Dutch Republic*,
Everyman ed., I, pp. 394-5; Champion, *Catherine de
Médicis présente à Charles IX son royaume*, pp. 262-93.

[30] *Papiers d'Etat*, IX, pp. 299,, 310, 315, 317 etc.

[31] *Elegies, Mascarades et Bergerie*, Paris, 1565. Critical

edition in Ronsard, *Oeuvres complètes*, XIII, ed. P. Laumonier, 1948. The collection dedicated to Elizabeth
contained Ronsard's verses for the Fontainebleau
festivals and a poem which relates to the Bayonne
Interview. It is not certain whether Ronsard was at
Bayonne, as he certainly was at Fontainebleau. See
Champion, *Ronsard*, pp. 215-6.

[32] *Papiers d'Etat*, IX, p. 311.

[33] The Huguenots believed that the Bayonne
Conference "indicated a desire on the part of the
King of Spain to associate the French Court with
his crusade against Protestantism" (*Cambridge Modern
History*, III, p. 8). This was true; but it was not true
that Catherine and Charles IX agreed to this policy
at Bayonne.

[34] On these festivals, see Prunières, *Ballet de cour*,
pp. 70-5 and his article "Ronsard et les fêtes de cour",
Revue musicale, VI, 1924, p. 41; Yates, *French Academies*, pp. 254-7.

[35] *Mémoires de l'Estat de France*, I, p. 31; Agrippa
D'Aubigné, *Oeuvres complètes*, ed. E. Réaume and F.
de Caussade, Paris, 1873-92, III, pp. 286-7.

[36] *Mémoires de l'Estat de France*, I, p. 263 verso.

[37] *Mémoires de l'Estat de France*, I, pp. 268-9;
D'Aubigné, *Histoire universelle*, ed. A. de Ruble, 1890,
III, p. 303, *Oeuvres, ed. cit.*, IX, p. 553.

[38] *Mémoires de l'Estat de France*, I, p. 271.

[39] Bibl.Nat., Mss. Clairambaut, no. 233, folios
3509-10. On the probable participation of the poets
and musicians of Baïf's Academy in entertainments
planned for this wedding, see Claude Le Jeune,
Airs (1608), ed. F. Lesure and D. P. Walker, introduction, p. xi.

[40] Bibl. Nat., Mss. Fr. 894, folios 101 ff.

[41] The first serious historian to state this seems to
have been J.-B. Adriani, who is quoted by D'Aubigné,
Histoire universelle, ed. cit., IV, pp. 89-90. The
rumour was widely current among Protestants all
over Europe; cf. *Cambridge Modern History*, III,
p. 20.

[42] On the significance of the date of the founding
of Baïf's Academy, see Yates, *French Academies*, pp.
209 ff.

[43] On the hope of a new conciliatory policy raised
by this marriage, see *Cambridge Modern History*, III,
p. 177, and on the reputation for tolerance of Maximilian II see J. Lecler, *Histoire de la tolérance au siècle
de la réforme*, Paris, 1955, II, pp. 264-5.

[44] On the activities of Louis of Nassau at this time
see, *inter alia*, Pirenne, *Histoire de la Belgique*, IV, p.
27 ff., Motley, *Dutch Republic*, Pt. III, chap. VI
(Everyman ed. II, pp. 262 ff.), Kervyn de Lettenhove,
Les Huguenots et les Gueux, II, pp. 289 ff.

[45] J.-A. de Thou, *Histoire universelle*, London, 1733,
VI, pp. 457-8

[46] P. Delaroche, *Trésor de numismatique et de glyp-
tique, Médailles françaises*, Paris, 1836, pl. XIX.

[47] Kervyn de Lettenhove, *Les Huguenots et les
Gueux*, II, p. 259

[48] *Histoire universelle, ed. cit.*, IV, p. 88. The "Stratagem" was a notorious work, widely circulated and
translated.

[49] *Mémoires de l'Estat de France sous Charles Neuviesme*, I, p. 271.

[50] *Album amicorum Joanni Rotarii*, Ghent University Library, Ms. G.3521, folio 53. Published by De
Busscher, *Recherches*, pp. 193-4.

[51] De Thou, *Hist. univ., ed. cit.*, VII, p. 2.

[52] See above, p. 40.

[53] J. Dorat, *Magnificentissimi spectaculi a Regina
Regum Matre in hortis suburbanis editi*, Paris, 1573. Cf.
Prunières, *Ballet de cour*, pp. 55-7.

[54] *Oeuvres*, ed. Merimée, X, p. 74.

[55] *Hist. universelle, ed. cit.*, IV, p. 179.

[56] *Oeuvres, ed. cit.*, X, p. 76.

[57] *Ibid., loc. cit.*

[58] A "grande salle" was expressly built for this
entertainment according to Brantôme (*Oeuvres, ed.
cit.*, X, p. 74); according to D'Aubigné (*Hist. univ.*,
IV, p. 178) an avenue was cut down to make way
for it. It was thus perhaps a temporary erection in
the Tuileries gardens.

[59] J. Ehrmann, "Caron et les tapisseries des
Valois", *Revue des Arts*, 1956, p. 13; "Dessins
d'Antoine Caron", *Bull. de la Soc. de l'Hist. de l'Art
Fr.*, 1956, pp. 117-8.

[60] N. Ivanoff, "Les Fêtes de Cour des Derniers
Valois d'après les tapisseries du Musée des Offices",
Revue du seizième siècle, XIX, 1932-3, p. 116 (referring
to Bibl. Nat., ms. Fr. 5102, f. 4).

[61] "Les nymphes descendirent (de la roche) pour
danser un ballet deux fois...et la pluspart de la nuict
fut passée au bal accoustumé". (*Hist. univ.*, IV, p.
178).

[62] See above, p. 59.

[63] The coat-of-arms, so faintly sketched in the
gardens of the Tuileries, is here distinctly recognisable as that of the Queen Mother. Compare her
coat-of-arms as it is sketched on the "Arthémise"
series of designs for tapestries. The vague type of
figure used to represent Catherine in that series is
similar to her appearance in these Caron drawings
and very different from the realistic figure in widow's
weeds substituted in the tapestries. The "Arthémise"
series, with which Caron was connected, is reproduced in M. Fenaille, *Histoire générale des tapisseries de
la manufacture des Gobelins*, Paris, 1903-7, I, pp. 113-99.

[64] See above, p. 40. Another possibility is that
it might refer to the magnificences which were held
in connection with Charles IX's entry into Paris in
1571.

[65] See H. de Noailles, *Henri de Valois et la Pologne*,
Paris, 1867, II, p. 387. Again, a festival in 1571 is
also a possibility for this drawing, or, of course, it

may belong to the famous series of 1564 (see above, p. 53).

[66] The text of this entry is in *Régistres des delibe-rations du Bureau de la Ville de Paris*, ed. P. Guérin, Paris, 1891, VII, pp. 91 ff. Cf. De Noailles, *Op. cit.*, II, pp. 377 ff. ; Yates, "Antoine Caron's Paintings for Triumphal Arches", *Journal of the Warburg and Courtauld Institutes*, XIV, 1951, pp. 133-4.

[67] See above, p. 14 and Pl. 7, a, b.

[68] See J. Ehrmann, "Dessins d'Antoine Caron", *Bull. de la Soc. de l'Hist. de l'Art Fr.*, 1956, p. 118. The tapestries in which the pattern appears are the "Légende de Notre Dame du Sablon" and "La Communion d'Herkenbald". In the former it is on the carpet beneath the image of the Virgin of Sablon, which, according to the legend, was brought to a Duke of Brabant by a woman of Antwerp who had had a vision commanding her to do this; in the latter, the pattern is on the head of Herkenbald's bed. For information and full bibliography concerning these tapestries, see M. Crick-Kuntziger, *Catalogue des tapisseries*, Musées Royaux d'Art et d'Histoire de Bruxelles, pp. 27-8, 31-4, pls. 16 and 20.

[69] De Noailles, *Op. cit.*, II, p. 350. This is the same man as the Polish prince who was accompanied to Oxford by Sir Philip Sidney in 1583, and for whose entertainment a public debate was arranged in which Giordano Bruno took part. See Yates, *John Florio*, Cambridge, 1934, pp. 88-9.

[70] We have wondered whether the Netherlandish pattern on the robe of the head Polish ambassador might allude to the lion and ducal crown of Brabant, thus making him representative both of the offer of the crown of Poland to Henri and of the offer of the Duchy of Brabant to his brother. We have not, however, been able to trace any traditional meaning for this pattern, The pattern is also used in the "Barriers" Tapestry; see below, p. 97.

[71] See J. Lecler, *Histoire de la tolérance au siècle de la réforme*, Paris, 1955, I, pp. 364-74, 375-9.

[72] Quoted by De Noailles, *Op. cit.*, II, p. 101.

[73] *Ibid.*, II, pp. 124 ff.; *Cambridge Modern History*, III, p. 86.

[74] De Noailles, *Op. cit.*, II, pp. 349-50; *Mémoires de l'Estat de France sous Charles Neuviesme*, III, p. 2.

[75] De Noailles, *Op. cit.*, II, pp. 368 ff.; *Mémoires de l'Estat de France sous Charles Neuviesme*, III, pp. 3 ff.

[76] *Oeuvres*, ed. Merimée, X, p. 189.

[77] *Ibid.*, *loc. cit.*

[78] *Ibid.*, pp. 204-5.

[79] *Ibid.*, p. 197.

[80] *Régistres du Bureau de la Ville de Paris*, VII, pp. 109 ff.; De Noailles, *Op. cit.*, II, p. 372.

[81] T. Godefroy, *Ceremonial François*, Paris, 1649, II, pp. 45-50.

[82] *Régistres*, VII, p. 121

[83] Motley, *Dutch Republic*, Everyman ed. II, pp. 390-7; Kervyn de Lettenhove, *Les Huguenots et les Gueux*, III, pp. 216 ff.

[84] *Mémoires de l'Estat de France sous Charles Neuviesme* III, p. 2 ff.

PART II, CHAPTER II
HENRI'S JOURNEY

[1] On the first part of the journey and those who accompanied Henri, see De Thou, *Hist. univ.*, VII, pp. 23-32; D'Aubigné, *Hist. univ.*, IV, pp. 187-200; Marguerite de Valois, *Mémoires*, ed. Michaud and Poujoulat, X, p. 410; Philippe Hurault, Comte de Cheverny, *Mémoires*, ed. Michaud and Poujoulat, XI, p. 14. Cf. De Noailles, *Op. cit.*, II, pp. 389 ff.; P. Champion, *Henri III roi de Pologne*, Paris, 1943.

[2] The chief source for it is the letters of Louis of Nassau, in *Archives de la Maison d'Orange-Nassau*, ed. Groen van Prinsterer, Leyden, 1841, IV. See also De Thou, VII, p. 28; D'Aubigné, IV, p. 194. Motley draws attention to the importance of the "secret interviews" at Blamont (*Dutch Republic*, Everyman ed. II, pp. 417, 424). Cf. also De Noailles, *Op. cit.*, II, pp. 390 ff.; Kervyn de Lettenhove, *Les Huguenots et les Gueux*, III, pp. 280-92.

[3] Originally by H. Bouchot, *Catherine de Médicis*, Paris, 1899, p. 98.

[4] Groen van Prinsterer, IV, pp. 81*-90*. Cf. Motley, *ed. cit.*, II, pp. 395-6.

[5] Groen van Prinsterer, IV, pp. 278-81; Cf. Motley, *ed. cit.*, II, pp. 417-8.

[6] Groen van Prinsterer, IV, p. 281; quoted as translated in R. Putnam, *William the Silent*, New York, 1911, p. 247; cf. Motley, *ed. cit.*, II, p. 424.

[7] De Thou, *Hist. univ.*, VII, pp. 28 ff.; Cf. De Noailles, *Op. cit.*, II, pp. 399 ff.; Champion, *Henri III roi de Pologne*, pp. 7 ff.

[8] D'Aubigné, *Hist. univ.*, IV, pp. 195-6; De Thou, *Hist. univ.*, VII, p. 28.

[9] Motley, *ed. cit.*, II, p. 424.

[10] See above, p. 29.

[11] *The Correspondence of Sir Philip Sidney and Hubert Languet*, trans. from the Latin by S. A. Pears, London, 1845, pp. 17, 46.

[12] Motley, *Dutch Republic*, ed. cit., II, p. 430; Putnam, *William the Silent*, pp. 253-70; C. V. Wedgwood, *William the Silent*, London, 1945, pp. 138-9.

[13] C. V. Wedgwood (*loc. cit.*) gives a moving account of William's agony at the loss of "mine own brethren whom I loved more than mine own life", as he calls them in his Apology.

[14] *Oeuvres*, ed. cit., X, p. 106.

[15] P. D. Roussel, *Histoire et description du Château d'Anet*, Paris, 1875, pp. 172 ff.; E. Lefevre, *Recherches historiques sur la Principauté d'Anet*, Chartres, 1862, pp. 23 ff.

[16] Charles IX, *La Chasse Royale*, ed. H. Chevreul,

Paris, 1863. The treatise was first published in 1625.

[17] *Lettres de Catherine de Médicis*, ed. H. de la Ferrière, Paris, 1891, IV, pp. 41-2; cf. P. Champion, *Charles IX et le contrôle de l'Espagne*, Paris, 1939, p. 358. D'Aumale had inherited Anet through his marriage with the daughter of Diane de Poitiers. He was, as Champion says, "fanatiquement Catholique".

PART II, CHAPTER III
FESTIVALS OF HENRI III

[1] The text and music of this performance is given in the illustrated publication, *Balet comique de la Royne*, Paris, 1582; cf. Prunières, *Ballet de cour*, pp. 82 ff.; Yates, *French Academies*, pp. 236-74. A manuscript programme for the magnificences as a whole exists, published and analysed in Yates, "Poésie et Musique dans les Magnificences au Mariage du Duc de Joyeuse, Paris, 1581" in *Musique et Poésie au XVIe Siècle*, Centre National de la Recherche Scientifique, Paris, 1954, pp. 241-63.

[2] *Balet comique*, p. I.

[3] Yates, article cited, pp. 244-5, where it is shown that the celebrated "Guerre de Claude Le Jeune" was written for this performance.

[4] Pierre de L'Estoile, *Mémoires-Journaux*, ed. Brunet and others, Paris, 1888, II, pp. 32-3.

[5] Yates, article cited, pp. 261-3.

[6] On the Queen Mother's participation in the Joyeuse festivals, see Abel Desjardins, *Négotiations de la France avec la Toscane*, Paris, 1859-75, IV, pp. 404-5,

[7] See Claude Le Jeune, *Airs* (1608), Rome, 1951, introduction by F. Lesure and D. P. Walker, pp. viii-ix.

[8] *Ibid.*, p. viii, and Yates, *French Academies*, p. 21.

[9] Cf. Yates, *French Academies*, pp. 219 ff.

[10] There is a set of drawings illustrating one of the processions, reproduced and discussed in Yates "Dramatic Religious Processions in the Late Sixteenth Century", *Annales Musicologiques*, Paris, II, 1954, pp. 215-70.

[11] On Henri's religious movement, see the article just cited and *French Academies*, pp. 213 ff.

[12] J. A. de Baïf, *Les Mimes, Enseignemens, et proverbes*, Paris, 1581 (*Oeuvres*, ed. Marty-Laveaux, V. pp. 9 ff); cf. *French Academies*, pp. 260-1.

[13] For the academic influence on the festivals, see *French Academies*, pp. 265 ff.

[14] See *French Academies*, pp. 156 ff, and "Dramatic Religious Processions", pp. 215 ff.

[15] Pierre de Vaissière, *Messieurs de Joyeuse*, Paris, 1926, pp. 120 ff.

[16] This print is reproduced in *French Academies*, Pl. 25, and the verses explaining it are quoted *ibid.*, pp. 332-3.

PART II, CHAPTER IV
FESTIVALS FOR ANJOU

[1] Cf. Viscount Dillon, "Barriers and Foot Combats", *Archaeological Journal*, LXI (1904), pp. 276-308.

[2] In spite of these various arguments, it remains possible that there was no French design behind the "Barriers" tapestry, that is to say, that this tapestry was entirely composed by Lucas de Heere. That a French "combat à la barriere" design existed is, however, attested by the inventory mentioned above, pp. 40-1.

[3] On this painting, see the articles by J. Ehrmann cited above, p. 4, note 4.

[4] Quoted from the manuscript programme for the Joyeuse Magnificences (Bibl. Nat., fr. 15, 831, f. 90) in Yates, "Poesie et Musique au Mariage du Duc de Joyeuse", *Musique et Poésie au XVIe Siècle*, p. 258.

[5] These are referred to by Jean Dorat in his poem on the wedding (*Oeuvres*, ed. Marty-Laveaux, pp. 23, 26); Cf. Yates, article cited, p. 259.

[6] *Recueil des choses notables*, p. 12 *recto* and *verso*. See above p. 59.

[7] Holinshed's *Chronicles*, ed. London, 1807-8, IV, pp. 434 ff.; Duc de Nevers, *Mémoires*, Paris, 1665, I, pp. 540 ff.; J. Nichols, *Progresses of Queen Elizabeth*, II, p. 336.

[8] Printed in Nichols, *Progresses*, II, pp. 310-29; Cf. E. Welsford, *The Court Masque*, Cambridge, 1927.

[9] On the relationship of two famous court entertainments in England to the Accession Day Tilts, see Yates, "Elizabethan Chivalry: The Romance of the Accession Day Tilts", *Journal of the Warburg and Courtauld Institutes*, XX, 1957, pp. 4-25.

[10] See above, pp. 33-4.

[11] The main source for these barriers is Nevers, *Mémoires*, I, pp. 555 ff. See also Nichols, *Progresses*, II, p. 336.

[12] Nevers, *Op. cit.*, I, p. 556.

[13] Kervyn de Lettenhove, *Les Huguenots et les Gueux*, VI, p. 149.

[14] Nichols, *Progresses*, II, pp. 344-5.

[15] *Ibid.*, p. 344.

[16] *Ibid.*, *loc. cit.*

[17] *La Joyeuse Entrée etc.*, Antwerp, Plantin, 1582 (for full title see above p. 34 note 54).

[18] *Progresses*, II, pp. 354-85. Our quotations from the text of this entry are from this English translation.

[19] *Progresses*, II, pp. 355-7; *Entrée*, pp. 12-14.

[20] *Progresses*, II, pp. 358-61; *Entrée*, pp. 16-19.

[21] *Progresses*, II, p. 363; *Entrée*, p. 20.

[22] *Progresses*, II, pp. 356-7; *Entrée*, p. 14.

[23] *Progresses*, II, p. 371; *Entrée*, pp. 29-30.

[24] *Progresses*, II, pp. 372-3; *Entrée*, pp. 31-2.

[25] *Progresses*, II, p. 367; *Entrée*, p. 25.

[26] See above, pp. 31-2.

[27] Reproduced in A. M. Hind, *Engraving in England*

in the Sixteenth and Seventeenth Centuries, Cambridge, 1952, I, Pl. 51.

[28] Reproduced in Putnam, *William the Silent*, p. 230. The Perseus theme was also used of Orange at his entry into Brussels in 1579; see Delen, *Histoire de la gravure dans les Anciens Pays Bas*, II, Les Graveurs Illustrateurs, pl. XXXIII.

[29] See G. T. van Ysselsteyn, *Geschiedenis der Tapijtweverijen in de Noordelijke Nederlanden*, I, pp. 263, 265, 300. The design by Carel van Mander the elder in 1600 is attested by a document. Dr. van Ysselsteyn compares the representation of Orange with engraved portraits by Goltzius (1581) and by Wiericx (these are reproduced in E. A. van Beresteyn, *Iconographie van Prins Willem I van Oranje*, Haarlem, 1933, pls. 18, 19).

[30] See above p. 70.

[31] *Progresses* II, p. 358; *Entrée*, p. 15.

[32] See above, pp. 35-6.

[33] For Sheffield's life, see the article *sub nom.* in the *Dictionary of National Biography*. His presence at Antwerp in 1582 is attested, not only by the *Joyeuse Entrée*, but also by William Camden in his *Annales* (London, 1615, p. 329).

[34] I am indebted to Mr. David Piper and to Professor E. K. Waterhouse for their help concerning the meagre iconography of Sheffield.

[35] John Pine, *The Tapestry Hangings of the House of Lords*, London, 1739 and 1753. Cf. Henry Yates Thompson, *Lord Howard of Effingham and the Spanish Armada*, Roxburgh Club, 1919; Van Ysselsteyn, *Op. cit.*, II, pp. xxxvii-xl.

[36] See C. Fairfax Murray, *Catalogue of the Pictures belonging to His Grace the Duke of Portland at Welbeck Abbey and in London*, London, 1894, no. 322.

[37] See A. M. Hind, *Engraving in England in the Sixteenth and Seventeenth Centuries*, Cambridge, 1955, II, Pl. 102 (c).

[38] *Correspondence of..Sidney and..Languet*, trans. Pears, p. 169. On Sidney and Orange see H. Fox Bourne, *Sir Philip Sidney*, London, 1893, pp. 127, 175; John Buxton, *Sir Philip Sidney and the English Renaissance*, London, 1954, pp. 34-5, 91-2, 138.

PART II, CHAPTER V
A LOST MOMENT IN HISTORY

[1] *Progresses of Queen Elizabeth*, II, pp. 383-4; *Entrée*, pp. 44-5.

[2] *Progresses*, II, p. 378; *Entrée*, p. 38.

[3] *Progresses*, II, pp. 382-3, 385; *Entrée*, pp. 42-3, 46.

[4] See above, pp. 10-11, 46.

[5] See above, pp. 87-8.

[6] J. A. Hessels, *Ecclesiae Londino-Batavae Archivum*, Cambridge, 1887, I, p. 52. Quoted by C. G. Stridbeck, "Combat between Carnival and Lent by Pieter Bruegel the Elder", *Journal of the Warburg and Courtauld Institutes*, XIX, 1956, pp. 96-109.

[7] See R. Boumans, "The Religious Views of Abraham Ortelius", *Journal of the Warburg and Courtauld Institutes*, XVII, 1954, pp. 374-7.

[8] Stridbeck, article cited.

[9] See above, p. 17.

[10] For example, the use of a revival of chivalry as a means of holding a people together amid the dangers and difficulties of the late sixteenth century; see my "Elizabethan Chivalry", *Journal of Warburg and Courtauld Institutes*, XX, 1957, pp. 22-4.

PART III, CHAPTER I
THE COLLAPSE

[1] There is a good account of the "furie française" and its sequel in the introduction to *Calendar of State Papers Foreign*, *1583*; cf. Motley, *Dutch Republic, ed. cit.*, III, pp. 402 ff.; Kervyn de Lettenhove, *Les Huguenots et les Gueux*, VI, pp. 361 ff.; Pirenne, *Hist. de la Belgique*, IV, pp. 182 ff.

[2] "A Briefe Declaration made by the Burgomaster, Aldermen, and Council of Antwerp touching the attempt against that city attempted the 17th of this month of January" in *Calendar of State Papers, Foreign*, *1583*, pp. 24-32. This English translation was made for Burghley from the pamphlet in Flemish printed by Plantin in 1583.

[3] *Cal. S. P. Foreign, 1583*, p. 71.

[4] *Ibid.*, pp. 84-5.

[5] *Ibid.*, p. 101. De Thou also says that Orange was unable to believe the news of Anjou's treachery until he saw "avec douleur que l'affaire etoit très-sérieuse" (*Hist. univ., ed. cit.*, IX, p. 38).

[6] D'Aubigné, *Hist. univ., ed. cit.*, VI, pp. 191, 193; also De Thou, *Hist. univ., ed. cit.*, IX, p. 182.

[7] Walsingham says that she wept every day for three weeks (*Cal. S. P. Foreign, 1583-4*, p. 572).

[8] De Busscher, *Recherches*, p. 40.

[9] Cf. P. Geyl, *The Revolt of the Netherlands*, London, 1932, pp. 274 ff.

[10] The description of it was published by Plantin in 1602; the decorations included an Elephant and a Giant.

[11] Cf. Yates, "Dramatic Religious Processions", *Annales Musicologiques*, II, 1954, pp. 217 ff.

[12] Cf. J.-H. Mariéjol, *Marguerite de Valois*, Paris, 1928, pp. 182 ff.

[13] This was the object of Epernon's journey to Navarre; cf. *Cambridge Modern History*, III, p. 38; Mariéjol, *Marguerite de Valois*, pp. 222 ff.

[14] *Cambridge Modern History*, III, pp. 37 ff.

[15] J. L. Motley, *History of the United Netherlands*, ed. of London, 1875, I, pp. 50-7.

[16] *Ibid.*, pp. 57-61.

[17] *Ibid.*, pp. 91-3, citing the report of the envoys.

[18] *Ibid.*, pp. 107 ff.

[19] De Thou, *Hist. univ., ed. cit.*, IX, p. 304.

[20] *Cal. S. P. Foreign, July 1583-July 1584*, pp. 611-14.

[21] Elias Ashmole, *History of the Order of the Garter*, London, 1672, pp. 406-11; cf. Yates," Dramatic Religious Processions", pp. 258-60.

[22] See R. Strong, "Festivals for the Garter Embassy at the Court of Henry III", *Journal of the Warburg and Courtauld Institutes*, XXII, 1959, pp. 60-70.

[23] The Spanish ambassador's deep disapproval had been apparent at Vespers; see article cited p. 66.

[24] Mariéjol, *Marguerite de Valois*, pp. 229 ff.

[25] See the Queen Mother's pathetic letter to Villeroy of May 22nd, 1585; *Lettres de Catherine de Médicis*, ed. Baguenault de Puchesse, VIII, pp. 291-2.

[26] See her anxious reports to Henri III in *Lettres*, VIII, p. 327; cf. Mariéjol, *Catherine de Médicis*, pp. 398 ff.

[27] Desjardins, *Négotiations de la France avec la Toscane*, IV, p 854; cf. Mariéjol, *Catherine*, pp. 405-6.

PART III, CHAPTER II

THE TAPESTRIES GO TO FLORENCE

[1] See J. Cartwright, *Christina of Denmark*, London, 1913, p. 490.

[2] Desjardins, *Négotiations de la France avec la Toscane*, IV, pp. 256-8.

[3] *Calendar of State Papers, Foreign, July 1583-July 1584*, p. 99.

[4] Protocollo di Ser Zanobi Paccali, 1589, Archivio Notarile Moderno, no. 1100 (folios unnumbered, the relevant documents are at the end of the volume). There is an exact copy of the list, and its preface, in Archivio Mediceo 6354 A, beginning at folio 368; and a copy of the list only, without the preface, in Guardaroba Mediceo, 152, folios 7-13. All these documents are in the Florentine Archives.

[5] This preamble is as follows:

"Al Nome di Dio. Amen

Inuentario di Robe che la Ser^ma Sig^ra Christiana Principessa di Loreno et Gran Duchessa di Toscana Nostra Signora dice hauer fatte portare et condurre di Francia le quale l'Ill^re Monsr Marchionne del Signor Martino Signor di Puylobier Maiordomo gia della Ser^ma et Christianissima Regina Madre del Re di Glorios. Mem. che ha dette robe in custodia, dice essere state donate, et date attualmente in uita dalla detta Christianissima Regina alla detta Ser^ma Gran Duchessa. Il quale Inuentario è stato fatto ne giorni infradetti nel Palazzo de Pitti del Ser^mo Gran Duca di Toscana dal Molto m^co et ecc^e Sr. Ascanio Rasi Dottore di Legge e Luogotenente Fiscale con l'interpositione del suo decreto per l'interesse de gl'assenti da gli stati del Ser^mo Gran Duca di Toscana, che si descriuera in fine, et con l'interuento di me Zanobi Paccalli cittadino e notario fiorentino per comandamento della detta Serenissima Gran Duchessa et in uirtu d'un rescritto fatto del Ser^mo Gran Duca

nostro signore sotto di 9 di maggio 1589 à pie d'un memoriale della prefata Ser^ma Gran Duchessa il qual memoriale insieme con il presente inuentario sara legato, et cucito in fine del mio protocollo segnato numero 33 del archivio et le quali robe sono state stimate mentre s'è fatto detto Inuentario come di sotto capo per capo si dira distintamente parte dalli sopradetti Benedetto Buonmattei, et Vinc^o suo figlio periti, et practici in fare simili stime, et chiamati ex off^o dal detto Signore Ascanio secondo il comandamento fattone da S. A. Ser^ma per il detto rescritto et parte dall' Ill^e Sr. Bernardo Vechietti gentilhuomo et senatore fiorentino, et dal m^co Sr. Giaches gioielliere di S. A. intendenti della ualuta delle robe stimate in uirtu d'un altro rescritto fatto per la medesima S. A. Serenissima sotto il medesimo memoriale sotto di Primo di Giugno 1589.

Comincia l'inuentario delle robe stimate delli detti Buonmattei a di 29 Maggio 1589."

(Archivio Notarile Moderno, 1100; Archivio Mediceo 6354 A, f. 368).

This preface has been published in a French translation by J. Ehrmann, "Dessins d'Antoine Caron", *Bull. de la Soc. de l'Hist. de l'Art Fr.*, 1956, pp. 124-5.

[6] Quoted from the Archivio Notarile Moderno, no. 1100. The entry is published in a French translation by Ehrmann, *loc. cit.*

There are three copies of this description of the tapestries in the Florentine archives; the original is the one in the Archivio Notarile Moderno; in the copy of this in Archivio Mediceo 6354 A the description of the tapestries is on folio 368 *verso*; in the copy in Guardaroba Mediceo, 152, it is on folio 7.

[7] Her discovery is unpublished, but is recorded in the fiches concerning the Valois Tapestries which she compiled and which the authorities of the Uffizi Gallery kindly allowed me to consult.

The priority of Cecilia Lisi in making this discovery is mentioned by Ehrmann, article cited, p. 122.

[8] C. Rigoni, *Catalogo della R. Galleria degli Arazzi*, Florence-Rome, 1884, pp. 67-9.

[9] This list immediately precedes the list of the objects given to Christina in the Queen Mother's life-time in all the three documentary sources. The preamble to it is precisely the same as the one quoted in note 5 above, except for the words "lasciate per testamento" instead of the words "donate e date attualmente in uita".

[10] Catherine's will is printed in her *Lettres*, ed. Baguenault de Puchesse, IX, pp. 494-8.

[11] This inventory is in Bibl. Nat. Fonds Latin, 14359. It was published, with a critical introduction, by E. Bonnaffée, *Inventaire des meubles de Catherine de Médicis en 1589*, Paris, 1874.

[12] *Inventaire*, ed. Bonnaffée, pp. 31, 47.

[13] *Ibid.*, p. 53.

[14] *Ibid., loc. cit.*

[15] The concierge of the house said that some "meubles ne sçait quelz" had been taken out of the house by two ladies by command of the Princess of Lorraine (*Inventaire, ed. cit.*, pp. 52, 53). These were evidently distinct from the "ameublement", and perhaps it was the goods smuggled out by these two women which were listed at Florence as those left to Christina "per testamento". Both the lists at Florence may thus represent property which was in Catherine's house but which was taken out before the inventory was made. There is a copy of that inventory, corresponding pretty closely to the text as printed by Bonnaffée, in Archivio Mediceo 6354A folio 173 ff. These documents at Florence are thus indispensable for the study of Catherine's collections.

[16] *Inventaire*, ed Bonnaffée, p. 56.

[17] *Ibid.*, p. 57.

[18] *Ibid.*, p. 160.

[19] Desjardins, *Négotiations*, IV, pp. 874 ff.

[20] *Ibid.*, p. 877.

[21] The original of this contract is in Archivio Mediceo 4742; this bulky volume of documents is entitled "Scritture diverse intorno al matrimonio di Ferdinando I e Cristina di Lorena, 1587-9" and contains ample material for a full elucidation of the negotiations concerning this marriage.

[22] Desjardins, *Négotiations*, IV, p. 878.

[23] *Ibid., loc. cit.*

[24] *Ibid., loc. cit.*

[25] *Ibid.*, p. 879.

[26] *Ibid.*, p. 852.

[27] *Ibid., loc. cit.*

[28] *Ibid.*, p. 880.

[29] *Ibid., loc. cit.*

[30] *Ibid.*, p. 881.

[31] Lenoncourt, as her father's representative, accompanied Christina to Florence; see Cartwright, *Christina of Denmark*, p. 508. (Christina of Denmark, the subject of Julia Cartwright's excellent book, was Christina of Lorraine's *other* grandmother, the mother of Duke Charles.)

[32] Desjardins, *Négotiations*, IV, p. 880.

[33] *Ibid.*, p. 862.

[34] *Ibid.*, p. 881.

[35] See above, p. 122.

[36] See Catherine's *Lettres*, ed. Baguenault de Puchesse, X, p. 250. Melchior de St. Martin, seigneur de Puylobier, became maître d'hôtel to Catherine in 1573. His name of "Melchior" is garbled into "Marchionne' in the Italian documents; see above p. 121, note 5.

[37] R. Gualterotti, *Descrizione del regale apparato fatto nella nobile citta di Firenze, per la venuta, e per le nozze della serenissima madama Cristina di Loreno*, Florence, 1589.

[38] *Ibid.*, pp. 56 ff.

[39] *Ibid.*, pp. 65 ff.

[40] A. Warburg, "I costumi teatrali per gli Intermezzi del 1589", in *Gesammelte Schriften*, Leipzig, 1932, pp. 261-2.

[41] See Yates, *French Academies*, pp. 241-2.

[42] There is no good study of Ferdinand I who is a most important figure; for an outline, see *Enciclopedia Italiana, sub nom.*

[43] Michelangelo Buonarroti, *Descrizione delle felicissime nozze della Christianissima Maestà di Madama Maria Medici*, Florence, 1600, sig. B 2 *recto*.

[44] C. Rigoni, *Catalogo della R. Galleria degli Arazzi*, Florence-Rome, 1884, introduction, p. xx.

[45] A. Gotti, *Le Gallerie di Firenze*, Florence, 1872, p. 258.

[46] *Ibid*, pp. 254-5.

[47] The fiches of the manuscript catalogue at the Uffizi note which of the tapestries were "nel deposito" at the Palazzo della Crocetta.

[48] Rigoni, *Op. cit.*, pp. 35-8.

INDEX

PLATES I-XII

II

TOURNAMENT

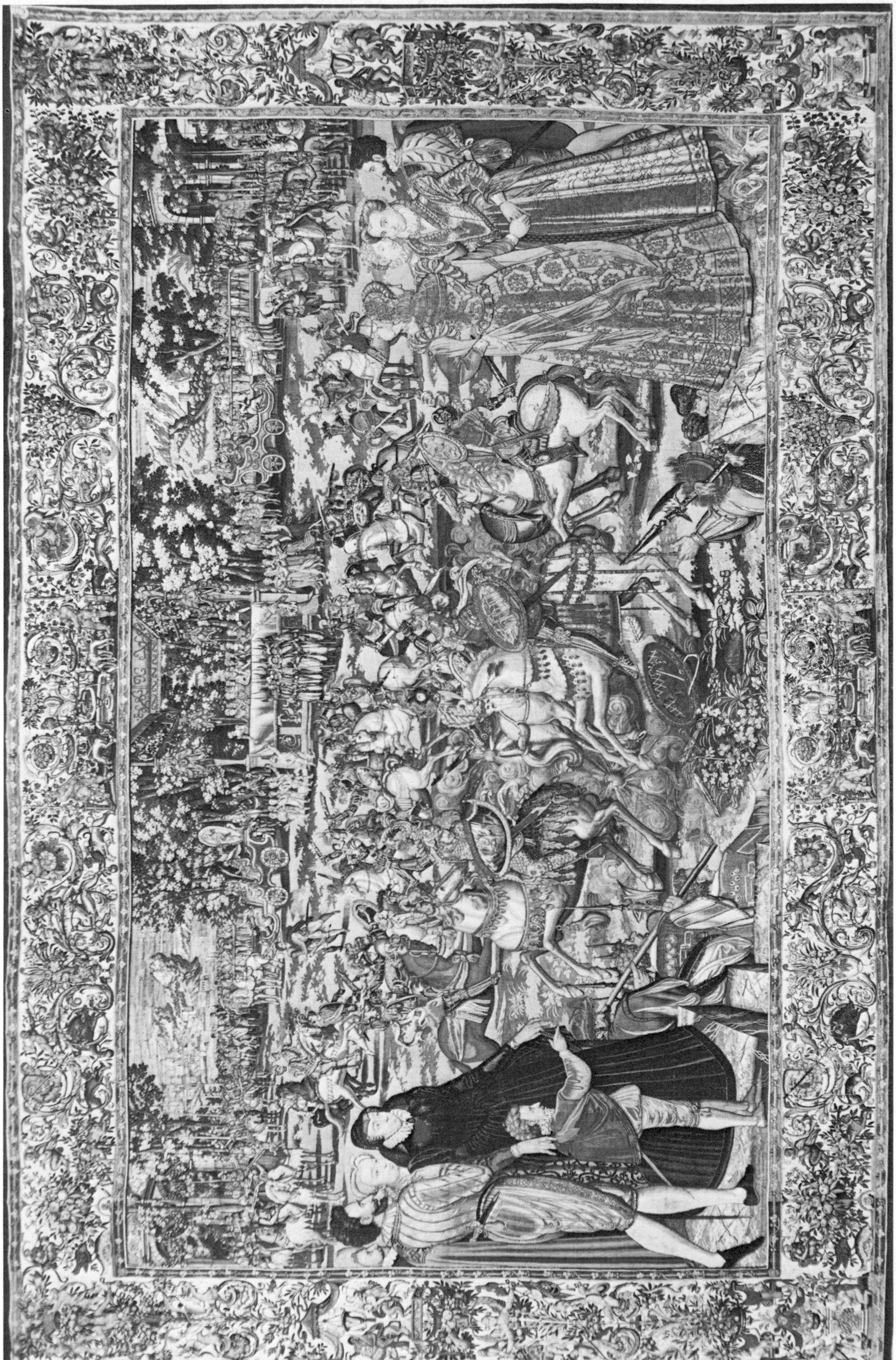

a   Antoine Caron, Festival at Fontainebleau

b   Antoine Caron, Tournament at Bayonne

a   Antoine Caron, Festival at Bayonne

b   Antoine Caron, Festival for the Polish Ambassadors

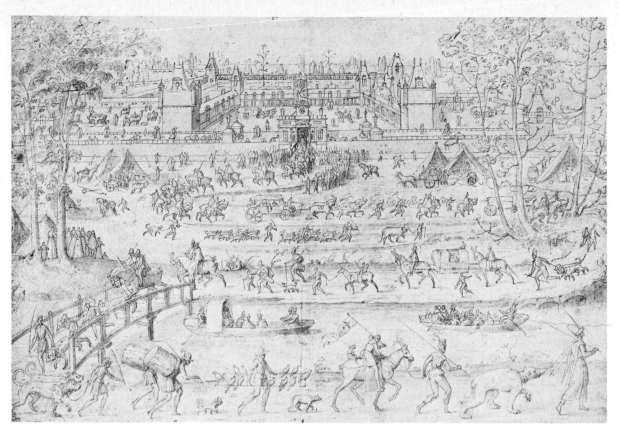

a   Antoine Caron, Hunting Scene at the Château d'Anet

b   Antoine Caron, Running at the Quintain

XII

Antoine Caron, Night Festival with an Elephant. Painting